The Political Economy

Also by Ngaire Woods

EXPLAINING INTERNATIONAL RELATIONS SINCE 1945

INEQUALITY, GLOBALIZATION AND WORLD POLITICS
(co-edited with Andrew Hurrell)

The Political Economy of Globalization

Edited by
Ngaire Woods

St Martin's Press
New York

THE POLITICAL ECONOMY OF GLOBALIZATION
Selection, editorial matter and Chapters 1 and 8 copyright © Ngaire Woods 2000
Individual chapters (in order) copyright © John H. Dunning; Diana Tussie and
Ngaire Woods; Benjamin Cohen; Geoffrey Garrett; Thomas Biersteker;
Jan Aart Scholte 2000

St. Martin's Press, Scholarly and Reference Division,
175 Fifth Avenue, New York, N.Y. 10010

First published in the United States of America in 2000

Printed in Hong Kong

ISBN   0–312–23319–1 (cloth)
ISBN   0–312–23321–3 (paper)

Library of Congress Cataloging-in-Publication Data
The political economy of globalization/Ngaire Woods.
p. cm
"Earlier versions of chapters 1 to 6 appeared in Oxford development studies, vol. 26,
issue 1"–acknowledgments p.
Includes bibliographical references and index.
ISBN 0–312–23319–1 (cloth: alk. paper) – ISBN 0–312–23321–3 (pbk:alk. paper)
1. International economic relations. 2. International relations. 3. World politics–1989–
I. Woods, Ngaire

HF1359.P655 2000
337–dc21   99–086149

For Tui

Contents

Notes on the Contributors   viii

Preface   x

1   **The Political Economy of Globalization**   1
    Ngaire Woods

2   **The New Geography of Foreign Direct Investment**   20
    John H. Dunning

3   **Trade, Regionalism and the Threat to
    Multilateralism**   54
    Diana Tussie and Ngaire Woods

4   **Money in a Globalized World**   77
    Benjamin Cohen

5   **Globalization and National Autonomy**   107
    Geoffrey Garrett

6   **Globalization as a Mode of Thinking in Major
    Institutional Actors**   147
    Thomas Biersteker

7   **Global Civil Society**   173
    Jan Aart Scholte

8   **Globalization and International Institutions**   202
    Ngaire Woods

Index   224

Notes on the Contributors

Thomas Biersteker is Henry R. Luce Professor of Transnational Organization and Director of the Thomas Watson Institute for International Studies at Brown University. His recent publications include *State Sovereignty as a Social Construct* (1996) with Cynthia Weber. His present research addresses globalization and its implications for states and other institutional actors.

Benjamin Cohen is Louis G. Lancaster Professor of International Political Economy at the University of California, Santa Barbara. His recent publications include *The Geography of Money* (1998). His research continues to focus on the politics of international money and finance.

John H. Dunning is Professor of International Business at Rutgers University and Emeritus Professor at the University of Reading. His recent publications include *Multinational Enterprises and the Global Economy* (1993). His present research focuses on economic and strategic theories of multinational enterprise activity.

Geoffrey Garrett is Professor of Political Science and Director of the Program in Ethics, Politics and Economics at Yale University. His recent publications include *Partisan Politics in the Global Economy* (1998). His present research is on the interaction between globalization and domestic politics and the emerging institutional architecture of the European Union.

Jan Aart Scholte is Reader in International Studies at the University of Warwick. His recent publications include the *International Relations of Social Change* (1993). His present research explores the involvement of civil society in global finance and in particular, civil society responses to IMF-sponsored restructuring.

Diana Tussie is Senior Research Fellow at the Facultad Latinoamericana de Ciencias Sociales, Buenos Aires. Her recent publications include *The Developing Countries in World Trade: Policies and Bargaining Strategies* (1993) with David Glover. Her present research covers both international trade and regionalism, and multilateral development banks and good governance.

Ngaire Woods is Fellow in Politics and International Relations at University College, Oxford. Her recent publications include *Inequality, Globalization and World Politics* (1999) with Andrew Hurrell. Her present research focuses on global economic governance and examines the politics of the IMF and the World Bank.

Preface

The idea for this book first emerged when, in my teaching and research into globalization, I became aware of how difficult it was to find texts which combined both a careful analysis of the evidence, and an examination of the political economy of globalization, not just with reference to specific economic issues, but in the broader context of international political and economic relations. It took further form when I was invited to guest-edit a special issue of *Oxford Development Studies*.

Editing the book has given me and the contributors an opportunity to present our assessment of the political economy of globalization in a more wide-ranging but at the same time more integrated way. The result is a text which we hope provides a clear set of concepts for considering globalization and its impact; detailed evidence about the practical impact of globalization – such as on foreign investment and on states' capacities to frame their own economic policies; and fresh arguments about the implications of globalization – be it on the role of money in the world economy, or on the emergence of a global civil society.

I am very grateful to my publisher, Steven Kennedy, not just for his careful shepherding of the project, but also for his ideas about the content and form of the book. Earlier versions of Chapters 1 to 6 appeared in *Oxford Development Studies*, vol. 26, issue 1 (a special issue on globalization). I am grateful, along with other contributors and the publishers to Carfax Publishing, Taylor & Francis Ltd, for permission for publication of the revised versions included here. Finally, I would like to thank Kerstin Gehmlich for excellent work in indexing the volume and Keith Povey for enlightened copy-editing.

NCAIRE WOODS

x

1 The Political Economy of Globalization

NGAIRE WOODS

Globalization has become a particularly fashionable way to analyse changes in the international economy and in world politics. Advances in technology and modern communications are said to have unleashed new contacts and intercourse among peoples, social movements, transnational corporations, and governments. The result is a set of processes which have affected national and international politics in an extraordinary way. The chapters of this volume debate the nature and implications of this transformation.

The term political economy is used advisedly for it has been used to describe a number of different things in political science and international relations: from the application of rational individualism to the study of politics, to debates over policy with an economic dimension.[1] In this volume, the term is used to describe the changing relationship between political systems (both national and international) and economic forces.[2] In other words, the volume is concerned with how policy-makers are being affected by economic forces, as well as how they themselves affect these forces. Following in the classical tradition of political economy, the chapters also address the moral debates about globalization, starting with the question '*cui bono?*' 'In whose interest?' or 'Who benefits?', and touching upon the possible ramifications for opportunity and inequality among a wide range of actors in a globalizing world.[3]

In order to understand what is new about globalization, we need carefully to distinguish two aspects of change: a quantitative dimension and a qualitative one. Quantitatively, globalization refers to an increase in trade, capital movements, investments and people across borders. Some refer to these new forces as 'transnationalism' and

1

'interdependence'. Yet as many sceptics point out, there is little that is new here. Transnationalism and interdependence were buzzwords not only twenty years ago,[4] but even eighty years ago, not to mention in the nineteenth century. For example, Norman Angell in 1912 wrote of the impact of 'rapid post, the instantaneous dissemination of financial and commercial information by means of telegraphy, and generally the incredible progress of rapidity in communication'. For Angell, the result was

> a financial interdependence of the capitals of the world, so complex that disturbance in New York involves financial and commercial disturbance in London, and, if sufficiently grave, compels the financiers of London to co-operate with those of New York to put an end to the crisis, not as a matter of altruism, but as a matter of commercial self-protection.[5]

Although trade, capital and the movement of peoples are all assumed to have increased exponentially since early this century, this assumption is misleading. For 17 countries for which there are data, transfers in goods, capital or people have not increased dramatically. In 1913 exports as a share of GDP from these countries accounted for 12.9 per cent of GDP as opposed to 14.5 per cent in 1993. Similarly, capital transfers as a share of industrial country GDP are still smaller than in the 1890s. Furthermore, whilst in earlier eras of globalization there was a large movement of people around the world, today immigration is far more restricted.[6]

So what is new about globalization at the end of the twentieth century? The answer lies in qualitative changes in international politics. In other words, changes in the way people and groups think and identify themselves, and changes in the way states, firms, and other actors perceive and pursue their interests. These changes are highlighted in successive chapters of this book, where they are also linked to economic trends and specific political phenomena.

This chapter serves to define the core elements of globalization and critically to assess key presumptions made about its impact. For example, it is widely argued that globalization is eroding state sovereignty. Yet this chapter suggests that the impact of globalization differs not just according to the sector of the economy being examined (as the overall argument of this book demonstrates) but also according to the character of each state. Strong states have not only influenced the nature and pace of globalization but, equally, have controlled their own integration into the world economy. Their sovereignty may well be qualitatively changing, but it is surely not being eroded. Weak states, by contrast, risk being further weakened by globalization. At the same time, however, globalization is opening up new kinds of governance (such as regional institutions) and adding new actors to the process (such as non-governmental organizations, and transnational arbiters and regulators). These developments may well be opening up new opportunities as well as challenges to even the weakest states in the system.

Core elements of 'globalization'

Globalization, in the sense that the term is used throughout this volume, comprises three interconnected elements: the expansion of markets; challenges to the state and institutions; and the rise of new social and political movements. These do not represent alternative definitions or competing theories. Rather, they reflect different aspects of globalization which are worth elaborating.

The expansion of markets

A first core aspect of globalization is the transformation of global economic activity. Technological change and government deregulation have permitted the establishment of transnational networks in production, trade and finance. Some have gone so far as to call this the new 'borderless' world.[7] The new 'production' network describes firms and multinational enterprises (MNEs) who use advanced means of communication, and new, flexible techniques of production so as to spread their activities across the globe. In trade, globalization refers to the fact that the quantity and speed of goods and services traded across the globe has increased, and so too has the geographical spread of participants, the strength and depth of institutions which facilitate trade, and the impact of trade on domestic economic arrangements.

Finally, in finance, globalization has been facilitated by new financial instruments which permit a wider range of services to be bought and sold across the world economy. Overall financial globalization is characterized by an increasing speed, quantity, geographical spread, and impact of international finance – the creation of what can rightly be called a global financial system. One consequence, as argued in Chapter 4, is that national currencies – for so long thought of as a corner-stone of sovereignty – have become deterritorialized, leaving governments to compete in a global marketplace for the control and useage of their currency.

It is important to recall that technology alone has not driven this expansion in global markets. Rather, technological advances, hand-in-hand with governments' policies, have produced the effects noted above. For example, the increased globalization of finance which occurred in the 1970s was made possible by state decisions to grant more freedom to market operators and to abolish postwar capital controls. Equally importantly, at this time states chose to refrain from imposing more effective capital controls.[8]

The transformation of politics

A second element of globalization is political. At the extreme, some argue that a new 'global politics' is emerging which, like the 'borderless world economy', is characterized by a global political order in which states' political boundaries become much less impor-tant.[9] In the old system, sovereign states interacted with each other according to rules which they – as states – agreed upon. In the new interconnected global political order, political power and political activity are said to extend across the boundaries of nation-states.[10] Without accepting the view that all politics has become 'global', several significant changes can be noted in political power and authority. These changes are due both to technological advances in communications, and to policy changes as governments and other actors reconceive their interests and their legitimate realm of authority.

In the first place, 'global issues' have emerged which require states to coordinate policy-making at levels above the nation-state. These issues include human rights, environmental degradation, and nuclear safety. Furthermore, the same technologies and policies which make new kinds of economic activity possible also facilitate the spread of transnational crime, weapons, drugs and illegal immigrants. The nature of these developments is such that no one state can effectively regulate on its own. Likewise, economic globalization requires new forms of regulation. For this reason, the globalization of politics describes a shift in decision-making up to either the regional or the international level. At the regional level, the past decade has seen a flourishing of new arrangements – for example, virtually every country in the world is now part of some regional trade agreement. So too, at the international level, there has been an increase not just in the number of institutions, but also in the depth and breadth of issues they are being required to address. These shifts in decision-making do not necessarily imply an erosion of existing state power and authority. Rather, what has changed is the way (and the fora) in which states use their power and authority – with states now choosing to participate in regimes in which they make decisions in coordination or cooperation with other states.

Accompanying the increase in regional and international decision-making, is a change in the way governments interact. Modern communications systems mean that national (or even sub-national) decision-makers can interact horizontally with officials in other countries. Where previously international relations were conducted through diplomatic channels or high-level meetings, officials at all levels of govenment may now communicate directly across borders with one another.[11] This is likely both to strengthen and to reflect strong regional ties – as in the European case.

It is not only governments that are interacting horizontally. A multitude of non-state actors are interacting in a similar way, including multinational enterprises, non-governmental organizations, and sub-national groups such as trade unions or indigenous minorities. The increasing linkages among these groups have strengthened their international presence, making these non-state actors another aspect of globalized politics.

Finally, globalization is inducing not just a shift in decision-making upwards towards regional and international fora, but at the same time a shift downwards to sub-national fora. In other words, globalization is inducing not just an increase in supranational decision-making, but at the same time a decentralization of decision-making within countries. One example is in Europe where sub-national regions have gradually increased their status within the institutions of the European Union. Indeed the increasing recognition of sub-national regions has been an important part of developing democratic representation and accountability in the EU. Similarly, the World Bank and other multilateral development banks have pursued more accountable and participatory programs in the developing world, through a more decentralized approach, which has encouraged local levels of governance.[12]

The emergence of new social and political movements

Globalization affects more than markets and states. It is altering the lives of people across the globe and affecting their culture and values. New communications systems mean that media, music, books, international ideas and values can all be disseminated in a global and virtually instantaneous manner. This is producing what some describe as a 'global culture'. Such a description, however, ignores the way in which globalization is simultaneously producing very different kinds of reactions and cultures. For example, whilst Western values and ideas (along with food chains) have spread into Russia and the Middle East, in both these regions of the world there has also been a strong reassertion of 'counter' national or religious identity – with strong nationalism in Russia and a dramatic rise in political Islam in the Middle East. These 'reactions' and 'rebellions' against Westernization are in turn assisted by the new technologies which make communication and networking across borders possible – such as the transnational networks built up around political Islam.[13]

A common feature of both Westernization and reactions against it are groups and movements organizing themselves using new technology and new ways of connecting across borders – described by some as a new 'global civil society'. More modestly, what is new is the extent to which territorial location, territorial distance and territorial borders have lost their determining influence. Modern technology means that people can connect in a space unbounded by territory. Distance can be covered in effectively no time and territorial frontiers present no particular impediment. As a result, transnationally organized groups can identify in a new way, forming around a premise of supraterritorial solidarity instead of within national bounds whether it be around class, gender, religious faith, or profession.[14]

Common to all elements of globalization is the sense that activities previously undertaken within national boundaries can be undertaken globally or regionally – to some extent 'deterritorialized'. This is equally true of, firms' research and development, the usage of national currencies, some global political issues, and social movements. The central question this raises is: upon whom do these changes impact?

The impact of globalization

The impact of globalization is the source of endless debate. In particular, debates revolve around competing interpretations of effects on investment, capital flows, jobs, profits, and welfare. One major assumption is that globalization reduces the capacity of states to promote welfare objectives within their own boundaries. This matter is addressed more fully in Chapter 5 but here it is worth a preliminary examination.

The technological advances driving globalization, it is often argued, enable multinational enterprises to behave in a more efficiency-maximizing way. This means they can respond faster and more radically to changes in wage and tax costs shifting their production, for example, to cheaper locations. Such responses compel governments to deregulate in their competition for investment – a competition described by some as a 'race to the bottom' as governments dismantle regulatory structures which keep wages and taxes high.[15] Some say that this deregulation results primarily in greater 'allocative efficiency', less government, lower costs, higher profits and greater job opportunities. Others point to the accompanying disadvantages of lower wages, declining welfare standards, and increasing inequality. Yet each of these arguments about the implications of globalization is misleading.

In the first place, there is little evidence that governments in fact seek multinational enterprises (MNEs) and foreign investment by deregulating so as to lower wages and lower taxes on capital.[16] In the second place, in a globalizing world MNEs are not attracted by lower wages and lower taxes.[17] Rather, their own competitiveness and the attractiveness of investment locations depend much more on the requirements of knowledge-intensive production. In summary, the initial premises of the view that globalization will result in a dismantling of the state as we know it are factually unsubstantiated, even if they appear to be intuitively attractive.

Clearly then, the impact of globalization needs to be analysed, paying careful attention to the facts as well as to potential explanatory theories – as the chapters of this volume attempt to do. In this context, it is worth noting some of the broad groupings of winners and losers from globalization in industry, in the workforce, in societies, and in international society.

In industry, firms which do not enjoy the kinds of organizational advantages described in Chapter 2, are likely to lose out to competitors who do. Furthermore, firms who previously relied on government investment (for example, in those situations where governments wished to spread economic growth more evenly across a country, or to protect jobs through subsidizing 'national producers') are likely to lose out over time, for whilst not all government intervention is being reduced by globalization, this kind of investment certainly is.

In the workforce, it is widely thought that workers who rely upon government-set minimum wages or working conditions will lose out since such government policies become anachronistic in a new era of global competition. Yet it is worth noting that in the past two years the British government has introduced a minimum wage, and the French government has legislated to reduce the working week to 35 hours: and these two countries are recipients of the largest flows of inward investment in Europe (see Table 2.2). Of course, similar arguments cannot be made about conditions in developing countries (see below). Furthermore, many workers do suffer – at least in the short term – from the effects of globalization. Even the most optimistic accounts of economic integration and transformation accept that workers who are not mobile, or whose skills are not transferable, may suffer in a globalizing world economy. For example, in industrialized countries the evidence suggests that low-skilled workers are already paying the price.[18]

In societies across the world there are many winners and losers from the different elements of globalization and from the combination of economic, political and social effects. Existing evidence suggests that as governments have liberalized policies so as to integrate more fully into the world economy, almost without exception economic inequality has increased.[19] As regards political rights and freedoms, globalization does not have a much better record. Not so long ago it was hoped that new standards of human rights and democracy would spread through networks enhanced by globalization – indeed, industrialized countries throughout the late 1980s and early 1990s dreamt of exporting a combination of open-market economics and democracy. Yet the experience of the last decade suggests that political change does not necessarily follow smoothly and conveniently behind economic integration: the expansion of markets does not automatically expand the number of countries embracing democracy. In many developing countries, economic liberalization requires policy choices or priorities which are sometimes at odds with a parallel urge to democratize.[20]

Globalization has also affected politics among states, creating winners and losers at the international level. In one study, the result is described as a world comprising a 'zone of peace' and a 'zone of turmoil'.[21] In the wealthy industrialized countries, globalization may well be producing a 'giant pluralist security community',[22] and a cohesive republican order 'centred on economic growth, democratic governance and liberal tolerance'.[23] However, in the zone of turmoil, a different politics is emerging. As weak governments try to deal with increasing economic inequality and political, religious, and tribal backlashes to globalization mentioned above, the result in many cases is a further weakening of the state and democracy, and a heightening of turmoil and poverty.[24]

At the international level, globalization provides some smaller states with new opportunities, but also highlights the existing power and advantages of large and powerful states. As Chapter 8 argues, increasing transnational economic activity requires global rules, regulations, and enforcement at the international level. Furthermore, it creates the need for an enforcer of the rules. For this reason, economic globalization casts a spotlight on the largest and most powerful states in the global economy – most particularly, the United States – and the role that such a state might play in ensuring international institutions are effective. It is worth adding here that the role of such a powerful state lies not just in enforcing rules, but also in generating and forming ostensibly 'universal' ideas and consensus about what the international rules should be. In 1994 John Williamson and Stephan Haggard argued that: 'At least in intellectual terms, we today live in one world rather than three.'[25] That 'one' intellectual world (of policy liberalization and democratization) is seen by many not so much as a sign of global convergence but rather as a sign of US dominance.

Globalization involves economic, political and social processes, all of which play into the emergence of new winners and losers. Increased communications technology, travel and contact present new opportunities for many seeking emancipation or positive change. However, at the same time, a central concern about globalization is that it will exacerbate inequalities so as to render groups within developing countries, and groups of countries themselves, both poorer economically, and politically less able to influence the rules of the game.[26] Clearly, the impact of globalization will depend in most cases on the strength and adaptability of the state, not just as a locus of power and authority, but also as a locus of representation and democracy.

Globalization and the demise of the nation-state?

In political science, the most debated of all the propositions about globalization is the notion that it is eroding the sovereignty and autonomy of the state. Since 'the state' is the core unit of analysis in much political science and most international relations, the question is a crucial one. On the one hand, 'the borderless world economy', 'global politics', and 'global civil society' (as discussed above) all describe a world in which the sovereignty of the state and the capacities of any government are being eroded. In reaction to this claim, there exists an equal and opposite literature arguing that, in spite of claims to the contrary, the state lives on and that some elements of globalization even reinforce the role of government.[27]

In fact, the impact of globalization varies, and one particular determinant is state strength.[28] All states are affected by globalization insofar as it alters their possibilities and opportunities. However, a much greater erosion of autonomy is occurring in respect of weak states than strong.

'Strong' states, in this context, have a capacity to influence the rules of the international economy, and/or a capacity to control their own integration into the world economy. The United States and other industrialized countries, for example, have played a crucial role in shaping globalization. These countries' decisions to deregulate and liberalize in various ways instigated the flows of currency, goods, services, and multinational activity across borders which we associate with globalization. In finance, as mentioned above, decisions taken by the United States and European states in the 1960s and early 1970s laid the foundations for the globalization of money and capital flows.

At the same time, globalization imposes limits even on strong states. A key example is the way international capital markets can exact a swift and devastating punishment on any government undertaking inappropriate monetary or exchange-rate policy policy: as the United Kingdom, Italy and Brazil have all experienced. Yet the extent to which markets punish other kinds of policies undertaken by strong states is often overstated. For example, there is no evidence that maintaining the welfare state is an offence which the markets will punish. On the contrary, the globalization of markets has been undertaken mostly by governments who have simultaenously increased their welfare states. The logic is that a government opening up to world trade has needed to 'buffer' its citizens from the dislocations and vulnerabilities of world markets in order to avert political protests and reactions against the global economy, such as that which occurred in the 1930s.[29]

'Strong' states are also those which can control – to some degree – the nature and speed of their integration into the world economy. For example, some states have managed to slow down or to control the speed and terms on which they have integrated in world capital markets. Often these states are also ferocious guardians of their independence in foreign policy, human rights and security issues, as well as their own domestic political arrangements. Such relatively 'strong' states include not just industrialized countries such as France and the United Kingdom, but also a wide variety of developing countries from the likes of Brazil to Malaysia, China, Iraq, and Iran. What is striking about these 'strong' states with the exception of the United Kingdom, is that each has propounded a powerful national ideology and rationale for rejecting what some call 'anglo-american capitalism'. In other words, they come ready-armed to the world economy with ideas of their own to stave off what Robert Wade has called 'coercive liberalism'.[30] In all of these cases, globalization is having a powerful effect, as is evidenced by the restructuring of national and private industries in France, the past decade of economic liberalization in Brazil, and in a radically different way, through international coercive interventions in Iraq. Yet at the same time, each of these countries either uses or at least seriously contemplates using capital controls. So too, each retains high protective barriers in important sectors of the economy. Their capacity to do this depends upon a matrix of factors which includes their size, resources, geostrategic advantages, and economic strength, and equally their national ideology and the domestic power of the state – be it coercive or consensual.

By contrast, weak states suffer from a lack of choice in their international economic relations. They have little or no influence in the creation and enforcement of rules in the system and they have exercised little control over their own integration into the world economy. Rather, in the aftermath of the debt crisis of the 1980s, many weak states opened up their economies, liberalized and deregulated, more as a result of the 'coercive liberalization' mentioned above, than of democratic policy choices. In the 1990s, as Dani Rodrik has described, this continues with 'forced harmonization', whereby, for instance, in the case of trade negotiations on intellectual property, developing countries were coerced into an agreement which transfers 'billions of dollars' worth of monopoly profits from poor countries to rich countries under the guise of protecting the property rights of inventors'.[31]

Weak states have been further weakened by an inability to deal with the political and social turmoil and rebellion resulting from globalization. Often economic liberalization and deregulation have been accompanied by a reduction in the role of the state – in both the economy and society, in the developing world (whilst in industrialized countries over the past two decades of globalization, a solid core of governmental activity has remained untouched – and untouchable – such as the National Health Service in the United Kingdom). In developing countries where governments were often weak to begin with, 'rolling back the state', in order to enhance global competitiveness has left a vacuum of political authority. This has been clearly demonstrated around the Southern and Eastern Mediterranean where after state subsidies and basic services were cut back during the 1980s, Islamic groups and other non-state actors quickly stepped in to substitute for the government: providing health care, soup kitchens, education and other social services. The substitution, however, had deeper implications for the state since many non-state actors did not just provide social goods, rather they mounted a direct challenge to the authority and legitimacy of the state.

In summary, the impact of globalization on the sovereignty and autonomy of states has varied according to state strength. It also varies across issue area, as the chapters described below demonstrate.

The political economy of globalization

The remaining chapters of this book survey the implications of globalization in seven different spheres of activity in the international political economy: multinational enterprises and investment; international trade and regionalism; global finance and money; national decision-making; actors' modes of thinking; global civil society, and international institutions. In each case the implications of globalization for specific actors and processes are analysed.

Chapter 2 examines major changes in foreign direct investment (FDI). The 1990s witnessed a spectacular increase in investment to Asia (South, East and Southeast Asia), as well as to Central and Eastern Europe, modest increases to Japan and the EU, and relatively smaller gains to all other areas of the world. So what explains these changes? In part, they are due to country-sector and firm-specific factors. However, they also reflect a transformation in the activities of firms who can now spread their activities across the globe. Globalization means that the most successful multinational enterprises (MNEs) are those with strong 'core competencies', that is, those that are good at management, organizing production, gaining access to markets, and research and development (R&D). MNEs in a globalizing world economy have also changed what they are looking for when they invest abroad. In the 1970s they sought natural resources, low-cost labour, and access to markets that attracted foreign direct investment. In the 1990s, MNEs are looking for skilled or semi-skilled labour, good physical infrastructure, government policies which are market-friendly, minimal distance-related transactions costs, and (in some sectors and countries) for 'clustering' which creates benefits such as a specialized pool of labour – as evidenced in export-processing zones. The result is that foreign direct investment flows have changed and, contrary to the view so popular in the 1980s, across-the-board liberalization and deregulation will not suffice to attract MNEs.

Chapter 3 examines the impact of globalization on political relations in the global trading system. Up until the 1980s, the international trade negotiations and rules were dominated by the industrialized countries, who evolved a pattern of liberalization and protectionism which worked greatly to their advantage. That regime now faces a host of new members as developing countries have liberalized and those nations of the former 'Soviet bloc' have entered the world economy. Furthermore, trade is no longer what it used to be. For example, the transnational activities of firms (as described above) mean that many goods and services no longer cross from a firm in one country to a firm in another, rather they are transferred *within* multinational enterprises operating in different countries. These changes in the membership and nature of world trade have led many to expect to see a strengthening in multilateralism – that is, a strengthening of the institutions of management and coordination of trade at the international level. Yet this is not necessarily the case. Rather, a third and possibly more powerful change is reconfiguring international trade relations. The emergence of powerful regional trade blocs may well prove an obstacle to the development of strong international institutions, in spite of the relatively recently created World Trade Organization (WTO). It is also possible, however, that regions cast in an open and politically inclusive way may reinforce multilateralism and lead to a more equitable political framework for managing world trade.

Chapter 4 examines globalization in finance and in particular the relationship between states and national currencies. For decades national currencies have been one of the hallmarks of state sovereignty – with governments jealously maintaining the value and guarding control over their own currencies, at least in part for reasons of national pride. Yet as financial markets have become more closely integrated into a global financial system, so the relationship between a national government and a national currency has been transformed. In the global financial system, currencies have become substitutable. As a result governments now compete to see that their currency is used in a maximal number of transactions and places. At the same time, governments have lost the control they once had over both the useage and the value of their currency. The 1997 financial crises in East Asia highlighted the kinds of constraints governments now face. In East Asia, no affected government was able to maintain confidence in the value of their currency as financial crises spread across the region. This forced governments of the region to examine alternatives such as currency boards, monetary union, and capital controls as ways to manage national currencies in a system which otherwise splits the state from its national currency.

Chapter 5 counterbalances the argument about the loss of monetary sovereignty by demonstrating that globalization poses fewer constraints on economic policy – at least in industrialized countries (OECD) – than is commonly thought. In the first place, the theory that globalization takes choices away from governments, forcing them to dismantle the welfare state, is shown to be a weak one. Certainly a large welfare state implies extra costs to business. However, it is wrong to assume that the business sector in industrialized countries can force governments to change national arrangements such as the welfare state, which are popular among citizens. Furthermore, even in the event of a crisis or where macreconomic performance deteriorates significantly such that governments face an incentive to act, there are other substantial obstacles to institutional reform. This theoretical argument is strongly supported by the evidence of government policies in OECD countries. Globalization has not resulted in OECD governments 'throwing open' all barriers and borders. Rather many countries have opened to trade but far less to capital markets. More specifically, there is no evidence that a policy 'race to the bottom' has occurred whereby globalization has forced the dismantling of welfare states. Finally, the evidence does show a deterioration in macroeconomic performance in OECD countries over past two decades but this can be explained in terms of factors other than globalization.

Chapter 6 presents the essence of globalization as a basic change in the way major institutional actors think and operate across the globe. This is evidenced not just by firms and the way in which they have developed networks of global production locations and investment strategies that spread corportate risk and tax liability on a global scale, and by international investors who have become global, but equally by other actors. The growth of global activities of nongovernmental organizations, for example, and the depth of activity of inter-state organizations reveal new ways in which international actors conceive of their identity and *raison d'être*. Similarly, governments and states today have redrawn the areas in which they claim sovereignty, as well as the grounds on which they justify intervention. All of this illustrates a change in modes of thinking and operation which have mixed effects on international relations. The effect of inequality among states and other actors, for example, is difficult to generalize. Globalization can be shown to exacerbate inequalities between states and within states as deregulation, austerity, and shifting investment take their toll. However, there is also evidence to suggest that globalization offers new opportunities even to weak states through dispersed production, broader markets, and flexible accumulation. Finally, the depth of globalization – its impact not just on modes of operation but also on thinking – means that, even though some aspects of the process could be slowed, it would be a gargantuan task to attempt to reverse it.

Chapter 7 addresses the rise of global civil society, defining it as civic activity which has one or more of the following characteristics: it addresses transworld issues (such as climate change or AIDS); it involves transborder communication (such as electronic media and computer networks); it has a global organization (whether centralized or via a network); and it works on the premise of supraterritorial solidarity (such as along lines or race, sexual orientation or a cosmopolitan conception of citizenship). Clearly, globalization has made all the above activities easier and more universal, and as a result global civil society has expanded rapidly over the past couple of decades. The impact on politics has been to create multilayered political loyalties as well as to broaden the scope of democratic practice by adding new channels of popular participation, consultation, debate and representation. Yet the effects are not all necessarily positive. The same globalized media used by laudable international groups may also be used by the unlaudable – be that transnational crime, racism or intolerant fundamentalists. And even where groups have worthy aims, they may well pursue misguided policies – miscalculating client needs or misreading public sentiments and thus producing negative consequences. Perhaps more seriously, global civil society suffers from problems of representation and accountability. Unlike governments, non-governmental organizations cannot claim to have been elected nor to be subject to formal public scrutiny. Nevertheless, global civil society represents an important way in which citizens all over the globe can legitimately seek to influence policies taken at an international or global level.

Chapter 8 addresses international institutions and analyses how states are attempting at an international level to manage globalization. The critical challenge is whether international institutions can be used better to coordinate and regulate a new more intrusive and 'domestic' set of issues than was previously the case. Multilateral institutions are now being asked to bulldoze into domestic politics, so as to implement international codes concerning issues ranging from human rights to the regulation of intellectual property. To be effective, they need to get compliance not just from governments but from citizens. Yet they will not achieve deep compliance while they rely on short-term incentives to governments and the coercion of powerful states. Yet the prospect of international organizations using a more participatory and egalitarian style of governance is unlikely. Ongoing inter-state competition for power and influence, the inability of powerful states to give up their own special privileges within international organizations, and organized vested interests within countries, together present a formidable obstacle to change.

Conclusion

Overall, the chapters of this book present a measured scepticism, based on both theory and evidence, about simple optimistic or pessimistic accounts of globalization. Globalization is not simply an encroachment of markets into the sovereignty of states. States, markets and other actors are involved in a process which is shaping the nature and pace of globalization. While some forms of state sovereignty are eroded (such as in respect of formal monetary policy), new arenas of power and competition are opened up. These include regional organizations, international agencies, and competition among currencies. At the same time, globalization is changing not just what states, firms and people *do*, it is also changing how they see themselves, and what they want. It is not leading to global convergence: in the case of multinational enterprises, firms are making more nuanced and complex calculations about how to organize and where to produce. In the case of peoples, some groups and societies are integrating more closely into a Western-defined world, others are defining and promulgating alternative identities and values. In the political realm, while states, firms and other actors lose autonomy in some areas, they are gaining influence in others. Yet the gains and losses are unequally divided among strong and weak states. Internationally, globalization may well further empower those states which shaped globalization in the first place – reinforcing their capacity to regulate its ongoing impact.

Notes

1. For a useful, concise overview see Peter A. Gourevitch, 'Political Economy', in Joel Krieger (ed.), *The Oxford Companion to Politics of the World* (Oxford: Oxford University Press, 1993) pp. 715–19.

2. For an account of the impact of globalization on global justice, see Richard Devetak and Richard Higgott, 'Justice Unbound: Globalization, States and Transformation of the Social Bond', *International Affairs*, 3 (1999) 483–500.

3. For a study focused specifically on the effects of globalization on inequality see Andrew Hurrell and Ngaire Woods (eds), *Globalization, Inequality, and World Politics* (Oxford: Oxford University Press, 1999).

4. Richard N. Cooper, *The Economics of Interdependence: Economic Policy in the Atlantic Community* (New York: McGraw-Hill for the Council on Foreign Relations, 1968); Robert O. Keohane and Joseph S. Nye, *Transnational Relations and World Politics* (Cambridge: Harvard University Press, 1971).

5. Norman Angell, *The Great Illusion: a study of the relation of military power in nations to their economic and social advantage* (London: Heinemann, 1912), p. 50.

6. UNDP, *Human Development Report* (New York: OUP for the United Nations Development Programme, 1997), p. 83.

7. K. Ohmae, *The Borderless World* (London: Collins, 1990); K. Ohmae, *The End of the Nation State* (New York: Free Press, 1995); W. Greider, *One World, Ready or Not: The Manic Logic of Global Capitalism* (New York: Simon & Schuster, 1997).

8. Eric Helleiner, *States and the Reemergence of Global Finance: From Bretton Woods to the 1990s* (New York: Cornell University Press, 1994); and see Chapter 8 of this book.

9. Anthony McGrew and P. G. Lewis (eds), *Global Politics* (Cambridge: Polity Press, 1992); T. Nierop, *Systems and Regions in Global Politics: An Empirical Study of Diplomacy, International Organization and Trade 1950–1991* (Chichester: John Wiley, 1994).

10. David Held, Anthony McGrew, David Goldblatt and Jonathan Perraton, *Global Transformations: Politics, Economics and Culture* (Cambridge: Polity Press, 1999), p. 49.

11. In the case of Britain, this is well portrayed by M. Clarke, *Britain's External Relations* (London: Macmillan, 1992).

12. Ngaire Woods, 'Good Governance in International Organizations', *Global Governance*, 5 (1999) 39–61 at p. 56.

13. Dale Eickelman and James Piscatori, *Muslim Politics* (Princeton: Princeton University Press, 1996).

14. P. Waterman, *Globalization, Social Movements, and the New Internationalisms* (London: Mansell, 1998).

15. See Chapter 5 of this volume.

16. See Chapter 5.

17. See Chapter 2.

18. Adrian Wood, *North–South Trade, Employment and Inequality: Changing Fortunes in a Skill-Driven World* (Oxford: Oxford University Press, 1994).

19. Frances Steward and Albert Berry, 'Globalization, Liberalization, and Inequality: Expectations and Experience', in Hurrell and Woods, *Inequality, Globalization and World Politics*, pp. 150–86.

20. Stephan Haggard and Steven Webb, *Voting for Reform* (Washington, DC: World Bank, 1994).

21. Max Singer and Aaron Wildavsky, *The Real World Order: Zones of Peace, Zones of Turmoil* (New Jersey: Chatham House, 1993).

22. Barry Buzan, *The European Security Order Recast: Scenarios for the Post-Cold War Era* (London: Pinter, 1990).

23. Dan Deudney and John Ikenberry, 'The Logic of the West', *World Policy Journal*, 10 (1993) 17–25.

24. Andrew Hurrell and Ngaire Woods, 'Globalization and Inequality', *Millenium*, 24, 3 (1995) 447–70.
25. John Williamson and Stephan Haggard, 'The Political Conditions for Economic Reform', in *The Political Economy of Policy Reform* (Washington: International Institute for Economics, 1994), p. 530.
26. Hurrell and Woods, 'Inequality and Globalization'.
27. Paul Hirst and Grahame Thompson, *Globalization in Question* (Oxford: Polity Press and Blackwells Publishers, 1996); Robert Wade, 'Globalization and its Limits: Reports of the Death of the National Economy are Greatly Exaggerated', in Suzanne Berger and Ronald Dore (eds), *National Diversity and Global Capitalism* (Ithaca: Cornell University Press, 1996).
28. For a discussion of strong and weak states see: Joel Migdal, *Strong Societies and Weak States: State–Society Relations and State Capabilities in the Third World* (Princeton NJ; Princeton University Press, 1988); Paul A. Cammack, *Strong States, Weak States, and Third World Development* (Manchester Papers in Politics 9/92, Department of Government, Victoria University of Manchester, 1992); Michael Handel, *Weak States in the International System* (London: Frank Cass, 1990).
29. This two-level process of globalization and state-welfarism has been called 'embedded liberalism': John Ruggie, 'International Regimes, Transactions and Change: Embedded Liberalism in the Postwar Economic Order', in Stephen Krasner (ed.), *International Regimes* (Ithaca: Cornell University Press, 1983); and see Chapter 5.
30. Robert Wade, 'National power, Coercive Liberalism and "Global Finance"', in Robert Art and Robert Jervis (eds), *International Politics: Enduring Concepts and Contemporary Issues* (New York: Addison/Wesley Longman, forthcoming).
31. Dani Rodrik, *The New Global Economy and Developing Countries: Making Openness Work* (Washington, DC: Overseas Development Council, 1999), p. 148.

2 Globalization and the New Geography of Foreign Direct Investment

JOHN H. DUNNING

Over the past two decades, developments in the global economy have deeply affected the pattern of foreign investment (FDI) by multinational enterprises (MNEs),[1] giving rise to a spectacular increase in investment to Asia and to Central and Eastern Europe, modest increases to Japan and the EU, and relatively smaller gains to all other areas of the world.[2] This chapter describes these shifts in investment and explores the underlying causes of change. The evidence presented suggests that MNEs have altered their patterns of investment in response to three factors: changes in their own competitiveness; alterations in what they seek from countries in which they invest; and a transformation in the way they link production to local markets. These factors are strongly interrelated and can be defined more technically as:

(i)   the competitive or ownership-specific (O) advantages of firms;
(ii) the competitive or location-specific (L) advantages of countries; and
(iii) the modalities by which firms coordinate their mobile O-specific advantages with the immobile L specific advantages of countries (for example, whether firms choose to buy or sell assets, or rights to assets through intermediate product markets and/or network relationships, or whether they prefer to internalize (I) the market for these assets or rights).[3]

The chapter argues that recent international political and economic events, together with technological advances, have influenced the configuration of OLI advantages facing MNEs, and thereby changed the geography of FDI.[4] It is also suggested that these same events have caused a fundamental – and possibly an irreversible – shift in the relative significance of the individual O, L and I variables as they influence both the strategy of MNEs toward FDI and the location of their value-added activities.[5] In making this argument, attention is given first to the distinction between the perceived need of firms to exploit (for example, capture the economic rent) on existing O specific advantages, and their need to protect or augment these advantages.[6] Attention is also given to the growing importance of high-value FDI, as witnessed by, for example, the significant expansion of research and development (R&D) activities undertaken by the foreign affiliates of MNEs, particularly, but not exclusively, in advanced industrial countries.[7]

The chapter proceeds in the following way. The following section describes the changes in the geography of FDI inflows between two periods – 1975–80 and 1990–96. Then we offer some explanations for the changes identified. Following this, there is a discussion of how the new geography of MNE activity varies according to the strategy of the investing firms, the activities in which they engage and the countries from which they originate. The conclusion summarizes the main findings of the chapter.

The New Geography of Foreign Direct Investment

Table 2.1 sets out the changing distribution of the flows of FDI by region and country of destination between the second half of the 1970s and the first six years of the 1990s.[8] For the first period, a six-year annual average is used, and, for the second, a seven-year annual average, of flows, which is a sufficiently long period to even out any 'lumpy' merger and acquisition (M&A) activity. FDI flow, rather than stock data are used, mainly because the former are regularly compiled by the IMF and UNCTAD,[9] and are reasonably comparable over time.

Table 2.1 suggests there have been quite significant shifts in the geography of FDI over the past two decades. A comparison of the data in Columns 2 and 4, as well as that set out in Column 5, shows

TABLE 2.1 The Distribution of Foreign Direct Investment Inflows by Host Region and Country 1975–80 and 1990–96 (US $ millions)

	1975–80 Annual average	%	1990–96 Annual average	%	Index of FDI growth 1975–80 = 100
Total inflows	32 183	100.0	234 724	100.0	729.3
Developed Economies	24 642	76.6	153 381	65.3	622.4
Western Europe	13 874	43.1	92 295	39.3	665.2
of which: European Union[a]	13 190	41.0	83 947	35.8	636.4
North America	8 757	27.2	50 942	21.7	581.7
of which: US	7 895	24.5	44 757	19.1	566.9
Japan	152	0.5	1 013	0.4	666.7
Other Developed Economies	1 859	5.7	9 169	3.9	493.2
of which: Australia	1 271	3.9	5 805	2.5	456.7
Developing Economies	7 539	23.4	74 778	31.9	991.9
Africa	810	2.5	3 498	1.5	431.9
Latin America & Caribbean	4 014	12.5	22 536	9.6	561.4
of which: South America	2 377	7.4	12 824	5.5	539.5
Asia	2 489	7.7	48 075	20.5	931.5
of which: South, East & South East Asia	1 971	6.1	45 857	19.5	2326.6
West and Central Asia[b]	518	1.6	2 217	0.9	428.1
Other Developing Economies[c]	226	0.7	668	0.3	295.8
Central and Eastern Europe	3	Neg.	6 565	2.8	218847.6

Notes:
[a] Includes the 12 member countries of the European Union in 1994.
[b] Including the Middle Eastern countries.
[c] The Pacific and developing Europe.
Neg. = negligible.

Sources: UNCTC, *Transnational Corporations and World Development* (New York, UN 1988); UNCTAD, *World Investment Report 1995: Transnational Corporations and Competitiveness* (New York and Geneva, UN 1995); UNCTAD, *World Investment Report 1998* (Geneva and New York: United Nations 1998).

that, of the major regions of the world, South, East and Southeast Asia and Central and Eastern Europe have spectacularly increased their share of inbound investment, while Japan and the European Union (EU)[10] have posted more modest gains. On the other hand, while other developed economies the Americas, West Asia and Africa have also recorded absolute increases in inward investment – and in the case of the US, substantial increases[11] – they have lost some of their earlier attractions, relative to those of other regions or countries.[12]

Table 2.2 gives details of the leading recipients of inward direct investment in the two periods in developed and developing countries. Overall in 1975–80, the ten largest recipient countries accounted for 74.1 per cent of all FDI flows; with just over one-half being directed to the United States, the United Kingdom, France and the Netherlands. By the first half of the 1990s, this geographical concentration had decreased to 66.5 per cent, although four leading countries, viz. the United States, the United Kingdom, France and China, still accounted for 46.4 per cent of the total FDI flows.

Table 2.2 also shows that, among the most significant changes in the distribution of inbound FDI between developing countries over the past two decades have been, first, the rise of China to the position of second largest recipient; and second, the declining drawing power of Brazil and one of the leading oil-exporting countries in the 1970s – Egypt. There has been some shifting in the ranking of the leading recipients of FDI. Among the developed countries, France, Spain and Canada have both increased their share of FDI over the past two decades, while, of the developing countries, Singapore, Argentina and Thailand have considerably strengthened their positions.

It is worth noting that there are some leading developed and developing economies which did not receive as much FDI as one might have expected. Japan is the most obvious example; it accounted for only 0.6 per cent inflows into the developed countries in 1975–80 and 0.9 per cent in 1990–96. Of the larger European countries, Italy received only one-quarter of the share of France in the first period and one-fifth in the second period, while some of the more populated newly industrial countries (NICs) of Asia – Indonesia, Korea, Taiwan and the Philippines – attracted only modest (though increasing) amounts of new capital inflows.

The cases of India and, even more spectacularly, some Central and East European countries, are interesting in that, although their share

TABLE 2.2 **The Largest Recipients of Inward FDI 1975–1980 and**

			Developed Countries		
Country	*1975/80* *$m*	*%*[b]	*Country*	*1990/96* *$m*	*%*
USA	7 894.0	32.0	USA	44 757.1	29.2
UK	5 795.4	21.1	UK	19 613.4	12.8
France	2 127.3	8.6	France	19 080.1	12.4
Netherlands	1 276.6	5.2	Belgium	10 012.1	6.5
Australia	1 271.4	5.2	Spain	8 579.3	35.6
Belgium[d]	1 203.1	4.9	Netherlands	7 770.9	5.1
Germany	1 052.6	4.3	Canada	6 185.3	4.0
Spain	970.5	3.9	Australia	6 118.9	4.0
Top 8	20 991.6	85.2	Top 8	12 2117.1	79.6
All	4 642.0	100.0	All	153 380.9	100.0

Notes:

[a] Bermuda was, in fact, ranked higher – sixth – but we have excluded the tax

[b] Of all developed country investment.

[c] Of all developing country investment.

[d] And Luxembourg.

Sources: UNCTC, *Transnational Corporations and World Development* (New York,
Competitiveness (New York and Geneva, UN 1995); UNCTAD, *World Investment*

In the years 1975–1980, the ten largest recipients of FDI identified in the above
for 68.8%. In the former period, Japan accounted for only 0.6% of all inflows into

of total inward FDI remains very small, the rate of growth of
investment directed to these countries over the last two decades has
been well above average.[13] On balance, however, there has been a
slight trend towards a more even geographical distribution of FDI. In
the case of developed countries, the standard deviation around the
mean amount of inbound FDI of $1265 million in the 1975–80 period
was $1995 million; and for developing countries around a mean of
$195 million, it was $354 million. The corresponding means and
standard deviation for the average annual amount of FDI in the
1990–94 period were $6609 million and $8848 million for developed
countries, and $950 million and $1335 for developing countries.

Explaining the changes in the geography of MNE activity

In explaining the changes in the geographical composition of FDI
over the last 20 years, it is worth first considering the main changes in

1990–1996 (annual averages)

Country	1975/80 $m	%[c]	Country	1990/96 $m	%[c]
		Developing Countries[a]			
Brazil	1 835.8	24.4	China	22 424.7	30.0
Mexico	1 023.5	13.5	Singapore	7 081.7	9.5
Malaysia	524.3	7.0	Mexico	5 622.1	7.5
Singapore	502.0	36.7	Malaysia	34 289.0	35.7
Egypt	376.1	5.0	Argentina	3 690.3	34.9
Iran	315.5	4.2	Brazil	3 222.7	4.3
Indonesia	289.9	3.8	Indonesia	2 842.6	3.8
Hong Kong	241.1	3.2	Thailand	2 179.9	2.9
Top 8	5 108.2	67.8	Top 8	51 353.0	68.7
All	7 539.1	100.0	All	74 777.6	100.0

haven from our rankings.

UN 1988); UNCTAD, *World Investment Report 1995: Transnational Corporations and Report 1998* (Geneva and New York: United Nations 1998).

table accounted for 74.1% of all FDI inflows, and in 1990–1994 they accounted developing countries; and in the latter for 1.0%.

the global political and economic scenario over this period. Although there is no clear watershed date which initiated the changes, the beginning of the administrations of Margaret Thatcher in the UK (in 1979) and Ronald Reagan in the US (in 1980) offers as good as a dividing line between the two eras of FDI as any other. As these changes are fairly well known, they are summarized in Table 2.3, which lists them sequentially, even though many of the changes are interdependent of each other. Overall the argument is that their combined effects on (a) the mobile competitive advantages of enterprises and (b) the immobile locational attractions of countries, have altered the organization and geography of MNE activity.

The changing value of firms' competitive advantages (O)

Prior to the late 1970s, the main competitive advantages possessed by the foreign affiliates of MNEs over their indigenous counterparts (some of which, themselves, were MNEs) were their privileged access

TABLE 2.3   Some Features of the Changing World Economic Scenario: Late 1970s to Mid-1990s

---

1. The renaissance of the market economy, as the predominant form of economic organization by most countries. Along with such renaissance has come the liberalization, deregulation and privatization of markets which have lowered the artificial or man-made costs of the movement of goods, services and assets.

2. In the light of 1, the reorientation of the macroeconomic and macro-organizational philosophies of national governments towards more market-enabling and less market-distorting policies – at least as far as wealth-creating activities are concerned.

3. The coming on-stream of a new generation of technological advances, and particularly those in telecommunications, which has hastened the trend towards knowledge-based capitalism; and which, for the most part, has lowered the costs of transversing space, and of assets, goods and people.

4. In the light of 1–3 above, the promotion of many regional economic schemes (notably the completion of the internal market in Europe, NAFTA, and ASEAN).

5. In the light of 1–4 above, the growing competition among firms – including firms of different nationalities. In a real sense, regional and global competition for resources and markets is replacing national competition – particularly in international industries

6. In the light of 1–5 above, firms have reorganized and restructured the range and composition of their value-added activities. Sometimes this has resulted in down-sizing and disinternalization of intermediate product markets; in other cases, it has prompted more mergers and acquisitions so that firms can better capture the benefits of economies of scale and scope; and acquire competitive-enhancing assets.

7. Partly as a consequence of 1–6, and the emergence of China, the newly industrializing countries (NICs) and some Central European economies, as important actors in the global market economy – each of which has different propensities both to be invested in – by foreign firms and to engage in outward foreign investment, the geography of FDI has undergone some major changes since the mid-1970s.

---

to specific intangible assets. In this chapter we use the letter 'O' to describe these 'competitive' or 'ownership' advantages which include the management and organization of a firm, its access to markets and its research and development.[14] For the most part, these core competencies of MNEs reflected the resource endowments of their home countries, rather than those of the host countries in which they operated. Few MNEs, at that time, practiced globally integrated production or marketing strategies, although, within the European Union, there was some product and process specialization, and some intra-firm trade, particularly among US affiliates. While the propensity of MNEs to increase the foreign component of their total value-added activities was leading to more sequential or efficiency-seeking FDI,[15] the majority of firms pursued multi-domestic strategies towards their global operations; and most foreign subsidiaries outside the resource-based and labour-intensive manufacturing sectors operated on a 'stand alone' basis and traded little with each other.

In the 1970s scenario, insofar as the geography of FDI reflected the distribution of the O-specific advantages among firms of different nationalities, these also tended to reflect the structure of the natural and created assets, and the markets, of their home countries. There is ample empirical evidence, both of the geography of outward FDI, and of that of recipient countries attracting inward FDI, to support this assertion.[16] Moreover, these same O-specific advantages help to explain at least some contemporary FDI – and particularly European and US FDI in Japan,[17] Japanese FDI in the US,[18] and that by Third World MNEs.[19]

Over the last two decades, the nature and character of the competitive advantages of MNEs has changed. In general, their country of ownership has become a less important determinant, and their degree of multinationality – which is a firm-specific variable – a more important one. Moreover, although part of the core-competencies of firms continues to be the exclusive or privileged possession of specific assets, it is the way in which these assets are governed and coordinated with the assets of other firms, and with the specific endowments of countries or regions in which they operate, which is increasingly driving the global strategy of MNEs, and the location of their various value added activities.

There are several benefits to the common governance of inter-related cross-border operations. These include lower transaction costs and greater coordinating benefits than those incurred or offered by external markets; and are particularly well demonstrated in the case of knowledge- or learning-based firms with multiple home bases.[20] It is these firms which are best positioned to benefit from the liberalization of markets and regional integration and to foster an international division of labour based not on the disposition of natural resources, but on that of created assets. The new geography of production has very different implications for the location of MNE activity. Earlier, determinants such as the quality and cost of natural resources and semi-skilled labour, are being replaced by factors such as the availability of a supportive and sophisticated physical and human infrastructure, and the ease of access to global markets.[21]

In, perhaps, no other area of value-added activity have the changing O-specific advantages of firms more affected the geography of FDI than that of research and development (R&D). Prior to the 1970s, there was comparatively little R&D – and particularly fundamental R&D – undertaken by MNEs outside their home countries.[22] Even where R&D was undertaken abroad, the predominant motive for foreign-based innovatory activity was to adapt home-based R&D and create peripheral products and processes – what Kuemmerle refers to as 'home-based exploiting R&D'.[23]

Over the last two decades, not only has the percentage of innovatory activity undertaken by MNEs outside their home countries risen sharply,[24] but the reasons for conducting such activity – at least in industrialized countries – have broadened to include both the creation of new core products and/or processes, and the acquisition of R&D facilities necessary to advance the productivity of domestic R&D or, as Kuemmerle puts it, to 'augment home-based R&D'.[25] Such a strategy has deep implications for investment patterns. Indeed, it suggests a more concentrated geographical pattern of FDI so as to take advantage of clusters of technological expertise and expense. Certainly, what little empirical evidence there is[26] supports this contention; and indicates that, in spite of the increase in the share of FDI directed to developing countries in recent years, the share of R&D activity so directed by MNEs may well have fallen.[27] This is not to say that MNEs are undertaking less R&D in developing countries, but rather that innovation-related FDI has not followed the same locational pattern as has that of other kinds of FDI.

The changing locational advantages of countries (L)

As MNE activity has widened and deepened (from market-seeking and natural-resource-seeking FDI to efficiency and strategic-asset-seeking FDI[28]) firms have had to reappraise their locational strategies. At the same time, world economic events have had a direct impact on the structure and character of the competitive advantages of countries.

In the 1970s, the locational advantages of countries lay primarily in their favoured possession of natural resources and unskilled or semi-skilled labour, and their ease of access to markets for finished products. These L-specific endowments attracted inbound foreign investors seeking to add value to their competitive (or mobile O-specific) advantages. Traditional location theory tended to classify the variables affecting the siting of foreign production into three groups, viz. those which were cost-related, revenue-related and profit-related.[29] Naturally, the advantages enjoyed by a particular country were also affected by government-imposed taxes or subsidies.[30]

In some sectors, and for rationalized (that is, efficiency-seeking) FDI, factors such as transaction costs and benefits were also of some importance; and particularly those which offered firms the opportunity to exploit the economies of scale and scope, and to capture the benefits of the common governance of related activities. Furthermore, in the high-technology and knowledge-intensive sectors, MNE affiliates, already well-established in host countries, were attracted more by knowledge-intensive labour than by low-cost labour. This was because knowledge-intensive labour added value to the O-specific assets being transferred from their home countries. The advantages were even greater where the affiliates were responsible for complete product lines of their own. These same firms also made stronger demands on the local physical infrastructure, especially transport and communications, and frequently valued the presence of sub-national clusters of value-added activities related to their own.

Over the last two decades, this latter type of FDI activity has become increasingly significant. In part this is due to the increasing multinationality of many foreign investors which has encouraged subsidiaries to engage in vertical or horizontal specialization. The change in investment pattern is also due to the elimination, or reduction, of distance-related transaction costs (see Chapter 6), especially between countries which are part of a customs union or free trade area, such as the European Union. The result is that the growth of intra-firm, intra-regional trade has well outpaced that of inter-firm inter-regional trade.[31] In the 1990s, FDI is determined less by the country-specific costs of factor endowments or size of local markets, and more by those variables which facilitate firm and/or plant economies of scale and scope;[32] and the effective exploitation of regional and/or global markets.

Most efficiency-seeking FDI in developing countries tends to be vertically integrated, with investors seeking locations which offer an adequate supply of cost-effective semi-skilled or skilled labour, a good physical infrastructure, government policies which are market-friendly, and minimal distance-related transaction costs. Further-more, 'clustering' may also offer a locational attraction, particularly in countries whose overall industrial base leaves something to be desired. 'Clustering' (or 'agglomeration economies'), first explicitly identified by Alfred Marshall (1920), enables the participating firms to draw upon a common infrastructure, a specialized pool of labour or customers, develop mutually beneficial relations with their suppli-ers, and learn from local producer associations and their competitors. Hence, the development of export-processing or free-trade zones, and the deliberate attempts by local or central governments to facilitate industrial districts of one kind or another.[33] Examples of such economic activity in developing countries abound.[34] They are parti-cularly numerous in those countries now attracting the bulk of new FDI in East Asia, – China, South Korea, Malaysia and Indonesia, and in Singapore, which, in effect, is a 'city-state'.

By contrast, most horizontally integrated FDI is concentrated in the advanced industrial economies; and it is in these economies – and particularly in some of the knowledge-intensive sectors – that one observes not only regional clusters of economic activity, but that FDI is especially drawn to these clusters. Again, there are many examples of recently formed clusters.[35] They include, in the US, an agglomera-tion of biotechnology and semiconductor firms in the Silicon Valley/ Bay area of California, and pharmaceutical and telecommunications firms in New Jersey; a range of high-technology firms along the M4 corridor in the UK (particularly between Slough and Swindon), and financial services in the City of London; and in Japan, the clustering of the prime R&D plants and semiconductor firms in the Tokyo or Osaka metropolitan regions.[36]

There has, however, been another reaction of firms to recent economic events – and particularly the liberalization of markets and technological advances – which has also affected FDI in indus-trial countries. That has been the dramatic increase in the number of cross-border mergers and acquisitions (M&As) and strategic alliances specifically aimed at protecting or enhancing the global profitability and/or market share of the participating firms. Between 1985 and 1996, for example, it is estimated that worldwide cross-border M&As accounted for around 55 per cent of FDI outflows; and nearly four-fifths of those between developed countries.[37] Similarly, the number of international inter-firm technology agreements concluded annually doubled between 1980–83 and 1992–96.[38]

In the 1990s, firms wishing to sustain or augment their existing competitive advantages will tend to acquire, or merge with, firms in other locations with a broadly similar, or more sophisticated, structure of natural and created assets. Certainly, this applies to M&As and alliances designed to strengthen or complement the technological base of investing companies, or to accelerate the innovating process. Such asset-seeking ventures, together with the desire for access to unfamiliar markets, have accounted for a great majority of all cross-border liaisons in recent years.[39]

By contrast, in the newly emerging markets, notably China, wholly- or jointly-owned 'greenfield' ventures have been the main mode of entry by MNEs. According to UNCTAD, over the last decade only one-fifth of cross-border M&As activities took place in developing countries; although this ratio is now sharply increasing.[40] Indeed, one suspects – although there are few hard facts to support this suspicion – there has been more strategic-asset-seeking FDI by Korean, Taiwanese, Malaysian, Thai and Brazilian firms in Europe and the US than there has been of European and US MNEs in Asia or Latin America; and that this has been particularly the case in the first part of the 1990s.

Some changes in the modality of organizing the competitive advantages of firms

Finally, this section of the chapter briefly considers the extent to which the geography of FDI may have been affected by changes in the modes by which firms arrange their cross-border activities. It is argued that FDI as a vehicle for both exploiting and augmenting O-specific advantages has continued to rise in significance. However, the impact of new ways to coordinate firms' advantages has had much less impact. Recall that firms can coordinate their mobile O-specific advantages and the immobile location advantages of particular countries by choosing to buy or sell assets, or rights to assets through intermediate product markets and/or network relationships, or alternatively firms can internalize the market for these assets or rights. It is not clear, however, that these modalities are having much impact on the geography of the value-added activity of firms.[41] This is probably due to the much more relaxed attitude to the foreign ownership of domestic assets in other parts of the world, notably in the erstwhile socialist regimes and several Asian and Latin American countries – for example, Malaysia, Korea, Mexico and Chile. At the same time, the trend towards a reduction of intra-regional barriers to trade, and more integrated cross-border production networks – particularly by Japanese and other Asian MNEs in South and East Asia and by US MNEs in Latin America – is further accelerating the pace of FDI in these parts of the world. A summary of the suggested explanations for recent changes in the geography of FDI is presented in Table 2.4 (these conclusions have not as yet been subject to any formal statistical testing).

Some country, sectoral and firms-specific factors affecting the geography of FDI

There are some changes in the geography of FDI over this period which can be explained by a variety of firm-specific structural and strategic-related variables. For example, the share of China of in-bound FDI has increased because one of the major source countries – Hong Kong (which was still under British as opposed to Chinese rule over this period) – had increased its FDI in China relative to that of other countries. Similarly, where high-value banking and financial services are primarily located in advanced industrial countries, and MNE activity in such services is growing relative to that in other sectors, then, ceteris paribus, one would expect the geography of FDI as a whole to favour those countries. Developing countries, on the other hand, appear to be the main recipients of capital inflows arising from privatization schemes and a revival of interest by foreign firms in infra-structural development projects.[42]

Below, this chapter considers three kinds of changes which have affected the spatial distribution of FDI over the past two decades: the changing structure of capital-exporting countries; the changing composition of MNE advantages; and the changing characteristics and strategy of the leading MNEs.

The structure of source countries

As Table 2.5 shows, the main change in the geographical composition of the stock of outward direct investment between 1973 and the early 1996 was a 23.2 percentage point drop in the share of the US, which contrasted with a 3.4 percentage point increase in the share of Japan, an 11.2 percentage point increase in that of Western Europe and

TABLE 2.4 **The New Geography of FDI: Some Suggested Explanations Couched in Terms of the Changing OLI Configurations Facing Investing Firms**

	1975–80	*1990–96*
O advantages (of firms)	• Those associated with the possession of, or privileged access to, country-specific intangible assets, viz. technology, trademarks, managerial expertise, entrepreneurship; and access to factor, intermediate product or final goods markets	• Those associated with multinationality *per se* (Ot) • Organizational learning, and ability to seek out and exploit complementary assets • Ability to achieve an optimum portfolio of assets and to combine own O advantages with L-specific endowments of foreign countries

L advantages (of countries)	• Traditional L specific variables related to
	  i. domestic factor costs,
	  ii. market-size and growth, and
	  iii. transport costs and tariff or other economic and psychic barriers
	• Government imposed incentives or obstacles to FDI, including performance requirements.
	• A market facilitating macro-economic and/or macro-organizational environment offered by host governments.
	• A stable political and economic regime.
		• The provision of location-bound resources and capabilities which help firms both to exploit and to augment their existing competitive advantages
		• The continual upgrading of location bound assets so as to promote increasingly high-value FDI

I advantages (of firms)	• Those arising from the imperfect markets for specific intangible assets; and from learning experiences and governance of interrelated value-added activities, mainly in the domestic market.	• Those arising from the ownership and/or control of inter-related activities in different geographical areas. These include spreading of political and environmental risks, and the holistic integration of disparate functions and strategies

TABLE 2.5 Stocks of Foreign Direct Investment by Major Home Countries and Regions 1973–96 (US$ billions)

	1973		1980		1990		1996	
Developed Economies	205.0	98.5	508.0	98.8	1614.6	95.9	2830.9	90.9
Western Europe	82.6	39.7	236.6	46.0	853.9	50.7	1584.8	50.9
of which: UK	27.5	13.2	80.4	15.6	230.8	13.7	355.1	11.4
France	8.8	4.2	23.6	4.6	110.1	6.5	202.2	6.5
Germany	11.9	5.7	43.1	8.4	151.6	9.0	291.7	9.4
Italy	3.2	1.5	7.3	1.4	56.1	3.3	107.5	**3.5**
Netherlands	15.8	7.6	42.1	8.2	109.1	**6.5**	**192.8**	**6.2**
Sweden	3.0	1.4	5.6	1.1	49.5	2.9	70.9	2.3
Switzerland	7.1	3.4	21.5	4.2	65.7	3.9	144.7	4.6
Other	5.5	2.6	13.0	2.5	81.0	4.8	173.4	5.6
North America	109.1	52.4	242.8	47.2	514.1	30.5	917.7	29.5
of which: US	101.3	48.7	220.2	42.8	435.2	25.8	793.0	25.5
Canada	7.8	3.7	22.6	4.4	78.9	4.7	124.7	4.0
Japan	10.3	4.9	19.6	3.8	204.7	12.2	258.6	8.3
Other Developed Countries	2.9	0.4	6.8	1.3	41.9	2.5	69.8	2.2
of which: Australia	1.0	0.5	2.3	0.4	30.1	1.8	46.0	1.5
Developing Economies	3.0[a]	1.4	6.1	1.2	69.4	4.1	281.6	9.0
Central and Eastern Europe	neg.	neg.	0.1	neg.	0.2	neg.	3.3	0.1
Total	208.1	100.0	514.2	100.0	1684.1	100.0	3115.8	100.0

Note:
Neg. = negligible
[a] Calculated by deducting FDI outflows 1974–1979 from 1980 stock data (UNCTC, 1988).

Sources: UNCTC *Transnational Corporations and World Development* (New York, UN 1988); UNCTAD, *World Investment Report 1988* (Geneva and New York: United Nations 1998).

other developed market economies, and a 7.6 percentage point increase in that of developing countries. Of the other developed countries, most increased their share of outbound FDI – and France, Germany, Italy, Australia, Spain and Belgium substantially so – but a few, notably the Netherlands, South Africa and the UK decreased theirs.

Two questions now arise. The first is: how does FDI from countries whose overall share has increased differ from the FDI of countries whose overall share has decreased? The second question is: how far has this difference influenced the overall geography of FDI between 1975–80 and 1990–96?

Table 2.6 sets out some details on the geography of FDI of Western Europe, Japan and the US[43] for the latter half of the 1970s and for the first six years of the 1990s. What do they show? First, in both periods, they depict some major differences in the geography of FDI of the three regions or countries. Between 1975 and 1980, Japanese MNEs directed a considerably higher proportion of their investments to developing countries, and especially Asia, than did their European or US counterparts; by contrast, their share of the increased stock of FDI in Western Europe was less than one-quarter of that of either US or European firms.[44]

Second, and perhaps more interestingly, one observes very different changes in the geography of FDI of the three major investors since the late 1970s While Japanese MNEs have increased their foreign activities most sharply in the developed countries (and particularly in the US in the 1980s and Europe in the 1990s), US MNEs have reoriented their interests away from other developed countries. European investors, on the other hand, have been increasingly attracted to locations nearer home, especially since the initiation of the Internal Market Program of the European Union.[45] Although not documented in Table 2.6, there was also a reorientation of FDI by Third World countries away from other developing countries – towards the advanced industrialized countries, in the 1980s;[46] but in the 1990s, other developing countries, and especially China, have absorbed the great bulk of such investment.[47]

Third, when comparing the spatial distribution of FDI of the three regions with that of all countries, it needs to be appreciated that the relative weight of the three regions as sources of FDI has shifted. As Table 2.5 has shown, taken as a group, Western Europe, Japan and the developing countries have increased their share of all FDI. Since

TABLE 2.6 Geographical Distribution of Changes in Outward FDI Stock 1975–80 and FDI Flows 1990–96 USA, Western Europe and Japan

	1975–80				1990–96			
	USA	Western Europe[a]	Japan	All Countries[b]	USA	Western Europe[f]	Japan	All Countries[b]
Developed Countries	78.2	81.1	45.7	76.6	63.1	62.8	65.5	77.2
Western Europe	48.4	40.7	39.2	43.1	49.2	45.7	15.5	8.5
(of which UK)	15.9	n.a.	n.a.	16.9	–16.9	–5.7	–7.0	–9.4
North America	20.4	32.8[c]	26.9[c]	327.2	7.9	15.4	46.3	20.3
(of which USA)	–	–32.8	–26.9	–24.5	–	–14.2	–44.7	–18.1
Japan	3.0	0.7	–	0.5	1.6	0.5	–	4.4
Other developed countries	6.4	13.7[d]	9.6[d]	5.7	4.5	1.1	3.7	7.0
(of which Australia and New Zealand)	–3.4	–10.5	neg.	–3.9	–4.3	–0.9	–3.5	–2.6
Developing Countries	21.8	18.9	53.9	23.4	5.9	6.8	4.2	1.5
Asia	2.8	6.3	27.7	6.2	9.8	2.1	24.0	15.2
(of which China)	–neg.	–neg.	–neg.	–neg.	–1.0	–0.2	–6.8	–5.1
Latin America	14.1	7.7	15.4	12.5	22.8	12.5	38.4	35.2
Africa	n.a.	n.a.	n.a.	2.5	30.3	30.7	0.4	0.9
Other	4.9[e]	4.8[e]	10.8[e]	2.2	3.0	6.1	1.4	30.1
Central & Eastern Europe	neg.	0.1	0.3	neg.	1.0	0.5	0.2	1.4
Total	100.0	100.0	100.0	100.0	100.0	100.0	100.0	100.0
[Share of each region in total FI stock 1980 and 1996]	[42.0]	[45.0]	[3.7]	[100.0]	[25.4]	[50.9]	[8.3]	[100.0]

Sources: 1975–80 – changes in both stocks: UNCTC, *Transnational Corporations.* 1990–94 FDI flows: OECD, *International Direct Investment.*

Notes to Table 2.6:

^a UK, Germany and the Netherlands in 1980 accounted for between 70% and 75% of the total Western European outward FDI stock. The UK data are for 1974–1980 and the German data are for 1976–1980.

^b FDI flows of all countries for both periods. These data are not directly comparable with changes in stock data, and occasionally anomalies occur, e.g. as in the case of the Japanese data, where the US Department of Commerce estimates of changes in stock are considerably in excess of those derived by the IMF from Japanese balance of payments accounts.

^c US data.

^d Including Canada.

^e Including Africa and unallocated.

^f For UK, Germany, France, Italy, Netherlands, Switzerland and Sweden which accounted for 79.3% of the Western European outward FDI stock in 1996.

neg. = negligible

n.a. = not applicable

in both periods, Japan and the Asian developing countries directed a much greater proportion of their FDI to other Asian countries, it is not surprising that the percentage of total FDI going to Asian developing countries – and China in particular – has risen so sharply. On the other hand, as the structure of the Japanese economy has moved closer to that of the leading European economies over the last two decades, so the industrial composition of its FDI has changed.[48] Japanese FDI has favoured the advanced industrial countries as a location for both production and pre-production (that is, R&D) activities.

In conclusion, the data set out in Tables 2.5 and 2.6 suggest that the changing composition of total FDI reflects the changing geography of the leading source countries or regions, and their significance as foreign direct investors. Yet, to quite a large extent, these changes have cancelled themselves out. Thus, while Japanese investors have focused more attention on Europe and the US, US investors have been more attracted to the developing economies. Western European investors have continued to favour other industrialized nations, but some of the earlier appeal of the US has lessened, particularly since 1989. And, while China has emerged as one of the three top recipients of FDI since 1990, the greater part of this inflow has originated, not from First World MNEs, but from Chinese ethnic communities elsewhere in East Asia.

The industrial composition of MNE activity

As the previous paragraphs imply, patterns of Western European, US and Japanese MNE activity are, at least partly, due to the comparative resource endowments and market conditions of their home countries. Until very recently,[49] most scholars have opined that FDI is likely to be concentrated in sectors characterized by some combination of three features. These include:

(i)   capital and/or knowledge intensity;
(ii)   product differentiation; and
(iii)   the provision of services which, are supportive of other kinds of FDI, or information intensive, 'or are 'branded' in some way or another.

For much of the postwar period, the growth of FDI has been concentrated in these sectors – notably oil, autos, electronics and electrical equipment, office machinery, pharmaceuticals, packaged foods, banking and finance, business consultancies and trade-related services; and indeed until the late 1980s, the share of the sales of foreign affiliates to the global sales of MNEs in these sectors continued to rise. It is thus understandable that countries which display a dynamic comparative advantage in those activities have recorded the largest rise in their inbound FDI.

At the same time, over the last 20 years, a series of critical technological and organizational advances have affected not only the sectoral pattern of economic activity, but also the very system within which the production of goods and services takes place. The new production system is sometimes referred to as 'Toyota'ism' and describes a more flexible, lean and so-called 'organcentric' mode of production which scholars distinguish from the previous system of 'Fordism' or machine-centred, large-scale mass production.[50] These changes in systems of production, coupled with the growing porosity of national boundaries, the increasingly generic and non-specific nature of many innovations, and the convergence of learning capabilities among networking firms, tends to blur the distinction between economic activities likely to be trade- or FDI-intensive, and those which are not.

So far, these changes, which have been largely concentrated in the advanced industrial economies, have had only a limited effect on the geography of FDI. But, comparing the period 1990–96 with that of 1975–80, two important developments are evident. The first is the extension of the cross-border vertical division of labour to embrace higher-value activities, and to take advantage of speedier, more efficient and less costly transportation and communication networks. The contemporary textile and clothing industry is an excellent example of a sector which has embraced a wide range of cross-border organizational arrangements, the success of which rests on the application of the latest technological advances – for example, in computer-aided design and manufacturing techniques; in the near-instantaneous transfer of information, such as designs, specifications, process technologies and marketing schedules, by use of the internet, fax or e-mail. Other traditional sectors, such as building and con-struction, are also being upgraded and becoming more FDI-inten-sive. At the same time, the liberalization of markets and privatization schemes and the increasing tradability of many services[51] are resur-recting FDI as a delivery mode for a whole range of infrastructural products, notably telecommunications and public utilities, as well as those which were previously tightly regulated – such as banking and financial services, insurance and some professional services.

The second important development of the last decade is the growing significance of intermediate and final services to foreign direct investors. In 1980, for example, 39 per cent of the total FDI stock by US MNEs was in the tertiary sector, and 49 per cent in the manufacturing sector; and the corresponding percentages for (the leading) European and Japanese MNEs were 40 per cent and 37 per cent, and 47 per cent and 34 per cent, respectively. By 1996, the percentages of all FDI accounted for by the tertiary sector had risen to 54 per cent in the case of the US firms, 51 per cent in the case of European firms, and 66 per cent in the case of Japanese firms;[52] and, that of manufacturing had fallen to 35 per cent, 49 per cent and 27 per cent, respectively.[53] On average, between 1980 and 1995, services accounted for a little over three-fifths of all new MNE activity; and if one was also to include the services component of the goods produced in the manufacturing sector – and particularly knowledge-intensive goods – this proportion would probably rise to two-thirds, or even higher in the case of US MNE activity.

Statistical data on the geography of FDI in services are extremely patchy. We do know, however that the strongest growth in MNE activity in services over the last 20 years has been among the so-called

'Triad' nations (the European Union, the United States and Japan). In the case of the country attracting the largest amount of FDI over this period (that is, the US), the share of the increase in the FDI stock directed to the tertiary (or services-related) sector between 1986 and 1997 was 53 per cent.[54] Most of these new capital imports were from Western Europe and Japan; and they comprised both M&As and greenfield investments. Indeed, apart from in a few manufacturing sectors – notably autos and consumer electronics and electrical goods – Japanese MNEs have concentrated their foreign activities in financial, trading and transportation services and real estate.[55] Between 1986 and 1994, no less than 72 per cent of the increase in the FDI stock of Japanese firms was directed to the tertiary sector.[56] In the EU too, over the last decade, the share of intra- and extra-EU FDI in services – particularly high-value services – has increased quite dramatically.

In many developing countries, too, the growth of inbound tertiary (services sector) FDI has outpaced that of manufacturing FDI.[57] However, unlike services-related MNE activity in the developed countries (apart from that of first-time investors) much of that attracted to the developing world has taken the form of trade-enhancing activities, or infrastructural investment, both of which are frequently a prelude to FDI in the primary or secondary sectors. Thus, for example, since the late 1980s, in China and parts of Latin America, FDI inflows have been increasingly directed to privatization schemes in such services as electric power, telecommunications, hotels, and building and construction. Recent deregulation of some public utilities and parts of the financial services sector in India seems set to open the door to more services-related MNE activity in that country.

In conclusion, while the implementation of new production systems and the move towards knowledge-based capitalism in the advanced industrial economies is reorienting the locational preferences of MNEs towards these economies, the emergence of powerful new nations in the Third World, and the liberalization and privatization of the markets for infrastructure and trade-supporting services is resulting in a counteracting shift in the location of FDI towards the middle- and lower-income economies. At the moment, the net effect of these forces is favouring the industrialized countries, although one suspects that the current trend could well be reversed if, and when, the Third World countries increase their share of the world's output.

The changing profile of the leading MNEs

The third contextual variable likely to influence the geography of
FDI is that of the distinctive characteristics of the MNEs. Such
characteristics are of two main kinds. First, there are the structural
attributes of firms – their age, size, degree of multinationality,
product range, innovating capabilities, degree of vertical integration
and so on. Second, there are the strategic actions or reactions of firms
towards the ownership and management of their core competencies,
and the location of the value-added activities arising from, .or
associated with, these.

Because of space constraints, this section will offer a few carefully
selected facts about the geography of FDI of particular firms, and
some speculation about the reasons for them, and the extent to which
they might help explain the data set out in earlier tables. In order to
control – as best as we can – for (source) country and sector
differences, the analysis is limited to just six sectors: oil refining, food
products, chemicals, electronics, computers and autos. In respect of
the first two sectors, the FDI profile of US and European MNEs shall
be considered. In respect of the the third sector, European MNEs; the
fourth sector, Japanese and European MNEs; the fifth, US MNEs;
and the sixth, MNEs from the US, Europe and Japan. Table 2.7 sets
out the details using an index of multinationality devised by UN-
CTAD.[58]

Table 2.7 presents a mixed picture. Take first, the degree of
multinationality of US firms in 1996. In the petroleum sector, the
index varies from 23.4 per cent to 72.7 per cent, but there is a high
correlation between the degree of multinationality and size of enterprise (one of the structural variables earlier identified). The same is
true of the three top US auto producers, although the variation in the
degree of multinationality is somewhat less. In the food products and
computer sectors, the degree of multinationality does not seem to be
size-related; rather, in this instance, one suspects it is the distinctive
strategy of the firms – and particularly that of the chief executives of
the firms towards foreign markets, which is the more important
explanation. The multinationality index for European firms in food
products, chemicals and electronics sectors shows a fairly uniform
pattern, but here the size (that is, the population) of the investing
country enters into the picture. In the chemicals sector, for example,
Solvay, a Belgian firm and AKCO, a Dutch firm, exhibit well above

the average multinationality ratio of the eight firms considered; while, in the electronics sector, Philips, from the Netherlands, and ABB (Asea Brown Boveri, a Swiss/Swedish firm), exhibit very high ratios indeed. More generally, normalizing for size of country, the UNCTAD data show a positive correlation between size of firm and degree of multinationality; while, in Western Europe, normalizing for size of firm, there is a negative correlation between size of country and degree of multinationality.

The multinationality of Japanese firms partly reflects their lateness in the internalization process; and partly that their average size (in 1996) was generally smaller than that of their European and US counterparts. Apart from Sony, all the Japanese electronics MNEs recorded lower indices of multinationality than their European competitors. In the auto industry, however, each of the Japanese producers registered average or above-average degrees of multinationality compared to those of their US or European rivals.

Since the late 1970s, the growing significance of the foreign operations of the world's leading 100 industrial MNEs has largely mirrored that of the countries and sectors of which they are part. That of the Japanese firms has expanded the most (admittedly from a very low base), followed by that of Western European firms – and particularly those from Germany and France. On average, the degree of multinationality of US MNEs has changed very little – hovering around the 30 per cent level.[59]

However, within countries and sectors, some firms stand out above others in the aggressiveness with which they pursue their FDI strategies. Of those listed in Table 2.7, those worthy of especial mention (their names are printed in italics) include the (relatively) smaller US oil refining companies Amoco and Atlantic Richfield; Volkswagen, Volvo, Bosch and BMW among the European auto companies; Hoechst, Rhone Poulenc, BASF and Bayer among the European chemical companies; ABB and Siemens among the European electronics companies; and Matsushita, Sony and Toshiba among the Japanese electronics companies. In other sectors, Digital and IBM (US – computers), Philip Morris (US – tobacco), Glaxo (UK – pharmaceuticals), Grand Metropolitan (UK – food products) and Sara Lee (US – food products) each recorded substantial increases in their foreign participation ratios. It is, perhaps, worth observing that the growth in these ratios has been accomplished both by purchases of existing foreign firms – for instance, Grand Metropolitan's acquisition of General Mills in the US, and the merger between Asea and Brown Boveri to form ABB; and by aggressive 'greenfield' investments – those undertaken by IBM, BMW and the Japanese electronics and auto companies in Europe and the US.

By contrast, in the case of those firms in bold print in Table 2.7, the index of multinationality has either declined or not kept pace with the average of the sector of which they are part. As far as MNEs from small countries are concerned – Sandoz, Ciba Geigy, and Nestlé (Switzerland), Philips of Eindhoven (the Netherlands) and Solvay (Belgium), this is because the foreign component of their operations was already very substantial in the early 1980s. Other MNEs have refocused their attention on their domestic markets. For example, faced by intensive competition from their Japanese counterparts, US auto MNEs – and especially Ford and GM – completely reconfigured their domestic production systems in the late 1980s and early 1990s, and have since regained much of the US market they lost in earlier years. Domestic mergers and acquisitions have had an ambivalent effect, depending on the geography of the acquired firm's investment. Among the leading 100 MNEs whose index of multinationality has fallen, or has not kept pace with the average for their sector for this reason, are BAT Industries (UK – tobacco, cosmetics and insurance), AT&T (US – telecommunications, equipment and services), Xerox (US – scientific and photographic equipment) and RTR Nabisco (US – food and tobacco products).

What now of the consequences of these shifts in firms' FDI profiles on the geography of FDI? Data constraints enable us to perform only the most superficial exercise. However, by comparing changes in the geography of the sales, assets or employment of firms according to the extent to which they had increased their index of multinationality in particular sectors and countries, we can gain a hint of the contribution of firm-specific factors to the changing spatial distribution of FDI.

Data is taken from the 1980 and 1992 editions of the World Directory of MNEs[60] in order to calculate – insofar as the data allowed – the average rates of FDI growth for two groups of firms, in each of the main regions of the world. To obtain the two groups, we simply divided the total number of firms into two and took the top and bottom growers in each industry/country sub-group.

The results of the exercise were somewhat inconclusive. While there is some suggestion that the MNEs with above-average rates of

TABLE 2.7 A Selection of the Largest MNEs, Classified by Sector, Country, Size[a] and Index of Multinationality[b] (IM) 1985 and 1996

Petroleum Refining

		IM 1985	1996
(a) US			
Exxon	(4)	59.0	72.7
Mobil	(10)	57.2	62.3
Chevron[d]	(45)	n.a.	35.3
Texaco	**(51)**	**42.6**	**44.6**
Amoco	*(66)*	*16.8*	*25.5*
Atlantic Richfield	*(93)*	*5.0*	*23.4*
(b) European			
(UK/N) Royal Dutch Shell	(2)	60.0	66.6
(F) Elf Aquitaine	*(13)*	*43.0*	*56.6*
(UK) BP	(25)	66.3	75.8
(I) ENI	(27)	n.a.	63.8
(F) Total	(29)	n.a.	33.5

Food Products

		IM 1985	1996
(a) US			
Philip Morris	(28)	28.0	47.8
Pepsico	**(88)**	**29.8**	**30.4**
Sara Lee (1995)	(90)	26.3	51.7
RJR Nabisco (1995)	**(90)**	**31.9**	**34.4**
(b) European			
Nestlé	**(11)**	**98.0**	**95.3**
(UK/N) Unilever	(18)	n.a.	87.1
(UK) Grand Metropolitan	*(69)*	*38.0*	*76.2*

Chemicals

		IM 1985	1996
(a) European			
(G) *Bayer*	*(14)*	*50.0*	*79.9*
(G) *Hoechst*	*(15)*	*41.5*	*65.6*
(F) *Rhone Poulenc*	*(33)*	*32.9*	*67.4*
(C) **Ciba Geigy (1995)**	**(38)**	**66.5**	**58.2**
(G) *BASF*	*(35)*	*30.2*	*59.2*
(B) *Solvay*	*(83)*	*89.5*	*92.2*
(N) *Akco*	*(79)*	*5.0*	*73.2*
(Ny) Norsk Hydro (1994)	**(99)**	**73.6**	**43.5**

Electronics

		IM	
		1985	1996
(a) Japanese			
Matsushita	*(53)*	*5.5*	*28.3*
Sony	*(24)*	*20.7*	*60.5*
Hitachi	*(60)*	*15.0*	*20.0*
Toshiba	*(91)*	*6.0*	*24.0*
NEC (1995)	*(93)*	*7.5*	*18.6*
(b) European		1985	1996
(S) ABB[c]	*(12)*	*60.0*	*96.1*
(F) Alcatel Alsthom	*(23)*	*n.a.*	*62.9*
(N) Philips	**(20)**	**93.6**	**84.9**
(G) Siemens	*(22)*	*28.0*	*50.4*

Computers

		IB	
		1985	1996
(a) US			
IBM	(6)	41.5	54.3
Hewlett Packard	(41)	37.1	50.0
Digital (1994)	*(81)*	*38.0*	*57.2*

Autos

		IM	
		1985	1996
(a) US			
Ford	**(3)**	**41.0**	**37.7**
General Motors	**(5)**	**30.8**	**30.3**
Chrysler	(80)	16.0	16.3
(b) European		1985	1996
Volkswagen	*(8)*	*29.0*	*55.3*
Daimler Benz	*(19)*	*21.0*	*41.9*
Fiat	*(17)*	*25.0*	*38.2*
Renault	**(30)**	**31.8**	**43.2**
Volvo	*(67)*	*38.0*	*58.5*
Bosch	*(47)*	*25.0*	*62.4*
BMW	*(37)*	*15.0*	*59.1*
(c) Japan			
Toyota	*(7)*	*12.5*	*35.0*
Nissan	(16)	n.a.	50.4
Honda	*(36)*	*21.1*	*56.6*

Notes:

Italic: above average growth of IM. Bold: below average growth of IM. Plain text: around average growth of IM.

[a] Ranked (by size of foreign assets) of the 100 leading MNEs.

[b] Defined as the average of the percentage of global assets, sales and employment of MNEs accounted for by their foreign affiliates.

[c] Asea and Brown Boveri.

[d] Previously Standard Oil of California.

European country codes: B, Belgium; F, France; G, Germany; I, Italy; N, Netherlands; Ny, Norway; S, Sweden; C, Switzerland; UK, United Kingdom.

growth grew relatively faster in Europe and North America than MNEs with below-average rates of growth, this was not so in the case in developing countries; indeed, in Asia, the slower growing MNEs increased their share of total MNE activity.[61] However, since the number of sample observations was only very small (56), we believe more broader based research is necessary before any reasonable conclusions can be drawn about the role of firm-specific factors in influencing the changing geography of FDI.

Conclusion

The principal objective of this chapter has been to describe and offer some explanations for the changing geography of FDI between the second half of the 1970s and the first five years of the 1990s. The two periods were chosen to reflect the years immediately preceding the introduction of a series of critical and far-reaching economic, political and technological events; and those after the most dramatic of these events – such as the collapse of the command economic system of the Central and Eastern European economies – came into effect.

Our conclusions may be classified into two groups: first, those relating to the facts; and second, those relating to the explanation of the facts. In respect of the facts, the main changes in the geography of the leading investing regions or countries between 1975–80 and 1990–96 are, first, the emergence of China as the second largest recipient of FDI. This surge of inbound FDI to the Peoples Republic explains a large part of new MNE activity directed to the developing countries since the late 1970s. Second, and more significant than the changing share of North/South FDI flows, have been the changes in the distribution of North/North, and North/South flows. Thus, Western Europe – and, in particular, France and Spain – have gained as FDI recipients at the expense of Canada and the US; while the newly industrializing countries of South and East Asia have become more attractive locales relative to most countries in Latin America. Third, while Africa continues to be of marginal interest to foreign investors, Central and Eastern Europe, and especially the Visegràd countries,[62] have begun to emerge as quite important recipients. Fourth, some of the traditional resource-based recipients of FDI, viz. Canada and Australia, have lost ground to the faster growing industrialized countries. Fifth, inward FDI going to Japan has increased only marginally over the last two decades. Sixth, there has been a slight fall in the geographical concentration of FDI among developed countries; and a slight rise of that among developing countries. However, excluding China, there has been a sharp reduction in the concentration of FDI among developing countries.

In explaining these facts, five main factors have been highlighted. First, changes in the geography of FDI, and/or the degree of multi-nationality of the investing firms, can usefully be explained by viewing the impact of global political and economic events on the configuration of OLI advantages facing foreign investors or potential foreign investors. These events were identified in the first section of this chapter. It was then concluded that both the core competencies of firms and the locational advantages of countries had undergone a number of profound changes (as summarized in Table 2.4); as, indeed, had the organizational modalities by which firms spatially reconfigured the creation and usage of their core competencies. The chapter highlighted the rising importance of asset acquiring or augmenting FDI, particularly among 'Triad' countries; and of the need of firms to site their foreign activities in countries and/or regions which offered the quantity and quality of locational assets which best complemented their ownership-specific advantages. These develop-ments have affected the geography of FDI in as much as firms increasingly favour locations which offer a range of facilities – the nature of which will vary to the type of value-added activity under-taken by MNEs, and particularly its technological and knowledge intensity.

A second set of factors affecting the geography of FDI include the composition of the countries of origin, the nature of the economic activities undertaken, and the structure and strategies of the partici-pating firms. Between 1975–80 and 1990–96, the most significant growth in outward FDI was recorded by MNEs from Japan and from Third World countries (especially from ethnic Chinese communities). By contrast, the US MNEs achieved only a modest growth in their foreign activities. Since, as Table 2.3 shows, the geography of FDI by the faster and slower growers was quite different, especially within the developing economies, it is clear that part of the changes in its distribution can be put down to the differential rate of growth of the leading outward investors. A good case in point is China where three-quarters of the inward FDI over the past 15 years has origi-nated from other Asian countries. By contrast, the decreasing share of

US-owned MNE activity has meant a fall in the share of the total FDI directed to Latin America – an area in which US firms tend to invest more than those of MNEs from other countries.

A third factor affecting FDI is the sectoral composition of economic activity. However, these changes have had a more ambiguous affect on the geography of FDI. On the one hand, the growth of the technology and knowledge-intensive sectors and high-value-service sectors have encouraged more FDI in the most advanced economies. On the other hand, the liberalization of many infrastructural service sectors, and the need of fast-growing emerging economies for re-source-based and/or market-seeking FDI has revitalized Heckscher-Ohlin type investment flows. We also discussed some of the (no less ambiguous) implications of the relatively faster growth in services FDI for the geography of FDI; and also those of the trend towards more flexible production systems, which favour the growth of small and medium-size MNEs, and also the upgrading of both manufacturing and service activities in developing countries.

Finally, the chapter took a brief look at the implications for the geography of FDI of the different rates of growth of some of the leading MNEs from six industries and three groups of investing countries (or regions). While no satisfactory comprehensive explanation of the changing locational strategies of the faster-growing MNEs was offered, we concluded that: first, the larger firms of the leading 100 industrial MNEs generally demonstrated a higher index of multinationality than their smaller counterparts; and second, that firms with the lower indices of multinationality in 1980 tended to record higher-than-average rates of FDI growth over the following decade. Both of these facts tend to support the earlier proposition that the strategic response of MNEs to the emerging global economy has been increasingly to integrate their sourcing value-added and marketing activities, and to harness their resources and capabilities from throughout the world.

Notes

1. Throughout this chapter, FDI stocks or flows are used as proxies for the value added activities of firms which own or control such activities outside their national boundaries (i.e. MNEs). Though an imperfect measure of these activities, the FDI data, published by all the major countries in the world, are broadly comparable. This is not the case with other data, sales, net output or employment.

2. 1996 is the latest year for which detailed data on FDI stock and flows are available at the time of writing. These do not fully take into account the effects of the East Asian crisis nor the problems of the Russian economy. However, preliminary data for 1997 suggest that FDI inflows to South East and South Asia were 6.2% higher than those for 1996, which in turn were 16.6% above those for 1995. By contrast, foreign portfolio capital inflows dropped dramatically; indeed there was a net exodus of capital from the region in 1997. FDI outflows from the region in 1997 were also about marginally higher than those in 1996 ($50.2 billion cf. $47.4 billion). Rather surprisingly, FDI inflows into the Russian Federation more than doubled from $2.5 billion to $6.2 billion in 1997: UNCTAD, *World Investment Report 1998* (Geneva: United Nations, 1998).

3. The OLI configuration, explaining the extent and pattern of the foreign value-added activities was first put forward by the author in the mid-1970s. For a recent exposition of the eclectic paradigm of international production. See John H. Dunning, 'Reappraising the Eclectic Paradigm in the Age of Alliance Capitalism', *Journal of International Business Studies* 26:3 (1995) 461–91; John H. Dunning, *The Eclectic Paradigm as an Envelope for Economic and Strategic Theories of MNE Activity* (Newark, US and Reading, UK: mimeo, 1999).

4. Of course, there are other modalities than FDI in promoting the cross-border mobility of goods, services and assets. Indeed, it is likely – though this is very difficult to quantify- that non-equity strategic alliances and networking have become increasingly important vehicles for the transfer of assets, particularly intangible assets, over the past two decades. See particularly, in this connection, the work of John Hagedoorn and his colleagues at MERIT and the University of Limburg.

5. Dunning, 'Reappraising the eclectic paradigm' and *The Eclectic Paradigm*.

6. These latter I have termed strategic asset acquiring advantages: John H. Dunning, *Multinational Enterprises and the Global Economy* (Wokingham, UK: Addison Wesley, 1993). In the last decade, FDI of this kind – particularly that by firms investing in advanced industrialized countries by way of mergers and acquisitions – has become one of the dominant factors affecting the geography of FDI.

7. For further details, see the next section and also M. Kenney and R. Florida, 'The Organization and Geography of Japanese R&D: Results from a Survey of Japanese Electronics and Biotechnology Firms', *Research Policy* 23 (1993) 305–23; and M. Kenney, and R. Florida, 'The Globalization of Japanese R&D: the Economic Geography of Japanese R&D Investment in the US', *Economic Geography*, 70 (1994) 344–69.

8. The former period was chosen as this was immediately prior to the wave of liberalizing markets, and the current generation of technological advances.

9. See, for example, IMF, *Balance of Payments Yearbook* (Summary Tables) (Washington, DC; International Monetary Fund, various dates); and UNCTAD, *World Investment Report 1996, Transnational Corporations, Investment, Trade and International Arrangements* (Geneva: United Nations, 1996).

10. Previously called the European Community. The composition of the EU is taken to be that existing on 1 January 1995 for all years discussed in this chapter.

11. The US, in particular, substantially increased its share of worldwide FDI in the 1980s. Between 1983 and 1989 it accounted for 42.6% of all inflows, compared with 24.5% in 1975–80. However, between 1990 and 1996, its share fell back to 19.1%.

12. In the case of both Africa and West Asia, it was the oil-exporting countries which recorded the least gains, and, indeed, in the 1990s, the flow of new investment has been less than one-half that of the second half of the 1980s.

13. India, for example, recorded a ninefold increase in direct investment inflows between 1990–92 and 1994–96. The Central and Eastern European countries recorded a fivefold increase.

14. See Dunning, *Multinational Enterprises*, for the original formulation.

15. B. Kogut, 'Foreign Direct Investment as a Sequential Process', in C. P. Kindleberger and D. B. Audretsch (eds), *The Multinational Corporation in the 1980s* (Cambridge, MA: MIT Press, 1983) 38–56.

16. The kind of O advantages which scholars, in the 1970s, used to explain FDI are set out in Dunning, *Multinational Enterprises*, and R. Caves, *Multinational Firms and Economic Analysis*, 2nd edn (Cambridge: Cambridge University Press 1996). The ones which consistently offered the greatest explanatory power were proprietary knowledge and product differentiation, and access to markets.

17. John H. Dunning, 'The European Internal Market Program and Inbound Foreign Direct Investment', *Journal of Common Market Studies*, 35, 1 (1997) 1–30.

18. J. F. Hennart and Y. R. Park, 'Location, Governance and Strategic Determinants of Japanese Manufacturing Investment in the US', *Strategic Management Journal*, 15 (1994) 419–36.

19. John H. Dunning, R. Narula and R. Van Hoesel, 'Explaining International R&D alliances and the Role of Governements', *International Business Review*, 7, 4 (August 1998) 377–98.

20. Michael E. Porter, *The Competitive Advantage of Nations* (New York: The Free Press, 1990).

21. So-called O_t (t standing for transactions) in the literature.

22. Exceptions included R&D by MNEs from the UK, Canada and some smaller European nations, and in sectors such as food, beverages and pharmaceuticals, where local supply or demand conditions made it desirable for some R&D to be decentralized.

23. W. Kuemmerle, *The Drivers of Foreign Direct Investment into Research and Development: An Empirical Investigation* (Boston: Harvard Business School Working Paper No. 96:062, 1996), p. 9.

24. In 1993, US firms conducted 13% of their R&D outside their home countries; the Japanese were increasingly establishing R&D facilities in Europe; while in the US, foreign firms accounted for 15.5% of total R&D expenditures in 1991, compared with 4.8% in 1977: John H. Dunning and R. Narula, 'The R&D Activities of Foreign Firms in the US', *International Studies of Management and Organization*, 25, 1–2, Spring–Summer (1995) 39–75.

25. Kuemmerle, *The Drivers of Foreign Direct Investment*.

26. For example, investment by US MNEs in the UK. See John H. Dunning, *American Investment in British Manufacturing Industry* (London: George Allen and Unwin, reprinted by Arno Press, New York, 1958. Updated and revised edition published by Routledge (London and New York) in 1998).

27. One of the reasons for this is that part – and probably an important part – of the growth of foreign-based R&D has taken the form of acquisition rather than of 'greenfield' R&D. In the US, almost four-fifths of the total investment outlays by foreign direct investors in the 1980s was through the purchase of existing US businesses.

28. It is noted that there are certain parallels between the kind of FDI designed to acquire natural resources in the nineteenth and early twentieth century, and that designed to acquire created assets, notably technology, information and learning experience of the 1980s and 1990s. Both were (or are) aimed at facilitating, or enhancing, the use of the existing O advantages of the investing companies; and both were (or are) frequently prompted by aggressive, or defensive, production, marketing and innovatory strategies of large oligopolists.

29. S. E. Guisinger and associates, *Investment Incentives and Performance Requirements* (New York: Praeger, 1985).

30. UNCTAD, *World Investment Report 1995: Transnational Corporations and Competitiveness* (Geneva: United Nations, 1995).

31. UNCTAD, *World Investment Report 1995*; *World Investment Report 1996*; *World Investment Report 1998*.

32. For a recent review of the interaction between trade and location theory, see a special edition of the *Oxford Review of Economic Policy* 1:2 (Summer 1998). For an examination of the evolving relationship between modern trade and FDI theory, see John H. Dunning, 'What's Wrong – and Right – With Trade Theory?', *International Trade Journal*, IX:2 (1995) 153–202; J. R. Markusen, 'The Boundaries of Multinational Enterprises and the Theory of International Trade', *Journal of Economic Perspectives*; 9:2 (1995) 169–89; J. R. Markusen. and A. Venables, *Multinational Firms and the New Trade Theory* (Cambridge, MA.: NBER Working Paper No. 5036, February 1995); and for a discussion of the changing locational attributes sought after by MNEs, see R. Kozul-Wright and R. Rowthorn, 'Spoilt for Choice? Multinational Corporations and the Geography of International Production', *Oxford Review of Economic Policy*, 14, 2 (1998) 74–92, and John H. Dunning, Location and the Multinational Enterprise: a Neglected Factor', *Journal of International Business Studies*, 29, 1 (1998) 45–66.

33. For a description of the various kinds of industrial districts, see B. Harrison 'Industrial Districts: Old Wine in New Bottles', *Regional Studies*, 26, 5 (1992) 469–83; A. Gray, E. Golog and A. Markusen, *Big Firms, Long Arms, Wide Shoulders: The Hub and Spoke Industrial District in the Seattle* (New Brunswick, NJ: PRIE Working Paper No. 79, 1995); S. O. Park and A. R. Markusen, 'Generalizing New Industrial Districts: a Theoretical Agenda and an Application from a Non-Western Economy', *Environment and Planning*, A 27 (1995) 81–104; M. J. Enright, 'Regional Clusters and Firm Strategy', in A. D. Chandler Jr, P. Hagström and Ö. Sölvell (eds), *The Dynamic Firm, The Role of Technology, Strategy, Organization and Regions* (Oxford: Oxford University Press, 1998); A. L. Saxenian, *Regional Advantage: Culture and Competition in Silicon Valley and Route 128* (Cambridge, MA: Harvard University Press, 1994).

34. See, for example, S. O. Park and A. R. Markusen, *New Industrial Districts: A Critique and Extension from the Developing World* (paper presented at the Symposium of the IGU Commission on Industrial Change, Time Space, Competition and Contemporary Industrial Change, Florida, August 1992); Park and Markusen, 'Generalizing New Industrial Districts'; K. Ohmae, *The End of the Nation State: The Rise of Regional Economies* (London: Harper, 1995); V. N. Balasubramanyan and A. Balasubramanyan, *Software in South India* (The Management School, Lancaster University, 1996).

35. Industrial clusters are, of course, not confined to high-technology firms. Examples of the concentration of more traditional industries are to be found in M. E. Porter, *The Competitive Advantage of Nations* (New York: The Free

Press, 1990); M.J. Enright 'Regional Clusters', and 'The Globalization of Competion and the Localization of Competitive Advantage: Policies Towards Regional Clustering', in N. Hood and S. Young (eds), *The Globalization of Multinational Enterprise Activity* (London: Macmillan, 1999); B. Harrison, *Lean and Mean: The Changing Landscape of Corporate Power in the Age of Flexibility* (New York: Basic Books, 1994). However, one's sense is that, in the contemporary global economy, these clusters are becoming more, rather than less, important.

36   T. Arita and M. Fujita, *Local Agglomeration and Global Networks of the Semiconductor Industry: A Comparative Study of US and Japanese Firms* (University of Pennsylvania and Kyoto University: mimeo, 1996).

37.   UNCTAD, *World Investment Report 1994: Transnational Corporations, Employment and the Workplace* (Geneva: United Nations, 1994); *World Investment Report 1998* (Geneva: United Nations, 1998).

38.   From 280 to 631: UNCTAD, *World Investment Report 1998*. For further details of strategic alliances in higher technology sectors, see J. Hagedoorn, 'Strategic Technology Alliances and Modes of Cooperation in High Technology Industries', in G. Grabher (eds), *The Embedded Firm* (London and Boston: Routledge 1993) pp. 116–37; J. Hagedoorn, 'Trends and Patterns in Strategic Technology Partnering since the Early Seventies', *Review of Industrial Organization*, 11 (1996) 601–16; R. Narula and J.H. Dunning, 'Technocratic-Corporate Partnering, Extending Alliance Capitalism', in G. Boyd and J.H. Dunning (eds), *Structural Change and Cooperation in the Global Economy* (Cheltenham, UK and Northampton, MA, USA: Edward Elgar, 1999) 137–59.

39.   Hagedoorn, 'Strategic Technology Alliances' and 'Trends and Patterns'; Narula and Dunning, 'Technocratic-Corporate Partnering'.

40.   In 1996 and 1997 cross-border M&A sales involving developing countries amounted to $178 656 million compared with $133 729 in 1994–95 and $89 844 million in 1992–93: UNCTAD, *World Investment Report 1998*, p. 413.

41.   Note that the assertion that FDI continues to be a major mode for exploiting or acquiring the O-specific advantages of firms in no way negates the proposition that firms need to engage in more cooperative ventures in order to best protect or enhance these advantages. In practice, however, many of these cooperative ventures will be between institutions within particular countries rather than across countries.

42.   UNCTAD, *World Investment Report 1996*.

43.   These data are culled mainly from: OECD, *International Direct Investment Statistics Year Book 1998* (Paris: OECD, 1998)., UNCTC, *Transnational Corporations and World Development* (New York, UN, 1988); UNCTAD, *World Investment Report 1995: Transnational Corporations and Competitiveness* (New York and Geneva, UN, 1995); and UNCTAD, *World Investment Report 1998*. In turn, these data were initially obtained from those published by the IMF (various dates), based on balance-of-payments statistics and those directly provided by national authorities of FDI stocks and/or flows.

44.   Unlike its US and Japanese counterparts, Western Europe FDI includes intra-regional FDI – which, as the table reveals, has increased substantially over the last 20 years. Were such FDI excluded from the data, its pattern of FDI would look very different indeed.

45.   Dunning, 'The European Internal Market Program'.

46.   Dunning, van Hoesel, and Narula, 'Explaining the New Wave'.

47.   UNCTAD, *World Investment Report 1998*.

48. T. Ozawa, 'Japan: the Macro-IDP, Meso-IDPs and the Technology Development Path (TDP)', in J. H. Dunning, and R. Narula (eds), *Foreign Direct Investment and Governments* (London and New York: Routledge 1996) 142–73.

49. 'Very recently' reflects that it has only been in the last five years that substantial MNE activity has occurred in sectors in which there was previously no, or little, foreign investment. For an examination of the recent surge in FDI in infrastructure development, see UNCTAD, *World Investment Report 1996*.

50. For a description see one recent analysis of the interface between the new system and the globalization of economic activity is W. Ruigrok and R. Val Tulder, *The Logic of International Restructuring* (London and New York: Routledge, 1995).

51. The increasing tradability of services is a two-edged sword as far as FDI is concerned. On the one hand, it opens doors for trade in services previously closed; on the other, it facilitates the kind of FDI which itself makes for more intra-country (and intra-firm) trade in services.

52. 1994 data.

53. OECD, *International Direct Investment Statistics Year Book 1998*.

54. Ibid.

55. The retrenchment in Japanese FDI in the US since the early 1990s explains why between 1994 and 1997 the share of new FDI in the service sector fell to 47.8%: ibid.

56. UNCTAD, *World Investment Report 1993: Transnational Corporations and Integrated Production* (Geneva: United Nations, 1993); OECD, *International Direct Investment Statistics Year Book 1998*.

57. Although, as a proportion of total FDI, it is still below that of most developed countries. In 1993, for example, 33% of the stock of inbound FDI in Taiwan was in the tertiary sector (compared with 20% in 1980). The corresponding percentages for Korea were 37% and 21%: UNCTAD, *World Investment Report 1995*.

58. UNCTAD, *World Investment Report 1995*. This essentially represents an average of three measures of multi- or trans-nationality, viz. share of foreign sales to total sales, share of foreign assets to total assets, and share of total employment. This index was calculated for the top 100 MNEs in 1994, its total employment, ranked by their foreign assets.

59. OECD, *International Direct Investment Statistics Year Book 1998*.

60. John M. Stopford, *The World Directory of Multinational Enterprises*, 1992 edn (Basingstoke: Macmillan, 1992); John. M. Stopford, J. H. Dunning and K. O. Haberich, *The World Directory of Multinational Enterprises* (Basingstoke: Macmillan, 1980).

61. Thus, for example, the average ratio between the 1990 and the 1978 share of the sales (and or employment) of foreign affiliates in Europe, relative to all foreign sales of MNEs in the top half of the industry/country groupings, was 1.15; and for MNEs with a below-average share it was 1.05; corresponding ratios for North America were 1.97 and 1.31. For developing countries, the ratios for Asia were 0.94 and 1.35; and for Latin America 0.93 and 0.90. It will be observed that the time period chosen for this exercise was that in which the share of all FDI in the US increased sharply.

62. That is, the Czech Republic, Hungary and Poland. These countries accounted for 69% of the regions stock on inbound FDI in 1994: UNCTAD, *World Investment Report 1995*, p. 100.

3 Trade, Regionalism and the Threat to Multilateralism

DIANA TUSSIE and NGAIRE WOODS

Globalization is having a profound effect on the political economy of trade.[1] Over the past decade more countries than ever before have been persuaded to push aside protective barriers and further integrate into the world economy, attracted by the possibilities of world markets. These new entrants include a wide range of developing countries and the former Soviet or Eastern bloc economies. The result is a pattern of international trade which poses significant challenges to the multilateral regime which evolved under the auspices of the General Agreement on Trade and Tariffs (GATT) and continues under the World Trade Organization (the WTO).

Industrialized countries are under pressure to put principles into action. The United States, the European Union, Canada, and Japan (the so-called 'Quad' who dominated the GATT) have long argued that multilateral liberalization is of benefit to all countries yet maintained protection in sectors such as agriculture and textiles,[2] and used loopholes in international trade rules to limit other kinds of exports, including measures such as voluntary export restraints (VERs) and anti-dumping actions. These derogations from free trade have reinforced strong vested interests in these countries, which make liberalization difficult. Yet without stronger reform in these areas the credibility and legitimacy of the multilateral regime will be further diminished, and countries will turn to other kinds of trade arrangements.

Regionalism has grown astonishingly in trade relations over the past decade – from Southern Africa to North America. It is not clear that all forms of regionalism positively reinforce a more liberal international trade order, although some clearly may. Below, this chapter identifies the mixed effects of regionalism, demonstrating the ways in which it both reinforces and corrodes multilateralism.

Multilateralism is also challenged by another set of forces. Trade arrangements are increasingly vulnerable to shifts and crises in exchange rates, foreign investment and capital flows. This was highlighted by the East Asian crisis of 1997, where a financial crisis not only spread quickly across the region but severely affected trade flows. Net exports from Western Europe and North America to East Asia declined sharply as demand in the five most directly affected countries (Thailand, Indonesia, Malaysia, the Philippines and South Korea) fell. Overall, the value of imports into East Asia fell by one-third in the first nine months of 1998 compared with the same period a year earlier.[3] At the same time, the price-competitiveness of East Asian goods in North American and European markets rose due to their currency devaluations. For these reasons, the financial crisis of 1997 created new pressures for protectionism both in East Asia as well as in the region's industrialized country markets. Likewise, similar pressures emerged in the wake of the financial crisis in Brazil in 1998.

New pressures for protectionism, unilateralism, and regionalism in trade serve to remind us of the reason for setting up the postwar multilateral trade regime: to stave off protectionist and 'beggar-thy-neighbour' reactions to crises which proved so disastrous in the interwar years. In the 1990s, this rationale for multilateralism has, if anything, been strongly reinforced. Yet it is not clear that multilateralism is strengthening.

Many scholars of international relations assume that increasing economic openness, such as has been experienced over the past decade or so, should be conducive to an invigoration of multilateralism. In this 'liberal institutionalist' view, openness and multilateralism are part and parcel of the same process[4] with multilateralism strengthening and deepening as more countries integrate into the world economy and more markets converge.

Yet, as will be argued below, in some ways multilateralism may be losing primacy at precisely the time when more countries have become bound up with global trade relations. In practice, it may even be the case that globalization and multilateralism are diverging rather than reinforcing each other. Indeed, globalization may have slowed down the evolution of a multilateralist trading system over the last decade. This poses an important paradox for liberal institutionalists who propose that the two processes will move forwards together, and forces us to re-examine other theoretical explanations of the relationship between globalization and multilateralism in trade.

The first section of this chapter outlines the political relations which have underpinned the multilateral trading system since the end of the Second World War. The second section discusses how these relations have been transformed by globalization. The third section examines the consequences for multilateralism, highlighting in particular the challenge of emerging regional trade arrangements which are further detailed in section four. Section five discusses the positive and negative implications of this regionalism. The conclusion draws together our overall assessment of the factors shaping multilateralism at the beginning of the twenty-first century.

The political economy of the trading system

Over the past 50 years, international trade has been heavily dominated by the industrialized countries. In this section, the political and economic reasons and ramifications of this dominance will be examined so as to lay out a framework for understanding the impact globalization is having on the politics and the economic of world trade.

As colonial rule disintegrated in the 1950s and 1960s, international trade changed in two ways. First, the direction of trade shifted as industrialized countries began to trade more and more with each other and relatively less with their former colonies. Second, the composition of trade or the kinds of goods traded altered as industrialized countries exchanged capital-intensive goods with each other. In other words, rather than trading cars for raw materials (as trade theory might predict), international trade became increasingly an exchange of, say, Renaults for Fords. Indeed, since the 1960s about two-thirds of world trade in manufactures has been in chemical and engineering goods – goods with low labour or raw material input in relation to capital. Overall this trading system especially met the needs of a small group of Western industrialized countries, and often worked against the interests of most developing countries.[5]

Several closely related trends supported a concentration of trade among the industrialized countries. Greater capital mobility facilitated cross-border investment which in turn increased trade: indeed capital and goods flowed hand-in-hand, with trade following investments and vice versa. Some three-quarters of international investments were concentrated in the industrialized countries. Furthermore, trade amongst this group of countries intensified as producers began *partially* to specialize *within* particular sectors, rather than specializing absolutely. Competition among producers came to focus less on price and more on the quality and particular attributes of products (see Chapter 2). Firms and countries used technological advances to carve out particular market-niches owing more to the type of good produced than its price. Finally, the growth and activities of multinational enterprises drove this process, with firms internationalizing and thereby tapping into the benefits of international specialization *within* the firm: trading within the firm so as to maximize gains from international differences in production and technology.

Outside the hotbed of trading activity described above, trade did not flourish. Rather in sectors and countries where these transformations did not occur, trade encountered numerous policy obstacles.[6] Trade frictions flared, particularly between industrialized and newly industrializing countries. As mentioned above, these relations were not reinforced by criss-crossing investments, nor by intra-sectoral specializations. Although some international investment flowed into the industrial sectors of developing countries, it tended not to increase their export capacity. Rather foreign direct investment (FDI) tended to flow into sectors where it could profit from direct subsidies, tax exemptions, protection and other state interventions.

The rules of the trading system reflected the trends and industrialized country interests outlined above. Successive negotiations on the General Agreement on Trade and Tariffs (GATT) liberalized largely two-way trade in goods between countries with a production capacity and potential for intra- rather than inter-industry specialization. In other words, the rules made it easier for the above-mentioned trade in Renaults for Fords as opposed to cars for beef. Indeed, tariff reductions tended to proceed on a reciprocal basis, sector by sector, as initiated in the Kennedy Round of trade negotiations. By contrast, exports from the developing world to industrialized countries remained subject to high tariffs and non-tariff restrictions.[7] In quantitative terms, average OECD tariff levels were reduced from 40 per cent to 5 per cent in the four decades between the 1940 and the 1980s.

However, the least developed countries face tariffs 30 per cent higher than the average, and developing countries as a group face tariffs 10 per cent higher than the average. These figures reflect the fact that tariffs remain high on the goods developing countries produce such as textiles, leather and agricultural commodities.[8]

The GATT system was one which developing countries found very difficult to alter or to side-step. Producers in developing countries could not 'jump barriers' as could multinational enterprises (MNEs) in industrialized countries. The latter could 'jump' impediments to trade by using investment as an alternative to the export of goods. At the same time, within the industrialized world, joint-ventures were made possible by the internationalization of capital. This meant that firms and governments could enter into joint ventures which softened their rivalry.

Developing countries played their own part in cementing a double-system in international trade. They sought early on to derogate from GATT rules so as to enforce import substitution or economic planning programmes. Furthermore, they pressed for special discretionary treatment by former colonial powers rather than for universally applicable liberalization.[9]

In summary, for a number of decades international trade was shaped by a particular combination of liberalization and protection. Trade patterns were reinforced by capital flows and the freer mobility of capital relative to other factors of production. Yet while capital-intensive goods experienced greater dynamism and enjoyed the benefit of deeper tariff reductions, labour-intensive goods remained relatively protected, with below-average tariff reductions as well as a greater incidence of non-tariff regulations. This global trading system was not one in which developing or Eastern European countries had a great stake. Yet the stakes of these countries changed dramatically as of the 1980s.

The globalization of trade

Since the 1980s, trade has been altered by the internationalization of production, distribution and marketing of goods and services, as well as the increasing flows of capital and investment which underpin trade. Although sceptics have presented evidence demonstrating that more trade and investment took place before the First World War than at present,[10] nevertheless today's linkages are qualitatively different to those experienced in the earlier part of this century. These qualitative differences are worth noting, along with their effects on the political economy of trade relations.

In the past two decades, the trading system has been altered by the emergence of new participants. In the four decades running from 1945 to 1985 global economic expansion was taking place mainly within and among OECD countries. However, in the wake of the 1980s debt crisis, a large number of developing countries began to liberalize their economies, dismantling trade barriers, as well as domestic production subsidies. Subsequently, these countries enjoyed an increase in exports as well as imports, including more trade with OECD countries, and perhaps yet more markedly, an increase in trade with other developing countries.[11] As a result, these developing countries today have a much greater stake in the international trade regime and the application of its rules to their trading partners as well as to themselves. More recently, they have been joined by the former Soviet bloc countries who emerged at the end of the 1980s urgently seeking new markets and trade partners.

Alongside the addition of new participants in the world trading system, globalization at the end of the twentieth century involves an unprecedented degree of functional integration among otherwise internationally dismembered activities (see Chapters 2 and 7). This is made possible not just by the transit of goods in the world economy but by a new rapid flow of tangible and intangible forms of capital, resulting from changes in technology as well as changes in industrialized country policies. The growth of capital flows has been explosive, with an almost fourfold increase in FDI flows being recorded in the period 1985–95.[12] These kinds of flows have been shown to be correlated to increased trade.[13] They have also complicated trade negotiations, adding talks on trade-related investment measures and services to an already crowded agenda.

The broad implications of growing capital flows have emerged as governments have responded with more and more alacrity to global markets. In particular, governments have turned their policies towards what they think is necessary to attract foreign capital (see Chapter 5). In industrialized countries, governments have facilitated large FDI flows by privatizing state-owned companies and thereby sparking a slew of new joint ventures in a myriad of sectors encompassing previously state-owned, foreign and domestic firms. Such opening brings host countries into a web of multinational investments as new strategic alliances are created among firms.

In some developing or newly industrialized countries similar strategies have been undertaken. Big firms have seized the moment, adopting an accelerated strategy of internationalization. In 1995, around 15 per cent of the global FDI outflows ($33 bn) originated in developing countries. The need for economies of scale as well as a generally more benign financial environment has shaken companies to search for new markets abroad as a way to gain competitiveness and ensure access to markets. Leading examples in Latin America include Cemex of Mexico, Yacimientos Petroliferos Fiscales of Argentina, Endesa and Luksic of Chile. Altogether cross-border investments have expanded dramatically and with them trade in a number of services.

The opening up of large domestic companies to international capital, however, has not always had felicitous results. The dramatic inflows of capital into Korea and Thailand, for example, led to a severe crisis in 1997. Capital poured into these countries before appropriate financial sector institutions of supervision and regulation were in place. In Korea, the spotlight then turned on the governance of large corporations who were accused of corruption and mismanagement. In a crisis of confidence, short-term investors fled more quickly than they had arrived and international institutions were left attempting to concoct solutions for the region. The experience of the crisis, and of the attempted solution, has injected a sharp note of caution into arguments about investment and financial opening. Many developing countries have begun to question the wisdom of rapidly opening their economies to such potential turbulence.[14]

A further change associated with globalization in trade is a new pattern of growth and competition in the world economy. The flood of investments into some of the newly-more-integrated areas of the world led them to grow above world averages. Between 1989 and 1996 Latin America, Eastern Europe and East Asia grew quite vigorously, in contrast to the sluggish 2.5 per cent average annual growth in developed countries. The rate of growth of imports into Latin America and East Asia, as a result of the revolution in trade policy, was a remarkable 14 per cent per year since 1990, almost doubling world averages. These growth rates sharpened competition in certain sectors for the OECD countries and heightened their resolve to bring new issues onto the global trade agenda, such as services (for example, telecommunications, skilled labour movement, financial services and so on), a sector in which OECD countries hope to retain competitiveness. In other sectors, greater competition has brought issues of labour and environmental standards into sharper focus.[15]

Finally, new growth, investment and trading patterns have enhanced the stakes countries have in free trade arrangements at both the international and regional levels. Overall, globalization has brought new participants, new kinds of transnational exchanges, and new sets of relations into the international trade arena. While many states face new opportunities, they are also constrained by new vulnerabilities. All of these effects have profound consequences for multilateralism.

The challenges for multilateralism

A slightly flagging multilateral trade regime was recharged in 1986 by the launch of the Uruguay Round of talks. The stated objectives of the Round included: to bring both agriculture and textiles into the GATT; to limit the uses of safeguards (as a loophole for protectionism); to improve GATT discipline on all subsidies affecting trade; and to include the news issues of trade-related intellectual property rights and controversial investment measures, as well as services. The results of the round emerged when agreement was reached in December 1993.

In negotiations on agriculture, talks descended into an unseemly and acrimonious negotiation between the United States and the European Union, which was temporarily resolved in a compromise agreement.[16] Agreement was reached to launch negotiations on both trade-related intellectual property and trade-related investment measures (TRIPS and TRIMS). Perhaps the most powerful outcome of all was the establishment of a new stronger institution – the World Trade Organization (WTO) – for the surveillance of trade policies and the adjudication of trade disputes.

The WTO came into being on 1 January 1995 and, because of its improved dispute settlement mechanism, bolstered many hopes that a more rule-based approach to international trade rules was emerging. The institution, it was hoped, would stimulate and facilitate further liberalization in world trade in several ways. First, it could set an agenda which no individual government could afford to support in isolation. Second, through multilateral agreements, it could tie the hands of domestic policy-makers, giving them a fallback position when faced with demands from domestic groups. Finally, the institution could undercut the power of pro-protection interests by promulgating broader, public goods.[17]

The WTO is certainly a more powerful institution than its predecessor, the GATT. Perhaps the most important difference lies in the tightening and 'legalization' of disputes resolution mechanisms.[18] In the GATT, consensus was required in order for panel decisions on disputes to be accepted. In other words, any country could veto a panel decision. In the WTO, the onus has been reversed so that consensus is required to reject a panel decision on a dispute. The changes have led to quite a frenzy of countries availing themselves of the institution's dispute settlement.[19] Evidence of this 'leap to legalism'[20] is provided by the 60 disputes waiting in the pipeline for resolution, one-third of which have been initiated by smaller, less powerful countries.

The implications of a more effective and rule-based disputes mechanism are easily overstated. Political power within the WTO still lies with the 'Quad' (the United States, the European Union, Canada and Japan) who still enjoy enormous control over rules and outcomes. Perhaps more importantly, the WTO itself is only one of several fora in which trade policies are being detailed and implemented. The WTO has already been sidelined in several instances by unilateral, bilateral and regional decisions. The US imposition of extraterritorial sanctions on companies doing business with Cuba, Iran and Libya offers one example, and the ongoing alleged failure of the European Union to comply with WTO rulings on banana imports offers another. Finally, at the end of 1999 WTO members failed to reach agreement on an agenda for future trade talks.

The experience of the WTO to date highlights the fact that multilateralism depends upon the will of governments. In this sense, it is a very different dynamic to globalization. Globalization presents even passive states with both constraints and opportunities. By contrast, multilateralism requires states to act and to make deliberate policy choices. It is for this reason that the two processes do not necessarily advance hand-in-hand. Scholars who link globalization to increasing multilateralism argue that in a globalizing world states' choices will be guided by a recognition that long-term interests will be best advanced by greater cooperation. However, critics highlight intervening obstacles to multilateralism.

Perhaps the most powerful challenge to multilateralism lies in the problem of 'leadership'. Most theorists agree that leadership is essential for the creation of a multilateral regime: to set up rules and create a system in which the participants do not fear 'free-riding' or defection by others. The real debate is about the prospects for the regime once the hegemon either loses its relatively preponderant position, or changes its preferences in respect of the regime.

Some theorists have argued that institutions and rules can persist even after the hegemon loses the capacity or will to 'lead'.[21] Critics, however, propose that continuing 'leadership' by a preponderant state is necessary for a regime to continue. Hence, it was argued at the end of the 1980s that as US hegemony declined, so too the world economy would divide into regions.[22]

Since the end of the Cold War, it has become more difficult to make sense of existing theories. In the first place, it is not clear whether the US has emerged as more of a hegemon (that is, the world has become 'unipolar') or has declined in power relative to the European Union and Asian countries (or, in other words, the world has become 'multipolar'). In security issues, there is a strong argument for US preponderance: as evidenced by the Gulf War in 1991 and intervention in Kosovo in 1999. However, in the economic realm, the configuration of power is not so clear. On trade issues the European Union and the United States show a continuing capacity and willingness to confront one another: as shown by acrimonious disputes over bananas and beef hormones in 1999 and their disagreement at Seattle at the end of 1999. Given that the US does not enjoy its early Cold War preponderance in relation to Europe, multilateralism will require genuine and deeper agreement among these countries in order to proceed.

Furthermore, the experience of the 1990s underlined a relative weakness on the part of *both* the United States and Europe in the face of financial crises in other parts of the world. Crises in Mexico (1994–95), East Asia (1997), and Russia (1998) all demonstrated vulnerabilities of powerful economies fearing a 'systemic crisis' (see Chapter 8). Responses to these crises underlined both the need for the inclusion of new actors in multilateral arrangements (especially of emerging market governments), and at the same time underscored the continuing dominance of the US which took the lead in shaping the responses of the international community.

Even if the US has retained its powerful hegemonic position in the world trading system (let us assume for a moment that it has), the multilateral system requires not just a leader but also a certain kind of leadership. In other words, it is not enough for the US to maintain its dominant position. Of equal importance are the trade policy preferences emerging within the United States. These are worth analysing.

In the aftermath of the Second World War, the US was soon perceived as champion (and the necessary hegemonic supporter) of a global liberal trade order. Although, as put succinctly by Ruggie: 'it was less the fact of American *hegemony* that accounts for the explosion of multilateral arrangements than of *American* hegemony'.[23] Complementing its role as champion of international free trade, the US worked assiduously throughout the 1960s and 1970s to resist any efforts at closer regional ties, particularly in Latin America and Asia, which were seen as potential challenges to the American project and American predominance.[24]

In the past two decades, however, inward-looking interests have had a greater sway in the US. Trade policy has become more active and more regionalist. Protectionism has grown with the 'new protectionism' of the 1970s and with the 'aggressive unilateralism' of the 1980s.[25] At the same time, in the early 1980s, the US exhibited a new enthusiasm for regional initiatives. Moreover, this enthusiasm was largely due to a perception that regional arrangements offered an important alternative to multilateralism. As Jeffrey Frankel describes, in 1982 the US began to respond to European positions on multilateral trade talks with the view that 'if the multilateral road is obstructed, then we will just have to explore these other roads'.[26] The other roads included the US–Israel Free Trade Agreement, the Caribbean Basin Initiative, the Canada–US Free Trade Area (CUSFTA) and later the North American Free Trade Area (NAFTA). These shifts pose a strong challenge for multilateralism.

The change in US policy also casts a spotlight on the extent to which US policy is unilateral. The United States is the only country that has an extensively developed body of doctrine and practice favouring the extraterritorial application of its laws. Traditionally, US extraterritoriality involved matters related to anti-trust cases and export controls in the context of national security. Additionally, however, it can also be used to obtain the intellectual property protection of its liking, by-passing multilaterally-agreed-upon WTO standards and procedures. In effect, the US authorities still appear prepared to determine which are unlawful practices and who are outlaw countries.[27] For the United States a rule-based order has often meant the extension of American rules and procedures to the rest of the world.[28] This was a natural by-product of the hegemony enjoyed by the United States during the postwar years. However, this era is over. In the present, more globalized system, the US risks looking not so much like a leader (bearing the burden of providing collective goods to ensure that smaller players do not free-ride or defect) but as a heavy-rider on the system, eroding multilateralism through its own forceful rebellion against rules when they are not in its interests. In a more global economy, the litmus test of multilateralism rests crucially on the disposition of the United States to follow the rule of law -a law that it will not always be able to control.

Multilateralism is further challenged by the increase in the number of participants in the international trade regime. The conversion en masse to outward orientation has happened with equal speed and fascination in a great number of countries. In 1950 there were about 30 members – 'contracting parties' – to the GATT, as they were then called. Over five times that number are now members of the WTO. The dilemmas of large-number multilateralism have been described and analysed by Miles Kahler.[29] Greater numbers, he has demonstrated, diffuse influence and make collective decision-making difficult, heightening the uses of minilateral devices as participants grope towards agreement.

Even deeper than the problem of multilateralism with large numbers of states is the challenge of ensuring that all participants in the world trading regime have a strong stake in the system and are committed to its rules. In the past, dissatisfaction with the international economic order was expressed by withdrawing from active involvement: de-linking, industrial-planning, state-trading, quasi-autarky or heavy import substitution all expressed a discontent with the international order and a search for varying degrees of immunity from its effects. Later, a policy of obstructionism was used with the onset of the Uruguay Round as a loosely assorted coalition of developing countries led by Brazil and India attempted to bargain for reform.[30] In the 1990s, developing and other countries have largely decided to participate in the existing system and, where necessary, to undertake new kinds of bargaining strategies in order to bring about reform.[31] An inclusive system which sustains these countries' belief in their interests in multilateralism is now a requirement of the international trade regime. This is a tough order given the plurality of views about trade, as evidenced by disputes over 'fair' trade ranging through anti-dumping laws to environmental and labour standards.

In summary, the political process of managing an institutional arrangement for globalization will not be easy. It will suffer, as multilateralism always has, not so much from the lack of leadership but from the ebb and flow of US commitment to international institutions. The US has much to gain from an international trade regime and, indeed, it is within the United States that the vision of a global free trade area is being proposed.[32] The new 'big idea' is to create a timetable pushing the WTO towards the removal of all barriers by possibly 2020. However, protectionism within the United States, combined with a new enthusiasm for regional institutions may well continue to dilute US (and other countries') commitment to multilateralism in trade. The date 2020 highlights the role regional pacts are expected to play in pushing forwards a multilateral trade order, since this is the latest date for full liberalization within regions in the timetable of regional pacts (being the date APEC expects to reach free trade among all its members).

The free trade objective assumes that all regional pacts would grant 'most favoured nation' (MFN) treatment by a given date. Since (until recently) East Asia and Latin America have been expected to become the two most rapid growing parts of the world economy, in essence the vision of a global free trade area rests upon a 'grand bargain' among these two groups of countries, North America, Western Europe and Japan. The crucial question in all of this is: will regional trade arrangements play this positive role? And more specifically, in which areas will they be inclined to liberalization? And in which sectors will barriers to outsiders be retained?

The emergence of regionalism

The past two decades have seen a strengthening and deepening of regional trade arrangements as almost every country in the world has joined some kind of preferential trading arrangement.[33] The European Union (EU) has moved towards a single market. The North

American Free Trade Agreement (NAFTA) has cemented a free trade area between Canada, the United States and Mexico and is now further extending its membership. A larger, less formal arrangement has been consolidated by the Asia-Pacific Economic Cooperation group (APEC). In South America countries have joined MERCOSUR. In other parts of the world, the list includes: the Economic Community of West African States (ECOWAS), the Southern African Development Coordination Conference (SADCC), the Preferential Trade Area for Eastern and Southern African States (PTA), the Maghreb Union, the Association of Southeast Asian Nations (ASEAN), the South Asian Association for Regional Cooperation (SAARC), the Gulf Cooperation Council (GCC), the Latin American Integration Association (LAIA), and the Caribbean Community (CARICOM).

For many developing countries who felt excluded from GATT, regional arrangements provide an opportunity of the market access they always wished for but had never really extracted from multilateral negotiations. Furthermore, many countries have been helped by the unilateral liberalization of neighbours and the commitments undertaken in the context of regional trade agreements. Regionalism has provided an opportunity for meaninful reciprocal negotiations.

The impact of regional arrangements on trade flows and relations is the subject of heated debate among scholars.[34] An optimistic view of the consequences of regionalism is taken by those who argue that regional free trade arrangements are 'building blocks' towards global free trade. Regionalism, it is argued, facilitates liberalization since it is politically easier for countries to liberalize their trade barriers within a regional arrangement. Once they have done so, the argument continues, it becomes politically much easier to liberalize vis-à-vis the rest of the world. Likewise, the optimists highlight that regionalism has increased the depth of liberalization since regional free trade agreements frequently involve the integration or harmonization of a number of loosely assorted trade-related policies. This has led to negotiations at the international level on policies regarding intellectual property, as well as investment rules, labour rights, tax and competition policies, and the treatment of the environment. In other words, regionalism is assisting the passage from shallow to deep integration.[35]

The pessimistic view is that regionalism creates a stumbling block to multilateralized free trade, that 'open regionalism is nothing but an oxymoron'.[36] Once a region has established a free trade regime among its members, there will be an increasing temptation and opportunity for retaining barriers to non-members to induce tariff-jumping foreign investments. As Charles Oman has written, 'powerful OECD-based multinational firms that might once collectively have constituted a strong political force against regional protectionism in OECD countries can no longer be counted on to play that role'.[37] The argument is that once multinationals have established a presence within a major region, they will give more importance to lowering intra-regional trade barriers, rather than inter-regional barriers. Hence, the risk is that regionalism will facilitate rather than erode 'Fortress Europe' and other such regional islands of economic activity.

A third view of regional trading arrangements reminds us of the geography of regions, pointing out that the geographical proximity of neighbours plays a crucial role in the impact of any free trade arrangements.[38] Indeed, to some degree regional concentrations of trade flows may be due more to 'gravity' or market proximity than to formal trade arrangements. It is widely accepted, however, that formal agreements can have effects on confidence and induce foreign investment, as was seen in the case of NAFTA and MERCOSUR where the formal free trade agreement increased flows of investment as well as trade.

Empirically, the experience of the 1990s in most regions of the world has been one of increasing intra-regional trade. This is clear from IMF Direction of Trade statistics (see Table 3.1). Note that these figures have not been disaggregated so as directly to reveal the extent that formal trading arrangements may have increased trade. Nevertheless, they show a picture of increasingly concentrated intra-regional trade.

In summary, at the same time as regional trade agreements are flourishing in international economic relations, so too trade flows are also increasingly intra-regional. In Europe, the Western Hemisphere, Asia and Africa, the percentage of countries' exports and imports going to and from other countries within the region has grown over the past decade. The exception has been in the Middle East where a breakdown in political relations since the Gulf War (1990–91) has influenced trade. The implications of this new regionalism for the political economy of trade liberalization and hence for multilateralism are several fold.

TABLE 3.1 Trade within Regions in the 1990s

	1990	1991	1992	1993	1994	1995	1996	1997
Europe								
exports		23	23.5	27.6	33.8	35.5	35.8	35.7
imports		20.6	21.3	24.3	32.6	34.1	33.1	34.8
Western Hemisphere								
exports	16.2	16.7	18.8	20.1	20.2	20.1	20.3	
imports	17.6	16.5	17.1	17.2	16.9	17.8	17.5	
Asia								
exports	33.3	36	37.8	37.2	39.2	40.4	40.4	
imports	30.7	33.4	34.6	34.5	35	34.9	35.5	
Africa								
exports	7.3	7.4	8.2	8.5	9.2	10.7	10.1	
imports	7.9	7.5	7.8	7.9	9.0	10.0	11.0	
Middle East								
exports	8.2	7.5	7.1	7.3	7.4	6.5	5.8	
imports	8.2	7.1	7.1	8.1	8.7	7.4	6.5	

Note: % total exports and imports of a region moving between countries within that region.
Source: IMF, *Direction of Trade Statistics*, 1990–98.

The political economy of regionalism in trade

Regionalism in world trade has both positive and negative implications for liberalization and for multilateralism. On the negative side, there is a danger that the new regionalism will erode states' commitment to multilateralism and perpetuate a very partial and unequal form of liberalization. A first crucial question is how 'outsiders' to prosperous regions are treated and how this undermines or strengthens their commitment to multilateralism. The impact of the new regionalism on countries lying outside some regions has been very harsh. For example, countries bordering the European Union have found that regionally organized trading regime presenting a series of closed doors to them. The initial enthusiasm of former Eastern bloc countries to dismantle trade barriers has been replaced by a bitter recognition that the trade practices of most large industrialized countries are protectionist and restrictive, even though they are legal within GATT/WTO rules.[39] In this context, many countries bordering successful 'regions' such as the European Union or NAFTA are not only trying to gain entry but are also considering new regional areas of their own (as evidence, for example, by NAFTA's catalyzing of MERCOSUR and progress towards a free trade area of the Americas).[40]

A second problem for multilateralism is that regional trade institutions might be used by states as an alternative to multilateral institutions. Once powerful states have set up regulatory and legal institutions at the regional level, they may well start preferring to use these institutions even in disputes which should rightly go to the WTO – choosing the forum for dispute resolution according to what is most likely to serve their interests. Such behaviour erodes the 'rule of law' in international trade, suggesting different laws for different states according to their region and their power to influence regional fora. Furthermore, if powerful states focus attention inwards on their region and regional institutions, they are likely to neglect international fora and organizations. Although as yet there is little evidence of this, indeed Mexico and Canada are using the WTO against the United States, and Brazil is taking two cases against Argentina to the WTO.

These negative implications of regionalism do not overwhelm other considerations. It is worth noting (as shown by the figures on Table 3.1 above) that no country has a clearcut choice between regional trade and international trade. All regions depend heavily on other markets: the EU relies heavily on North American markets, as does Japan; NAFTA offers too small an arena of trade for the USA – indeed, the US impetus for the Uruguay Round was to open up access to foreign markets, to extend coverage to agriculture and services and to fix up areas like intellectual property and foreign investment.[42] At the same time, the evidence suggests that powerful states gain important bargaining leverage from participation in regional blocs. The United States, for example, used the threat of NAFTA and APEC to force other countries to take the Uruguay Round seriously.[42] Hence, regionalism is not in competition with multilateralism but it can increase the credibility of a threat of defection from the WTO of large players with a regional option.

On the positive side of the relationship between regionalism and multilateralism, it is worth noting that the new regionalism is being driven more by markets and less by policy, or by fiat or even enlightened bureaucrats. Few, if any, of the new associations (with the exception of Europe) are really a bloc. The new regionalism is more a product of the expansion of trade and cross-border investments among neighbouring countries after unilateral liberalization. Even MERCOSUR, when the car sector is excluded has led to more trade creation than diversion.[43]

Furthermore, the new regionalism bridges the traditional division - between industrialized and developing countries that had marked the GATT. This was expressed (as noted above) by one way exports (in a North–South or South–North direction) riddled with barriers of all kinds, and in messy efforts to compensate for the bias such as by allowing developing countries 'special and differential treatment' (whereby developing countries were not expected to provide fully reciprocal access to their markets and they were granted preferential access to industrialized countries' markets). Special and differential treatment proved to be no solution and, indeed, became a continuing source of friction as developing countries remained dissatisfied with the access they obtained, and industrialized countries grumbled about free-riding.

Regional free trade agreements tend not to make a distinction between types of countries or levels of development. Within NAFTA, Mexico has eliminated virtually all border restrictions – in agriculture as well as in industry – from 70 percent of its imports coming from the United States and Canada. The extension of NAFTA to Chile and the negotiations for the Free Trade Area of the Americas are expected to follow the same pattern – with little, if any, special and differential treatment.

Regionalism may well concentrate the regional power of already-powerful states. However, regional associations among small countries may also increase their power in multilateral trade negotiations since bargaining power has depended essentially on market size. A regional trading unit will tend to have more market power than any of its members alone. By decentralizing decision-making and strengthening *plurilateral* processes in a framework which gives even the weaker countries some say, the new regionalism can lead to the kind of multilateralism in which regional units will have stronger bargaining power. A small number of units engaging in inter-bloc negotiations would tend to make co-operative solutions more likely. In the words of President Cardoso referring to Mercosur, 'in the end, if the name of the game is reciprocity, it is necessary to have something to offer, and market size is the first prize'.[44]

All this supports the 'building block' view of the debate about regionalism and global free trade.[45] No regional unit seems to be inward-looking. Indeed, no regional unit can afford to be so, nor to grow apart from others. Markets are so deeply intertwined that no unit can afford to sacrifice intra-regional trade *at the expense of* inter-regional trade. No state has an interest in substituting regional for global trade. Regionalism rather reflects that countries are choosing to forge ahead faster or further than the multilateral track affords. The result is that trade between regions may not grow as fast as within them, but global trade will not necessarily deteriorate.

The implications of regionalism for multilateralism will ultimately depend upon the degree to which regionalism affects global economic integration and governance. The important issue is not so much the extent to which regional integration agreements in and of themselves multiply, but rather on their openness to other markets and their institutional structures. Open trading regions could provide the vehicle for much international production and exchange and building blocks towards a new, stronger multilateralism. It is conceivable that such regional institutions would be structured so as to give voice to a wider range of countries – permitting them to have a direct say at the regional level rather than remaining unheard at the international level. In this way, regionalism could provide a counterweight to the continuing dominance of powerful industrialized countries that has accompanied globalization.

Conclusion

Globalization in trade describes more than an increase in cross-border transactions. It refers to a transformation in the production, distribution and marketing of goods and services and an expansion of the international trade regime to include virtually all countries in the world economy. The result has been a pattern of world trade which is both global and highly transnational and in which some actors now conceive of their interests in these terms.

The transformation has not yet, however, been fully echoed by a major shift in the politics of international trade. The inequalities which marked negotiations and outcomes under the GATT system have largely remained: reductions in trade barriers are still weighted towards the goods and services produced in the industrialized countries, and these countries still dominate the multilateral negotiations. The multilateral system of rules and negotiations, however, is now seriously challenged not just by the large numbers of new entrants, but equally by the risk of insufficiently committed leadership, and by the rise of regionalism which offers outer-ring countries expectations of inclusion through broad duty-free access rather than through special and differential treatment.

The nature of emerging regionalism deeply affects multilateralism and the international trade regime. Three issues in particular will shape its impact on international trade. First, if regions remain open to outsiders, at best they are likely to become 'building blocks' towards a liberal multilateral regime; at worst they will be indifferent. In the second place, if rules within regional trade areas do not diverge from multilateral rules they can reinforce the multilateral system, yet when differencies abound, states might well use regional institutions as an alternative to the WTO regime when it suits them. The WTO would thus be hollowed out. Finally, regions may well prove to be a good vehicle for smaller countries to enjoy more of a voice in international trade – magnified by their combined market share and political power. At the same time, there is also the risk that such regional arrangements may offer powerful countries smaller multi-lateral fora in which they can dominate more decisively.

In conclusion, globalization sets new requirements for international political relations in trade. Yet the need for stronger cooperation and coordination among states is not necessarily strengthening multilateralism. Rather, some of the new requirements are being met at the regional level, and the impact of these arrangements is not yet fully apparent.

Notes

1. As described in Chapter 1, political economy is used in many senses in political science and international relations. In this chapter it is used to describe the political relations which underpin international trade arrangements. For a survey of a rational choice approach to examining issues of trade protectionism and rent-seeking, see Stephen Magee, 'The Political Economy of Trade Policy', in David Greenaway and Alan L. Winters, *Surveys in International Trade* (Oxford: Blackwell, 1994) pp. 139–76.
2. Diana Tussie, *Developing Countries and the World Trading System: A Challenge to the GATT* (London: Frances Pinter, 1987).
3. World Trade Organization, *Annual Report 1998* (Geneva: World Trade Organization, 1998).

4. John Ruggie, 'The Anatomy of an Institution', in John Ruggie (ed.), *Multilateralism Matters: The Theory and Practice of an Institutional Form* (New York: Columbia University Press, 1993).

5. Tussie, *Developing Countries*.

6. Ibid.

7. Ibid. J. De Castro, Determinants of Protection and Evolving Forms of North—South Trade, *UNCTAD Discussion Papers*, 26 (1989).

8. Textile and clothing, for example, accounts for 24% of Sub-Saharan African exports, 14% of Asian and 8% of Latin American and Caribbean exports: figures from UNDP, *Human Development Report 1997* (New York: Oxford University Press, 1997) p. 85.

9. Robert Hudec, *Developing Countries in the GATT Legal System* (Aldershot: Gower for the Trade Policy Research Centre, 1987).

10. Paul Krugman, *Pop Internationalism* (Cambridge, MA: The MIT Press, 1997).

11. Paul Krugman, 'Growing World Trade: Causes and Consequences', *Brookings Papers on Economic Activity*, 1 (1995), 5–25.

12. WTO, *Trade and Foreign Direct Investment*: Report of 16 October 1996 (Geneva: WTO, 1996). See also Chapter 4 of this volume.

13. Evidence that flows of FDI and trade are strongly correlated has been presented using the example of APEC economies by Industry Canada, *Foreign Direct Investment and APEC Economic Integration*, Working Paper 8 (Ottawa: Industry Canada, 1996).

14. Dani Rodrik, *The New Global Economy and Developing Countries: Making Openness Work* (Washington, DC: Overseas Development Council/Policy Essay No. 24, 1999).

15. On labour standards see the debate sparked by Adrian Wood, 'How Trade Hurt Unskilled Workers', *Journal of Economic Perspectives*, 9, 3 (1995) 57—80; and for a good summary of the debate over inclusion in the WTO see Jerome Duperrut, 'Social Clauses in International Trade', *Trade Monitor,* 15 (1996) who points to moral, employment and institutional reasons for these to be shifted to WTO from ILO. On environmental protection see Diana Tussie (ed.), *The Environment and International Trade Negotiations* (Buenos Aires: FLACSO, 1998); Kym Anderson, 'Environmental Standards and International Trade', in Michael Bruno and Boris Pleskovic (eds), *Annual World Bank Conference on Development Economics 1996* (Washington, DC: The World Bank).

16. William P. Avery (ed.), *World Agriculture and the GATT* (Boulder, CO: Lynne Rienner, 1993).

17. These are the kinds of effects which scholars predict flow from the creation of formal institutions: see Judith Goldstein, 'International Institutions and Domestic Politics: GATT, WTO and the Liberalization of International Trade', in Anne Krueger (ed.), *The WTO as an International Organization* (Chicago: Chicago University Press, 1998), 133–52.

18. John H. Jackson, 'Designing and Implementing Effective Dispute Settlement Procedures: WTO Dispute Settlement, Appraisal and Prospects', in Krueger, *The WTO*, 161–80.

19. Celso Lafer, 'O Sistema de Soluçao de Controvérsis da Organizaçao Mundial do Comércio', *Documentos, Debates, Estudos. Instituto Roberto Simonsen*, No. 3 (1996); and WTO website (http://www.wto.org).

20. Kendall Stiles, 'Negotiating Institutional Reform: The Uruguay Round, the GATT and the WTO', *Global Governance*, 2, 1 (1996) 119–48.

21. Robert Keohane, *After Hegemony: Cooperation and Discord in the World Political Economy* (Princeton, NJ: Princeton University Press, 1984).
22. Robert Gilpin, *The Political Economy of International Relations* (Princeton: Princeton University Press, 1987), p. 397.
23. John Ruggie, 'The Anatomy of an Institution', in J. Ruggie (ed.), *Multilateralism Matters: The Theory and Practice of an Institutional Form* (New York: Columbia University Press, 1993) p. 8.
24. The regional efforts of the 1960s were indeed signals of the discontent with a US-dominated 'multilateralist' world economy. For recent analyses of Latin America see R. Bloomfield and A. Lowenthal, 'Inter-American Institutions in a Time of Change', *International Journal* 45 (1990): 867–88; and M. Hirst, *Democracia, Seguridad e Integración: América Latina en un mundo en transición* (Buenos Aires: FLACSO, 1996). For Asia see T. J. Pempel, *Transpacific Torii: Japan and the Emerging Asian Regionalism* (Seattle: Manuscript in Jackson School of International Studies, University of Washington, 1995).
25. Jagdish N. Bhagwati, *Aggressive unilateralism: America's 301 trade policy and the world trading system* (London; Harvester Wheatsheaf, 1991).
26. Jeffrey Frankel, *Regional Trading Blocs in the World Economic System* (Washington, DC: Institute for International Economics, 1998).
27. M. Hart, 'Cooperation: Social Policy and Future Trade Negotiations', *Canada–US Law Journal*, 20 (1994).
28. Susan Strange reminds us of the way the powerful can use regimes in this way in her now classic '*Cave! hic Dragones*: a Critique of Regime Analysis', *International Organization*, 36 (1982) 479–96.
29. Miles Kahler, 'Multilateralism with Small and Large Numbers', in John Ruggie (ed.), *Multilateralism Matters: The Theory and Practice of an Institutional Form* (New York: Columbia University Press, 1993).
30. R. Kumar, 'Developing Country-Coalitions in International Trade Negotiations', in: D. Tussie and D. Glover (eds), *The Developing Countries in World Trade: Policies and Bargaining Strategies* (Boulder, CO: Lynne Rienner, 1993) 205–24.
31. Ngaire Woods and Amrita Narlikar, 'International Trade and the Emergence of New Inter-state Coalitions', Delivered at FLACSO/IRDC Seminar on 'Emerging Issues in International Trade Relations', Geneva 23–5 September 1998 (Oxford: Oxford University, 1998).
32. Fred Bergsten, 'Globalizing Free Trade', *Foreign Affairs*, 75, 3 (1996) 105–20.
33. World Trade Organization (1995); see Frankel, *Regional Trading Blocs*.
34. See, for a survey of analyses of regionalism and trade, Takatoshi Ito and Anne O. Krueger, *Regionalism versus Multilateral Trade Arrangements* (Chicago: University of Chicago Press, 1997).
35. R. Lawrence, 'Futures for the World Trading System: Implications for Developing Countries', in M. Agosin and D. Tussie (eds), *Trade and Growth: New Dilemmas in Trade Policy* (London: Macmillan, 1993) 43–68.
36. T. N. Srinivasan, 'Regionalism and the WTO: Is Nondiscrimination Passé?', in Krueger, *The WTO*, 329–52 at p. 340.
37. Charles Oman, 'Globalization, Regionalization, and Inequality', in Andrew Hurrell and Ngaire Woods, *Inequality, Globalization, and World Politics* (Oxford: Oxford University Press, 1999) 36–65 at pp. 57–8.
38. Paul Krugman, *Geography and Trade* (Cambridge, MA: MIT Press, 1991).
39. Jaroslaw Pietras, 'The Role of the WTO for Economies in Transition', in Krueger, *The WTO*, 353–64.

40. Cf. the view and the evidence that regionalism is being accompanied by stronger global interdependencies: J. Poon and K. Pandit, 'The Geographical Structure of Cross-National Trade-Flows and Region States', *Regional Studies*, 30, 3 (1996) 273–85.
41. John Odell and Barry Eichengreen, 'The United States, the ITO, and the WTO: Exit Options, Agent Slack, and Presidential Leadership', in Krueger, *The WTO*, pp. 181–212 at p. 183.
42. On NAFTA see Jeffrey Schott, *Free Trade Areas and US Trade Policy* (Washington, DC: Institute for International Economics, 1989) and Jarrod Wiener, *Making Rules in the Uruguay Round of the GATT* (Aldershot, UK: Dartmouth, 1995). On APEC see I. Destler, *American Trade Politics*, 3d edn (Washington, DC: Institute for International Economics, 1995); and Jeffrey Frankel, *Regional Trading Blocs in the World Economic System* (Washington, DC: Institute for International Economics, 1998).
43. Nigel Nagajaran, 'On the Evidence for Trade Creation for MERCOSUR', *Integration and Trade*, 2, 6 (1998) 3—30.
44. As quoted in Andrew Hurrell, 'Progressive Enmeshment, Hegemonic Imposition, or Coercive Socialisation?: Understanding Policy Change in Brazil' (Oxford: unpublished manuscript, 1996).
45. Lawrence, 'Futures'.

4 Money in a Globalized World

BENJAMIN J. COHEN

One of the hallmarks of globalization in the contemporary era is the ever closer integration of national financial markets. Over the last half century, as barriers to international investment have gradually evaporated, capital mobility has accelerated to heights unseen since the days before the First World War. Most informed observers agree that, as a result, the traditional relationship between states and markets has been fundamentally altered. But how, precisely? At issue is the role of the state in the management of money. What does the globalization of finance mean for the convention of national monetary sovereignty? On this crucial question, not surprisingly, views differ. Where some analysts still see a potent role for government, ostensibly the ultimate locus of legitimate rule, others discern only constraint on political authority and a transfer of power to private societal actors. Who now rules – states or markets? To say the least, consensus remains elusive.

The aim of this chapter is to update our understanding of how money is governed in an increasingly globalized world. This will be done by shifting focus from capital mobility alone to the broader issue of substitutability between national monies: or the accelerating competition among currencies across political borders, driven largely by market forces. My argument is that monetary sovereignty has been not so much lost as transformed by contemporary developments. Where once existed formal *monopoly*, with each state claiming absolute control over money within its own territory, we now find effective *oligopoly* – a finite number of autonomous suppliers, national governments, all vying ceaselessly to shape and manage demand. Globalized money, at its most basic, has become a political contest for market loyalty, posing extraordinarily difficult choices for policy-makers.

The organization of the chapter is as follows. Current thinking on the role of money in a globalized world is briefly surveyed in the first section, followed by an outline of the basic parameters of cross-border currency competition. The main benefits of national monetary sovereignty are then summarized. The fourth section then analyses at some length the contemporary challenge to monetary sovereignty posed by cross-border currency competition. Following this discussion, we take up the tricky question of how governments may respond to their growing loss of monetary control. The difficult choices involved are illustrated in the sixth section by a brief review of policy reactions in East Asia to the worldwide financial crisis that began in 1997. States, the chapter concludes, are still able today to exercise authority in currency matters, but only within the constraints of oligopolistic rivalry rather than as privileged local monopolists.

The Capital Mobility Hypothesis

That national monetary sovereignty has been significantly compromised by financial globalization is manifest. Indeed, critical explorations of the political implications of financial globalization have become a staple – one might even say a cliché – of the recent scholarly literature.[1] Overwhelmingly, analysts concur that governmental authority has to some extent been eroded by the remarkable increase of capital mobility in recent decades. Where consensus breaks down is over the question of degree. *How much* has public policy been constrained and what, if anything, can governments do about it?

The most popular view among specialists, labeled by David Andrews the Capital Mobility Hypothesis, is also the most pessimistic. In financial matters, it is said, states have become essentially impotent. Andrews summarizes the proposition as follows:

> The premise [is] that the constraints imposed on states by capital mobility are structural in nature, or at a minimum can usefully be construed as structural by analysts. That is to say, the degree of international capital mobility systematically constrains state behavior by rewarding some actions and punishing others.[2]

The underlying logic of the Capital Mobility Hypothesis is unexceptionable, deriving directly from the dilemma of what I have elsewhere termed the 'Unholy Trinity' – the intrinsic incompatibility of currency stability, capital mobility, and national monetary autonomy.[3] Unless governments are willing to tolerate a virtually unlimited degree of exchange-rate volatility, they must, in a financially integrated world, carefully tailor their policies to what is needed to avoid sudden or massive capital flows. The challenge to public authority is real, neither easy to withstand nor, typically, amenable to formal negotiation.

Dissent from the Capital Mobility Hypothesis typically takes two forms, either empirical or theoretical. At the empirical level, statistical evidence is cited to suggest that practical constraints on state behavior may in fact be rather less pronounced than suggested – particularly if one distinguishes between monetary policy, which does indeed tend to be negatively impacted, and fiscal policy, which could remain a potentially potent tool of policy.[4] At the theoretical level, debate focuses mainly on the issue of reversibility. Has the constraint on monetary sovereignty really become something akin to a structural feature of the international system? In fact, we are reminded, financial globalization was a direct consequence of decisions taken at the national level to promote competition and deregulate markets. As Eric Helleiner has written: 'The contemporary open global financial order could not have emerged without the support and blessing of states.'[5] What governments have wrought, therefore, they might also undo should they so choose. Summarizes Louis Pauly: 'Capital mobility constrains states, but not absolutely . . . States can still defy markets . . . The abrogation of the emergent regime of international capital mobility . . . may be unlikely and undesirable, but it is certainly not inconceivable.'[6]

Neither form of dissent, however, has put much of a dent in the popularity of the Capital Mobility Hypothesis, which remains the dominant paradigm for thinking about money in today's globalized world. Empirical caveats do not prove the proposition wrong, just less than complete. Theoretical arguments for reversibility, meanwhile, are challenged by real evidence of significant hysteresis in the development of financial markets. After several decades of worldwide liberalization and innovation, a vast network of private institutions and intermediaries has now come into existence that can be used – legally if possible, illegally when felt necessary – to evade intervention by public authorities. Though abrogation of the regime of capital mobility might still be conceivable in principle, it would not be easy and would surely be costly in practice.

But that hardly means that the Capital Mobility Hypothesis is without flaw. On the contrary, for all its insight and relevance, the proposition borders on caricature, seriously misrepresenting both the scope and the severity of the challenge to contemporary government. In fact, the view manages simultaneously both to *understate* and to *overstate* the constraints now imposed on the monetary powers of states.

Constraints are understated because a focus on capital mobility, emphasizing asset-market integration, highlights only one function of money: its use for store-of-value purposes. In fact, that is only part of the story. Change in currency markets has really been far more extensive, involving all the standard functions of money – not just the role of money as a private investment vehicle, but also its use as a unit of account and, most critically, as a transactions medium – thus penetrating to the very core of what is meant by national monetary sovereignty. Much more is involved here than just borrowing and lending or trades of financial claims. It is, indeed, a matter of the basic effectiveness of government itself.

At the same time, the challenge is overstated because a focus on capital mobility, stressing the preferences of currency users, highlights only one side of the market: the demand side. That too ignores an important part of the story, namely supply, which even in an increasingly globalized world remains largely the privilege of the state. Governments are still the principal source of the monies that are now exchanged so easily across political frontiers. Hence the state, though challenged, still retains a considerable influence of its own in the governance of monetary affairs. The real issue is how governments choose to respond to the accelerating cross-border circulation and competition of currencies.

Cross-border currency competition[7]

When addressing issues of global finance, we are accustomed to thinking of money as effectively insular: each currency sovereign within the territorial frontiers of a single country or monetary union. In fact, nothing could be further from the truth.

For a currency to be truly 'territorial', its functional domain would have to coincide precisely with the political jurisdiction of its issuing state – a very special case. The currency would have to exercise an exclusive claim to all the traditional roles of money within the domestic economy. There could be no other money accepted for transactions purposes or used for the denomination of contracts or financial assets. And the government would have to be able to exercise sole control over the operation of the monetary system, dominating market agents. In matters of commerce, the equivalent would be described as 'autarky': national self-sufficiency. In truth, however, autarky is no more commonly achieved in monetary matters than it is in trade.

As a practical matter, a surprising number of monies today have come to be employed widely outside their country of origin for transactions either between nations or within foreign states. The former is usually referred to as 'international' currency use (or currency 'internationalization'); the latter is typically described by the term 'currency substitution' and may be referred to as 'foreign-domestic use'.[8] Reciprocally, an even larger number of monies now routinely face growing competition at home from currencies originating abroad. It is simply wrong to deny that several currencies may circulate in the same state. In fact, the phenomenon is increasingly prevalent.

Both currency internationalization (CI) and currency substitution (CS) are a product of intense market rivalry – a kind of Darwinian process of natural selection, driven by the force of demand, in which some monies such as the US dollar or Deutschmark (DM) come to be viewed as more attractive than others for various commercial or financial purposes. Cross-border circulation of currencies was once quite common prior to the emergence of the modern state system. More recently, the practice has re-emerged, as declining barriers to monetary exchange have greatly expanded the array of effective currency choice. Competition between national monies is accelerating rapidly. As a result, the domains within which individual currencies serve the standard functions of money now diverge more and more sharply from the legal jurisdictions of issuing governments. Money has become effectively 'deterritorialized'.

Regrettably, the full dimensions of today's currency deterritorialization cannot be measured precisely. Since comprehensive statistics on global currency circulation do not exist, neither CI nor CS can be accurately or consistently documented with any degree of refinement. Partial indicators, however, may be gleaned from a variety of reliable sources.[9] Though space limitations prevent their detailed reproduction here, some brief recapitulation can serve to underscore the impressive orders of magnitude involved.

The clearest signal of the accelerated pace of CI is sent by the global foreign-exchange market where, according to the Bank for International Settlements,[10] average daily turnover has accelerated from $620 billion in 1989 (the first year for which such data are available) to close to $1.5 trillion nine years later – a rate of increase of nearly 30 per cent per annum. A parallel story also seems evident in international markets for other financial claims, including bank deposits and loans as well as bonds and stocks, all of which have grown at double-digit rates for years. Using data from a variety of sources, Thygesen *et al.*[11] recently calculated what they call 'global financial wealth': the world's total portfolio of private international investments. From just over $1 billion in 1981, aggregate cross-border holdings quadrupled to more than $4.5 billion by 1993 – an expansion far faster than that of world output or trade in goods and services.

The clearest signal of the accelerated pace of CS is sent by the rapid increase in the physical circulation of several major currencies, including especially the dollar, DM, and yen, outside their country of origin. For the dollar, an authoritative study by two Federal Reserve economists[12] puts the value of US bank notes in circulation abroad at between 55 and 70 per cent of the total outstanding stock – equivalent to perhaps $250 billion in 1995. The same study also reckons that as much as three-quarters of the annual increase of notes in recent years has gone directly abroad, up from less than one-half in the 1980s and under one-third in the 1970s. Appetite for the greenback is obviously growing. Using a comparable approach, Germany's Bundesbank[13] has estimated Deutschmark circulation outside Germany at about 30 to 40 per cent of total stock, equivalent to some DM 65–90 billion ($45–65 billion) at the end of 1994. The mark's successor, the European Union's new euro, is confidently expected to take over the DM's role in foreign-domestic use once euro notes enter circulation in 2002 and perhaps even to cut into the dollar's market share.[14] In Asia, Bank of Japan officials are privately reported to believe that of the total supply of yen bank notes, amounting to some $370 billion in 1993, as much as 10 per cent may now be located outside Japan.[15] Combining these diverse estimates suggests a minimum foreign circulation of the biggest currencies of at least $300 billion in all – by no means an inconsiderable sum and, judging from available evidence, apparently growing rapidly.

The evidence also appears to suggest that a very wide range of countries is affected by the phenomenon, even if the precise numbers involved remain somewhat shrouded in mystery. According to one authoritative source, in the mid-1990s foreign bank notes accounted for 20 per cent or more of the local money stock in as many as three dozen nations inhabited by at least one-third of the world's population.[16] The same source also suggests that, in total, as much as one-quarter to one-third of the world's circulating currency was recently located outside its country of issue.[17]

These numbers clearly confirm the growing importance of both international and foreign-domestic use of money. Two main messages stand out. First, the scale of cross-border currency use is manifestly extensive and growing rapidly, reflecting both the scope and intensity of market-driven competition. Monetary circulation really is no longer confined to the territories of issuing countries. Strict autarky in currency relations is indeed a special case.

Second, while the number of monies actually employed for either international or foreign-domestic purposes tends to be rather small, the number of those routinely facing rivalry at home from currencies abroad appears to be remarkably large. Deterritorialization also means that there is no longer a functional equivalence among national monies. Even though all currencies of sovereign states enjoy nominally equal status as a matter of international law, some monies – to paraphrase George Orwell – clearly are far more equal than others as a matter of practical reality. Some monies, particularly in the developing world and so-called transition economies, face what amounts to a massive competitive invasion from abroad; others, especially those of the wealthiest industrial countries, are effectively immune from foreign rivalry at home. The population of the currency universe is in fact distinctly stratified.

Topping the charts, quite obviously, is the dollar, which remains by far the world's most popular choice for both CI and CS. In effect, the dollar's functional domain spans the globe, from the Western Hemisphere (where the accepted synonym for currency substitution is 'dollarization') to the former Soviet bloc and much of the Middle East (where dollars circulate widely as a de facto parallel currency).

Next comes the DM – soon to be replaced by the euro – which clearly dominates currency relations within much of the European neighbourhood, including East Central Europe and the Balkans. And not far behind are the yen and a handful of other elite international monies such as the pound sterling and Swiss franc. Much lower ranked are the many currencies of poorer countries – forced to struggle continuously for the loyalty of local users.

Add these two messages together and a picture emerges that is strikingly at variance with the conventional imagery of strictly territorial money – a universe of increasingly intense competition as well as a distinct hierarchy among currencies. Individually, national monies confront market forces that are increasingly indifferent to the barriers posed by political frontiers. Collectively, therefore, governments face a challenge to their monetary sovereignty that is unprecedented in modern times.

Benefits of monetary sovereignty

Monetary sovereignty, of course, continues to exist as a constitutive rule. It is the exceptional government that does not still seek to preserve, as best it can, an effective monopoly over the issue and management of money within its own territory. Production of money may not be an essential attribute of state sovereignty. Along with the raising of armies and the levying of taxes, however, it has long been regarded as such. As one observer has commented, with just a touch of sarcasm: 'A government that does not control money is a limited government . . . No government likes to be limited . . . Governments simply must monopolize money if they are to control it and they must control it if they really are to be governments.'[18]

It is easy to see why a monetary monopoly is so highly prized. Genuine power resides in the privilege that money represents. Four main benefits are derived from a strictly territorial currency: first, a potent political symbol to promote a sense of national identity; second, a potentially powerful source of revenue to underwrite public expenditures; third, a possible instrument to manage the macroeconomic performance of the economy; and finally, a practical means to insulate the nation from foreign influence or constraint. Within each state, all four advantages privilege the interests of the government in relation to societal actors.

At the symbolic level, a territorial currency is particularly useful to rulers wary of internal division or dissent. Centralization of political authority is facilitated insofar as citizens all feel themselves bound together as members of a single social unit – all part of the same 'imagined community', in Benedict Anderson's apt phrase.[19] Anderson stresses that states are made not just through force but through loyalty, a voluntary commitment to a joint identity. The critical distinction between 'us' and 'them' can be heightened by all manner of tangible symbols: flags, anthems, postage stamps, public architecture, even national sports teams. Among the most potent of these tokens is money, as Italian central banker Tommaso Padoa-Schioppa has noted: 'John Stuart Mill once referred to the existence of a multiplicity of national moneys as a 'barbarism' . . . [O]ne could perhaps talk of a tribal system, with each tribe being attached to its own money and attributing it magical virtues . . . which no other tribe recognizes.'[20]

Money's 'magical virtues' serve to enhance a sense of national identity in two ways. First, because it is issued by the government or its central bank, a currency acts as a daily reminder to citizens of their connection to the state and oneness with it. Second, by virtue of its universal use on a daily basis, the currency underscores the fact that everyone is part of the same social entity – a role not unlike that of a single national language, which many governments also actively promote for nationalistic reasons. A common money helps to homogenize diverse and often antagonistic social groups.

A second benefit of a territorial currency is 'seigniorage' – the capacity a monetary monopoly gives national governments to augment public spending at will. Technically defined as the excess of the nominal value of a currency over its cost of production, seigniorage can be understood as an alternative source of revenue for the state, beyond what can be raised via taxation or by borrowing from financial markets. Public spending financed by money creation in effect appropriates real resources at the expense of the private sector, whose purchasing power is correspondingly reduced by the ensuing increase of inflation – a privilege for government if there ever was one. Because of the inflationary implications involved, the process is also known popularly as the 'inflation tax'.

Despite the economic disadvantages associated with inflation, the privilege of seigniorage makes sense from a political perspective as a kind of insurance policy against risk – an emergency source of revenue to cope with unexpected contingencies, up to and including war. Decades ago John Maynard Keynes wrote: 'A government can live by this means when it can live by no other.'[21] Generations later another British economist, Charles Goodhart, has described seigniorage as the 'revenue of last resort'[22] – the single most flexible instrument of taxation available to mobilize resources in the event of an sudden crisis or threat to national security. It would be the exceptional government that would *not* wish to retain something like the option of an inflation tax.

A third benefit derives from money's potential impact on 'real' economic performance – aggregate output and employment – as well as prices. So long as governments can maintain control of currency supply within their own territory, they have the capacity, in principle at least, to influence and perhaps even manage the overall pace of market activity. Money may be used to promote the broad prosperity and strength of the state as well as the government's own narrowly drawn fiscal requirements.

Currency territorialization equips government with two potent policy instruments. First is the money supply itself, which can be manipulated to increase or decrease levels of expenditure by domestic residents. The second is the exchange rate – the price of home currency in terms of foreign currency – which can be manipulated to increase or decrease spending in the national economy through induced shifts between home and foreign goods. Neither instrument is infallible, of course; nor is either likely to attain a truly sustained impact on economic activity over the proverbial long term, if recent theoretical developments are to be believed. But over the shorter time horizons that are of most interest to public officials, monetary and exchange-rate policies do manifest substantial influence as tools for macroeconomic management. It would be an exceptional government that would not wish to retain these weapons in its arsenal as well.

Finally, an important benefit is derived in a negative sense – from the enhanced ability a territorial money gives government to avoid dependence on some other provenance for this most critical of all economic resources. Currency territoriality draws a clear economic boundary between the state and the rest of the world, promoting political authority. The closer government is able to come to achieving national monetary autarky, the better it will be able to insulate itself from outside influence or constraint in formulating and implementing policy.

That sovereign states might use monetary relations coercively, given the opportunity, should come as no surprise. As Jonathan Kirshner recently reminded us: 'Monetary power is a remarkably efficient component of state power . . . the most potent instrument of economic coercion available to states in a position to exercise it.'[23] Money, after all, is simply command over real resources. If a nation can be denied access to the means needed to purchase vital goods and services, it is clearly vulnerable in political terms. The lesson is simple: If you want political autonomy, don't rely on someone else's money.

Winners and losers

From the above discussion, it is clear that we should not be surprised that states cling so resolutely to the idea of monetary sovereignty. What matters, however, is not formal principle but actual practice – and that depends not just on the supply of money but also on demand, over which governments today have decreasingly firm control. States exercise direct jurisdiction only over the stock of national currency in circulation. In an increasingly globalized world, not even the most authoritarian government can assure that its money will always be preferred to currencies originating elsewhere.

Deterritorialization, therefore, is bound to alter the distribution of resources and capabilities in monetary affairs, both between governments and between the public and private sectors. Clearly, critical shifts occur in the balance of power among states. Less obviously, but no less importantly, decisive changes ensue in the reciprocal interaction between governments and markets – changes that can have a profound impact on effective political authority in every state, whatever the competitiveness of its currency.

Political symbolism

Consider the political symbolism of money. If a territorial currency acts to cultivate a sense of national identity, deterritorialization might logically be expected to have more or less the reverse effect, loosening ties of loyalty to the state. In fact, however, consequences are rather less straightforward than would appear. In some cases, identification with the 'imagined community' may actually be reinforced rather than reduced by an erosion of monetary insularity. Governments may gain as well as lose, depending not only on the outcome of the Darwinian struggle between currencies but also on how official policies interact with the preferences of market actors.

Deterritorialization clearly does dilute the 'magical' qualities of money for governments with relatively uncompetitive currencies: monies whose authority at home is significantly compromised by more popular rivals abroad. The more a foreign currency comes to be used domestically in lieu of national money, for example, as a result of excessive inflation or a perceived devaluation risk, the less citizens feel inherently connected to the state or part of the same social entity. The critical distinction between 'us' and 'them' is gradually eroded. Worse, an instrument that was intended to symbolize the power and nobility of the nation becomes instead a daily reminder of inadequacy and impotence – not sound currency but 'funny money', an object of derision and disrespect. Governments that issue such money are not apt to command much respect either.

Looking to the most competitive currencies, on the other hand, deterritorialization appears more likely to enhance than to dilute a money's 'magical' qualities. A position of prominence in the hierarchy of currencies plainly promotes the issuing state's overall reputation in world affairs. Broad international circulation tends to become an important source of status and prestige – a highly visible sign of elevated rank in the community of nations. What people would not take pride in the esteem accorded one of its most tangible symbols?

Matters get more complicated, however, when governments attempt to intervene to modify or control market preferences. A weak currency, for instance, might also become a source of strength if a government is determined to do something – or, at least, to give the appearance of doing something – about a competitive challenge from abroad. In effect, monetary policy may be transformed into an exercise in political symbolism. A market-driven invasion of foreign money can be treated as the equivalent of an overt military aggression. Defence of the national currency may thus be promoted as the equivalent of a glorious stand on behalf of the 'imagined community' – the ultimate expression of *amor patriae*.

Conversely, a strong currency might also become a source of weakness, particularly if a government attempts to preserve an international role for a money whose popularity has begun to fade. No currency has ever enjoyed a permanent dominance in cross-border use. Once gained, though, the prestige of 'great-currency' status might quite understandably be difficult to surrender, even apart from any material benefits that may accrue. But just as a determined defence against an invading currency at home can inspire renewed confidence in a government, fruitless efforts to promote or revive a national money's fortunes abroad may well have the reverse effect, encouraging increased scepticism and even ridicule. Efforts to manipulate market demand in this manner are not always fated to succeed, as anyone with a memory of the last days of the old sterling area can testify.

Seigniorage

Impacts on the seigniorage privilege will also vary depending on the competitiveness of individual monies as well as the interaction of official policies with market preferences. For less competitive currencies, a government's capacity to appropriate resources via money creation is plainly compromised insofar as convenient substitutes for domestic currency become readily available from abroad. In effect, the base for levying an inflation tax is shrunk. As a consequence, state power to cope with unexpected contingencies is undoubtedly constrained.

But is state power correspondingly augmented for countries with more competitive monies? At first glance, there seems no doubt on that point either. The broader a currency's functional domain, the easier it should be for its issuing government to exploit the fiscal benefits of seigniorage. Not only is the domestic monetary monopoly protected, but now foreigners also can be turned into a source of revenue to the extent that they are willing to hold the money or use it outside the country of origin. Expanded cross-border circulation generates the equivalent of a subsidized or interest-free loan from abroad – an implicit transfer that represents a real-resource gain for the economy as a whole. Economists refer to this as 'international' seigniorage, in order to distinguish it clearly from the more traditional domestic variety. International seigniorage can be quite considerable in practice, as the historical experiences of both sterling and US dollar have amply demonstrated. But international seigniorage can be exploited only so long as a currency retains its competitive superiority in the marketplace – an advantage that can never be permanently guaranteed. In practice, therefore, the issuing state's seigniorage capacity may in time actually be decreased rather than increased.

The problem can be simply stated. As overseas circulation grows, foreigners may legitimately worry more about the possibility of future devaluation or even restrictions on the usability of their holdings. Hence, over time, the issuing government will have to pay increasing attention to competition from other currencies and to curb its appetite for the inflation tax accordingly. At a minimum, interest rates may have to be raised significantly to maintain the money's financial attractiveness. Ultimately, national policies will almost certainly be inhibited by the need to discourage sudden or substantial conversions through the exchange market.

In short, the power derived from the seigniorage privilege may be constrained for all countries, whatever the competitiveness of their currencies. In a world of accelerating cross-border use, no government can afford to ignore the preferences of market actors when reckoning how to finance its expenditures.

Macroeconomic management

Much the same can also be said about a government's capacity for macroeconomic management. Here too state power will be affected in all countries, and here too much will depend on how official policies interact with market preferences.

In this connection, the main impact of deterritorialization is felt in the mechanism for balance-of-payments financing. Economists have long contrasted the relative ease of adjustment to interregional imbalances *within* countries with the frequently greater difficulties associated with payments adjustments *between* countries. One major difference is the greater scope for equilibrating capital flows within an individual country in the event of transitory disturbances, owing to the existence of a stock of 'generalized' short-term financial claims that can be readily traded between surplus and deficit regions. The development of these generalized claims, in turn, has traditionally been attributed to the existence of a single national currency, which of course removes all exchange risk.

Such reasoning is obviously based on the conventional assumption of autarky in monetary relations. The same logic applies, however, even if that assumption is relaxed in recognition of the accelerating pace of cross-border currency use. The broader the functional domain

of a given money, the greater will be the effective range for equilibrating capital flows, taking the form of purchases and sales of
generalized claims denominated in that single currency. Other things
being equal, therefore, these flows should reduce the costs of adjustment for countries with the most competitive monies. Their macroeconomic policy flexibility should be effectively enhanced. Countries
with weaker currencies, by contrast, should find themselves less able
to rely on equilibrating capital flows in the adjustment process. With
confidence in their money lacking, their room for manoeuvre will be
correspondingly reduced.

Consequences for neither class of country, however, are entirely
unambiguous. For top-ranked states, domestic monetary policy could
conceivably be pegged to a misleading target, since a large but
indeterminate part of the money stock is in circulation abroad. Policy
might also be destabilized periodically by unanticipated variations of
foreign demand for the domestic currency or by a crisis threatening a
weaker client currency (as the dollar was threatened by the Mexican
peso crisis in late 1994). The gain of policy flexibility is by no means
costless. Likewise, for lower-ranked countries, implications vary
depending on how governments choose to respond to the reduction
of their room for manoeuvre. Little economic control is gained, and
much financial stability may be lost, if efforts to preserve monetary
autonomy are not regarded as credible by market actors. On the
other hand, a much healthier economic performance may be at-
tained, with lower costs of adjustment, if governments in effect submit
their nominal sovereignty, at least in part, to the strict discipline of
the marketplace. At a minimum, such states are obliged to take due
account of market sentiment in framing macroeconomic policy.

Monetary insulation

The story also seems much the same when we come to the fourth
benefit of a monetary monopoly: insulation from external influence.
In this respect too states with the most popular monies would appear
to gain disproportionately, insofar as expansion of a currency's
functional domain offers a potential means for coercing others.
Political power should be enhanced at the expense of lower-ranked
countries that become correspondingly more dependent on a foreign
money; but, in this connection also, results are highly sensitive to the
interplay of official policies and market preferences.

That hierarchy among currencies might influence the distribution of power between states is clear. The very notion of hierarchy is political in nature, suggesting varying degrees of reciprocal influence – differential impacts on the ability of governments to achieve goals at home or abroad. Internationally, the issuer of a widely circulated currency is in a position to exercise influence over others through its control of access to financial resources, directly or indirectly. Real resources may be gained through the privilege of international seigniorage; and the structure of the system may be shaped to persuade other governments that they have a vital stake in continued adherence to existing rules. Domestically, the country should be better insulated from outside influence or coercion in formulating and implementing policy. But here too leverage can be exploited only so long as the currency in question retains its competitive superiority in the marketplace. Once rival monies begin to emerge, the issuing country will find that its ability to manipulate the dependency of others may in fact be compromised. Prospective outcomes will very much depend on the reactions of market agents, who may either reinforce or nullify the impact of overtly coercive measures. The exercise of power, therefore, will increasingly demand a systematic cultivation of market sentiment. Equilibrating capital flows may continue to provide an extra degree of policy flexibility to deal with transitory payments shocks. Over time, however, state behaviour will be increasingly constrained by the need to discourage sudden or substantial conversions into other currencies. Ultimately effective political power, on balance, may well be decreased rather than increased.

Summary

How, then, can we summarize the impact of spreading cross-border competition on state authority? Some individual governments, particularly those with the most widely accepted monies, actually benefit in key respects, at least for a time. Moreover, their gains plainly come at the expense of states with less competitive currencies, shifting the traditional balance of power in their favour.

Not even the most top-ranked countries, however, are immune from market pressures forever. Over time, every one of the advantages of broad international acceptability is subject to erosion by the force of demand-driven competition. On balance, accordingly, it seems evident that in comparative terms the biggest winners are not governments at all, however popular their currencies may be, but rather a select set of private societal actors – specifically, those in the marketplace with the capacity and opportunity to choose among alternative monies. In the relationship between state and society, it is plainly the latter that is more favoured by deterritorialization. Governments everywhere are privileged less, elements of the private sector more.

In purely material terms, such societal actors attain a significant measure of efficiency gains: an improvement in the usefulness of money for all its principal functions. Cross-border substitutability also provides an effective refuge against abuse of the seigniorage privilege. Politically, the private sector achieves a degree of leverage over public policy that is unprecedented in modern times. The power of the state is clearly diminished.

The state as oligopolist

Does that mean that where once governments exercised monetary sovereignty, the private sector now categorically rules? The answer, it should be clear, is 'no' – not so long as states remain the principal source of the currencies that today compete so vigorously across national frontiers. The Darwinian struggle may be intense, but it is a struggle that, for now at least, is limited on the supply side almost exclusively to official national monies. Governments thus continue to play a role, albeit a lessened one, in the management of monetary affairs. The power of the state may be diminished. It has not, however, been extinguished.

Rivals to national monies do exist, of course, but for the present mostly take the form of very local private monies that are little different from institutionalized systems of barter.[24] One day a new and more threatening kind of competitor may well be generated in the developing world of cyberspace, if and when digital entries in computers – electronic cash or 'e-cash', as they are sometimes called – begin to substitute for bank notes and checking accounts as customary means of payment.[25] But even that threat will remain nothing more than hypothetical until e-cash, once introduced, can command the same general acceptability as conventional monies, a development that at the moment would appear still to be a long way over the horizon. Until that distant future, traditional state monies will continue to dominate the supply side of the market.

Thus not one but two sets of actors are intimately involved here: not just the users of money but also its producers – governments. Neither one side nor the other, therefore, is wholly in charge. Rather, as in any market setting, it is supply and demand together, interacting symbiotically, that determine final outcomes. The basic point was made many years ago by the renowned English economist Alfred Marshall, commenting on whether it is demand ('utility') or supply ('cost of production') that governs market results ('value'): 'We might as reasonably dispute whether it is the upper or the under blade of a pair of scissors that cuts a piece of paper, as whether value is governed by utility or cost of production.'[26]

Likewise, in our own time, we might as reasonably dispute whether it is the state or society that governs. In reality, as with Marshall's scissors, it is both, each playing a critical reciprocal role in an ongoing dialectical process. The real question is what, if anything, governments can do about their loss of monetary authority.

With deterritorialization, governments have been deprived of the monopoly control they once claimed over demand. This is as true for countries at the top of the currency hierarchy as it is at the bottom. The reason is that today many transactors now have an alternative: the happy option of currency choice. Few states, therefore, are any longer in a position to *enforce* an exclusive role for their own money within established political frontiers. Governments do, however, still dominate the supply side of the market, retaining jurisdiction over the issue of money. Hence they are in a position still to *influence* demand insofar as they can successfully compete, inside and across borders, for the allegiance of market agents. Power is retained to the extent that user preferences can be swayed.

In essence, therefore, the role of states today is not unlike that of competing firms in an oligopolistic industry – the state as oligopolist – and no one has ever accused oligopolists of a lack of practical authority. In a world of increasing interpenetration of monetary domains, all governments find themselves driven to join the competitive fray, to preserve or promote market share for their product. Like oligopolistic firms, governments assert influence by doing what they can, consciously or unconsciously, to shape and manage demand.

Commercial rivalry between states is nothing new, of course. Governments have always contested one another for markets and resources as part of the great game of world politics. Nor is the idea that all states must now vie to attract diverse market agents any longer particularly novel. More than a decade ago, the late Susan Strange had already noted how the spreading globalization of world markets was pushing governments into a new kind of geopolitical rivalry, 'competing for world market shares as the surest means to greater wealth'.[27] More recently, Philip Cerny crystallized the idea in his notion of the 'competition state' – governments 'driven by the imperatives of global competition to expand transnationalization'.[28] The competition state, however, participates in markets only indirectly, mainly as a catalyst to alter incentives confronting agents on both sides, supply as well as demand. What is unique about cross-border currency competition is that the state participates directly as the dominant actor on one side: the supply side. It is the government's own creation, its money, that must be marketed and promoted.

Oligopoly provides a particularly apt analogy in this regard because of its two key structural characteristics of interdependence and uncertainty. Both are inherent features of the traditional state system as well. In the inter-state system, as in an oligopolistic industry, actors are sufficiently few in number, so that the behaviour of any one has an appreciable effect on at least some of its competitors; in turn, the actions and reactions of other actors cannot be predicted with certainty. The result is an interdependence of decision-making that compels all states, like rival firms, to be noticeably preoccupied with considerations of long-term strategy. In this sense, producers of currency are essentially no different from producers of cars or computers.

Moreover, like producers of cars or computers, governments have been forced to implement their strategies via efforts to manage the demand side of the market – in effect, to 'sell' their product. Their targets are the users of money, at home or abroad. Their aim is to sustain or enhance a currency's functional domain, almost as if monies were like goods to be sold under registered trademarks. As economist Robert Aliber has quipped, 'the dollar and Coca-Cola are both brand names'.[29] In his words: 'Each national central bank produces its own brand of money . . . Each national money is a differentiated product . . . Each central bank has a marketing strategy to strengthen the demand for its particular brand of money.'[30]

The task, of course, may not be easy. What strategies are available to governments to market their brand of money? Broadly speaking, economic theory distinguishes between two contrasting approaches to the formulation of competitive strategy in an oligopolistic setting. Firm behaviour can be either defensive or offensive – that is, designed either to build defences against existing competitive forces; or, alternatively, to attack existing conditions in order to enhance market position. The former seeks to match the firm's strengths and weaknesses to its environment, taking the structure of the industry as given. The latter seeks to improve the firm's position in relation to its environment by actively influencing the balance of forces in the marketplace. Currency policy too can be either defensive or offensive, aiming either to preserve or promote market share.

In turn, each approach may be pursued either unilaterally or collusively, yielding a total of four possible broad strategies. These are:

(1) *Market leadership*: an aggressive unilateralist policy intended to maximize use of the national currency, analogous to predatory price leadership in an oligopoly.

(2) *Market alliance*: a collusive policy of sharing monetary sovereignty in a monetary or exchange-rate union of some kind, analogous to a tacit or explicit cartel.

(3) *Market preservation*: a status-quo policy intended to defend, rather than augment, a previously acquired market position.

(4) *Market followership*: an acquiescent policy of subordinating monetary sovereignty to a stronger foreign currency via some form of exchange-rate rule, analogous to passive price followership in an oligopoly.

Strategies, in turn, require tactics. For governments, again, two contrasting approaches are possible – either *persuasion* or *coercion*. Though neither approach is foolproof, either may help to influence overall demand for a currency. In practice, most governments have learned to make use of both, in varying combinations, since the two are not mutually exclusive.

Persuasion is of course the standard approach of the private sector, where coercion is presumably illegal. In an industrial oligopoly, rival firms may enhance the appeal of their products via price cuts, quality improvements, aggressive advertising, or any number of similar marketing devices. In the international arena, states can try to do the same by investing in their money's reputation, acting to reinforce the attractiveness of a currency for any or all of the usual monetary purposes. The idea is to enhance confidence in the money's continued usefulness and reliability – unfortunately, not something that can be accomplished quickly, and certainly not without considerable cost and effort. Resources thus must be expended persistently to establish and sustain a successful brand name.

Several means of persuasion are possible. Most narrowly, use of a money might be encouraged by higher interest rates, convertibility guarantees, or special tax advantages on selected liquid assets. More broadly, governments can try to promote acceptance by facilitating expansion of a currency's circulation, for example by sponsoring development of debt markets denominated in their own money. Most fundamentally, a currency's reputation may be buttressed by a credible commitment to 'sound' monetary management, a character- istic that is highly prized in the Darwinian struggle among monies. Rational transactors are unlikely to be attracted to the currency of a government that cannot resist the temptation to willfully exploit the seigniorage privilege. States that wish to avoid a flight from their currency thus must, in effect, practice a kind of fiscal self-denial – a 'patience for revenue', as one economist puts it[31] – voluntarily limiting issue of their own money.

One way to make such a commitment credible is by means of a currency board or firm exchange-rate rule: a strategy of followership. As many high-inflation states have discovered, in the former Soviet bloc as well as in the developing world, the so-called 'strong-currency option', borrowing credibility from a respected central bank else- where, may be the only route to building or restoring confidence in a feeble national currency. Alternatively, governments may seek to restore credibility more on their own, without direct subordination to a stronger foreign currency, by way of a convincing reform of macroeconomic policy at home – a strategy of market preservation instead of followership. Where possible, many states may prefer to cope directly with the discipline of the marketplace rather than to submit to the dominion of another government.

Complementing all this is the possibility of coercion – legally, the unique privilege of sovereign governments in the modern state system. True, oligopolistic actors in the private sector may also resort at times to high-pressure tactics, such as compulsory tying arrange- ments or exclusive marketing schemes, but only insofar as the law allows and never backed by a legitimate threat of force. States, on the other hand, are the ones who actually make the law and are the embodiment of coercive authority. The principle of political sovereignty permits governments, alone among economic agents, to rely on much more than just the art of persuasion to defend market position.

Indeed, coercion has long been a part of every government's arsenal in monetary affairs, going back to the monopolization of monetary powers that began in the nineteenth century. Most prevalent are legal-tender laws and so-called public receivability provisions. Legal tender is the term given to any money that a creditor is obligated to accept in settlement of a debt. Public receivability refers to what currency may be used for remittance of taxes or to satisfy other contractual obligations to the state. Also available is a broad range of other measures that might be used to regulate private financial activity, up to and including direct controls over cross-border capital flows or exchange transactions. It may not be true that conventional territorial currencies would disappear completely in the absence of legal restrictions, as some economists have argued, but it is evident that without such measures the demand for many national monies, particularly those most challenged by competition from abroad, would be significantly reduced – for some, perhaps even to the vanishing point. The Darwinian struggle has little sympathy for the weak.

Illustrations from East Asia

Nothing demonstrates the pitilessness of that struggle more than the financial crisis that swept over East Asia following devaluation of the Thai baht in mid-1997. Initially, as the first shockwaves of currency speculation hit the region, the impulse of governments was to go on the defensive, investing expensively in determined efforts to restore confidence in their currencies – the 'confidence game', as Paul Krugman ironically dubbed it.[32] The object of the game was market preservation, at almost any cost. User preferences, however, proved more resistant to tactics of persuasion than first anticipated, and governments that previously had taken pride in the competitiveness of their national monies suddenly found themselves unable to sustain market share. Strategies that once seemed adequate to manage demand now had to be re-evaluated in the light of a worldwide 'flight to quality' by mobile capital. The question was: Could anyone think of an effective alternative?

Currency boards?

For a few, the answer seemed obvious: Abandon any pretence of national monetary sovereignty and adopt instead a strategy of strict market followership in the form of a currency board, as already existed in Brunei and Hong Kong. Long promoted by a small coterie of specialists inspired by the writings of American economist Steve Hanke,[33] the currency-board idea enjoyed a brief vogue in Indonesia in early 1998 prior to the forced resignation of President Suharto in May. In February 1998, on Hanke's advice, the government announced it was moving ahead with plans to establish a currency-board system linked to the US dollar. Suharto himself referred to the project as an 'IMF-plus' program.[34]

In the end, however, the idea was abandoned under pressure from the Fund and other foreign creditors, who – with very good reason – sensed a disaster in the making. Certainly a currency board had not protected Hong Kong from the relentless pressures of destabilizing speculation. Given the level of uncertainty in Indonesia at the time, establishment of a currency board might well have led to a rush to buy dollars, generating sky-high interest rates that in turn could have crushed what was left of the country's banking system. The Indonesian government was soon persuaded that it first needed to strengthen financial markets, deal with foreign debts, and bolster central-bank reserves before it could even think of embarking on such a risky experiment. Accordingly, the plan was formally abandoned in late March, and no other country in the region has since indicated any interest in moving in the same direction.

Monetary union?

For others, the answer seemed to lie in a different direction – in abandoning monetary sovereignty not to a currency board but rather to a monetary union of some kind on the model of Europe's new euro. In short, go on the offensive with a forceful strategy of market alliance. Union would offer the benefit of numbers – and thus the hope that the whole might, in effect, be greater than the sum of the parts. Who could doubt, after all, that one joint money might be more attractive than a myriad of separate national currencies? Even before the crisis broke, the idea was already being actively explored by prominent scholars.[35] Once the region's troubles began, interest rapidly spread. In the words of one observer: 'Some kind of monetary regionalism in the region is . . . inevitable.'[36] According to another: 'Asia should . . . create an Asian Monetary Union.'[37] Official responses, however, were for the most part distinctly unenthusiastic.[38] For a variety of reasons, political as well as economic, no government was yet prepared to forsake completely its own brand of money.

In fact, it is evident that the political preconditions for monetary union in Asia were not yet in place. As I have written elsewhere, the lessons of history on this issue are clear.[39] To be sustainable, a joint currency among sovereign states requires one or the other of two prerequisites: either a local hegemon to enforce discipline or else a broad network of institutional linkages sufficient to neutralize the risks of free-riding or exit by any participant. Neither prerequisite was yet in evidence in Asia.

Certainly it was clear that Asian countries lacked a broad constellation of commitments of the sort that might have made a full surrender of monetary sovereignty immediately acceptable to each partner. The void was not for want of trying. Even before the crisis, regional central banks had begun to build institutional linkages in a series of low-profile forums designed to promote dialogue and mutual exchanges of information.[40] Such groupings, many hoped, might help weave precisely the sort of fabric of related ties that could one day support more ambitious strategies of monetary alliance. But despite such efforts there was still little tradition of true financial solidarity – to say nothing of political solidarity – across the region.

On the other hand, there obviously was a potential hegemon in the neighbourhood: Japan. Indeed, it is fair to say that no initiative toward monetary union in the region would have much chance at all without the active participation of Asia's dominant financial power. But were Asians yet prepared to bury historical suspicions of Japanese motivations and interests? Japan, despite its own economic travails, might well aspire to a strategy of market leadership, but it was not at all clear that others in the area would voluntarily follow. In fact, nothing approximating a formal yen bloc seemed politically acceptable to regional governments.

To be sure, that did not rule out less ambitious forms of joint collaboration with the Japanese, so long as Japan's hegemonic pretensions remained relatively muted. In early 1996, for example, as many as nine governments in the area were happy to sign up for a series of agreements committing the Bank of Japan to make yen credits available when needed to help stabilize exchange rates.[41] And in 1997, after the first shockwaves of crisis hit, they were even more enthusiastic about Tokyo's proposal for a new regional financial facility – what came to be called the Asian Monetary Fund (AMF) – to help protect national currencies against speculative attack.[42] The AMF proposal was by far the most ambitious effort by Japan to implement a strategy of market leadership in Asian finance. Although successfully blocked by the United States, which publicly expressed concern about a possible threat to the central role of the IMF in monetary affairs,[43] the idea continued to attract interest in Asia, and Tokyo persisted in seeking new ways to promote regional cooperation based on a more internationalized yen.[44] The process, however, is apt to be much more evolutionary than revolutionary in nature, offering little likelihood of significant change in the near term.

Capital controls?

A third possible answer lay in yet another direction: a reversal of currency deterritorialization via capital controls – in effect, a strategy of market preservation based more on coercion than persuasion. Though once widely favoured as a means of preserving monetary sovereignty, particularly in the first decades after the Second World War, capital controls had long since come to be derided as wrong-headed if not downright anachronistic – not only inefficient but, in an increasingly globalized world, perhaps unworkable as well. In the midst of the worst financial crisis since the Great Depression, however, the question could legitimately be asked: Could their disadvantages really be so much greater than their advantages? Influential voices were soon heard calling for a reconsideration of the case for controls, led by Paul Krugman and fellow-economist Jagdish Bhagwati. As Bhagwati wrote: 'When a crisis hits, the downside of free capital mobility arises . . . The gains from economic efficiency that would flow from free capital mobility, in a hypothetical crisis-free world, must be set against this loss if a wise decision is to be made.'[45]

Advocates of capital controls in the Asian region were inspired above all by the obvious example of China. Though hardly without tribulations of its own, including a near-bankrupt banking system, loss-making state industries, and rising unemployment, China was spared the worst ravages of the financial crisis. Where other economies were being pushed into recession, Chinese growth barely faltered; and where other regional currencies were being depreciated in value by anywhere from 10–20 per cent in Taiwan and Singapore to as much as (at one time) 80 per cent in Indonesia, the yuan held steady. One of the main reasons, clearly, was China's vast panoply of exchange and capital restrictions, which made it virtually impossible for users, domestic or foreign, to bet heavily on a devaluation. It seemed only natural, therefore, to ask whether similar limits might work for other countries as well.

The most dramatic response came from Malaysia, which in September 1998 imposed strict controls of its own over the convertibility of the national currency, the ringgit, for both trade and investment uses. Kuala Lumpur's new strategy was adopted quite self-consciously in emulation of the Chinese. Said one government minister: 'Malaysia's new currency controls are based on China's model.'[46]

In the first year of the crisis, the Malaysian economy had shrunk by close to 7 per cent, the value of the ringgit by 40 per cent, and the Kuala Lumpur stock market by 75 per cent. By the end of August 1998, the country's authoritarian leader, Prime Minister Mahathir Mohamad, was no longer prepared to tolerate the orthodox policies of his finance minister (and heir apparent) Anwar Ibrahim, who was fired and later jailed. Those policies, the Prime Minister believed, simply collaborated in a Western conspiracy to ruin the Malaysian economy. The time had come, he asserted, to take back control from international speculators, led by financier George Soros and 'the Jews.' Henceforth circulation of the ringgit would be carefully controlled, the exchange rate was to be rigidly fixed, and capital invested in the country would have to remain for at least one year before it could be repatriated. The idea was to provide room for more expansionary domestic policies than had otherwise seemed possible. Monetary policy was immediately eased, with interest rates cut sharply, and in October a new budget was brought in combining substantial tax cuts with heavy new public spending programs. 'The plan', Dr Mahathir told legislators, 'aims at freeing Malaysia from the grip of the Asian financial crisis and to place Malaysia's economy on a stronger footing.'[47]

That the Prime Minister's radical new controls would prove controversial was hardly surprising. Though easy to ridicule for his conspiratorial views, Dr Mahathir none-the-less posed a serious challenge for conventional views on monetary management, which took the primacy of capital mobility as a given. For decades, emerging nations had been lectured on the virtues of financial-market liberalization – yet here was a government that was doing just the reverse, despite the risks and potentially high costs involved. Moreover early signs, though mixed, suggested that Malaysia's economy might actually respond positively to the regime's expansionary policies. Although no other country immediately followed Dr Mahathir's lead, it was clear that his audacity could yet have a powerful demonstration effect. What if Malaysia should indeed recover more quickly as a result of its new wall of insulation against international speculation? The experiment was being carefully watched by regional governments.

Conclusion

States, we may thus conclude, face difficult choices in today's increasingly globalized world. Governments have not lost a role as a result of currency deterritorialization. They are still part of money's implicit system of governance. But, as the Asian financial crisis amply demonstrates, the traditional notion of monetary sovereignty has come to be increasingly and forcefully contested by competitive market forces. Governments have been compelled to adapt to a dramatic transformation of their status – from monopoly to oligopoly – and authority must now be exercised in fundamentally different ways if it is to stay at all effective.

Notes

1. For two recent surveys, see B. J. Cohen, 'Phoenix Risen: The Resurrection of Global Finance', *World Politics*, 48 (1996) 268–96; and D. M. Andrews and T. D. Willett, 'Financial Interdependence and the State: International Monetary Relations at Century's End', *International Organization*, 51 (1997) 479–511.
2. D. M. Andrews, 'Capital Mobility and State Autonomy: Toward a Structural Theory of International Monetary Relations', *International Studies Quarterly*, 38 (1994) 197, 204.

3. B.J. Cohen, 'The Triad and the Unholy Trinity: Lessons for the Pacific Region', in R. Higgott, R. Leaver, and J. Ravenhill (eds), *Pacific Economic Relations in the 1990s: Cooperation or Conflict?* (Boulder, CO: Lynne Rienner, 1993) 133–58.

4. See, for example, W.R. Clark and U.N. Reichert, 'International and Domestic Constraints on Political Business Cycle Behavior in OECD Economies', *International Organization*, 52 (1998) 87–120; G. Garrett, 'Global Markets and National Politics: Collision Course or Virtuous Circle?', *International Organization*, 52 (1998) 787–824; T. Oatley, 'How Constraining is Capital Mobility? The Partisan Hypothesis in an Open Economy', *American Journal of Political Science*, 43 (1999) 1003–27 and Chapter 5 of this volume.

5. E. Helleiner, *States and the Reemergence of Global Finance* (Ithaca, NY: Cornell University Press, 1994).

6. L.W. Pauly, 'Capital Mobility, State Autonomy and Political Legitimacy', *Journal of International Affairs*, 48 (1995) 373.

7. The discussion in this section is necessarily condensed. For more detail on the characteristics and implications of cross-border currency competition, see B.J. Cohen, *The Geography of Money* (Ithaca, NY: Cornell University Press, 1998).

8. Useful sources on currency internationalization include P.R. Krugman, 'The International Role of the Dollar', in P.R. Krugman, *Currencies and Crises* (Cambridge, MA: MIT Press, 1992) 165–83; and S.W. Black, 'The International Use of Currencies', in D.K. Das, *International Finance* (London: Routledge, 1993). General introductions to currency substitution include A. Giovannini and B. Turtelboom, 'Currency Substitution', in F. Van Der Ploeg, *The Handbook of International Macroeconomics* (Oxford: Basil Blackwell, 1994) 390–436; and P.D. Mizen and E.J. Pentecost, *The Macroeconomics of International Currencies: Theory, Policy and Evidence* (Brookfield, VT: Edward Elgar, 1996).

9. Representative samples can be found in Cohen, *The Geography of Money* and N. Thygesen *et al.*, *International Currency Competition and the Future Role of the Single European Currency* (London: Kluwer Law International, 1995).

10. Bank for International Settlements, *Central Bank Survey of Foreign Exchange and Derivatives Market Activity* (Basle: BIS, 1999).

11. Thygesen *et al*, *International Currency Competition*, p. 145.

12. R.D. Porter and R.A. Judson, 'The Location of US Currency: How Much is Abroad?', *Federal Reserve Bulletin*, 82 (1996) 883–903.

13. Bundesbank, 'The Circulation of Deutsche Mark Abroad', *Monthly Report*, 47 (1995) 65–71.

14. See, for example, K. Rogoff, 'Blessing or Curse? Foreign and Underground Demand for Euro Notes', in D. Begg, J. von Hagen, C. Wyplosz and K.F. Zimmerman, *EMU: Prospects and Challenges for the Euro* (Oxford: Blackwell, 1998).

15. D.D. Hale, 'Is It a Yen or a Dollar Crisis in the Currency Market?', *Washington Quarterly*, 18 (1995) 164.

16. R. Krueger and J. Ha, 'Measurement of Cocirculation of Currencies', in Mizen and Pentecost, *The Macroeconomics of International Currencies*, pp. 60–1.

17. Krueger and Ha, 'Measurement', p. 76.

18. D. O'Mahony, 'Past Justifications for Public Interventions', in P. Salin, *Currency Competition and Monetary Union* (The Hague: Martinus Nijhoff, 1984) p. 127.

19. B. Anderson, *Imagined Communities: Reflections on the Origins and Spread of Nationalism*, rev. edn (London: Verso, 1991).
20. T. Padoa-Schioppa, *Tripolarism: Regional and Global Economic Cooperation* (Washington, DC: Group of 30, 1993) p. 16. Padoa-Schioppa, once deputy governor of the Bank of Italy, is now one of the six members of the executive council of the European Central Bank.
21. J. M. Keynes, *Tract on Monetary Reform* (1924) reprinted in *The Collected Writings of John Maynard Keynes*, vol. 4 (London: Macmillan, 1971).
22. C. A. E. Goodhart, 'The Political Economy of Monetary Union', in P. B. Kenen, *Understanding Interdependence: The Macroeconomics of the Open Economy* (Princeton, NJ: Princeton University Press, 1995) p. 452.
23. J. Kirshner, *Currency and Coercion: The Political Economy of International Monetary Power* (Princeton, NJ: Princeton University Press, 1995) pp. 29, 31.
24. Literally hundreds of private monies exist around the world, particularly in English-speaking countries, but none trades in any significant amount across national frontiers. In Britain alone there are at least 45, many with exotic – not to say eccentric – names like beaks, bobbins, cockles, and kreds. For some discussion, see L. D. Solomon, *Rethinking Our Centralized Monetary System: The Case for a System of Local Currencies* (Westport, CN: Praeger, 1996).
25. For a prediction along these lines, see S. J. Kobrin, 'Electronic Cash and the End of National Markets', *Foreign Policy*, 107 (1997) 65–77. But for a contrary opinion, see E. Helleiner, 'Electronic Money: A Challenge to the Sovereign State?', *Journal of International Affairs*, 51 (1998) 387–409.
26. A. Marshall, *Principles of Economics*, 8th edn (New York: Macmillan, 1948).
27. S. Strange, 'The Persistent Myth of Lost Hegemony', *International Organization*, 41 (1987) 564.
28. P. G. Cerny, 'The Infrastructure of the Infrastructure? Toward 'Embedded Financial Orthodoxy' in the International Political Economy', in R. P. Palan and B. Gills, *Transcending the State-Global Divide: A Neostructuralist Agenda in International Relations* (Boulder, CO: Lynne Rienner) p. 225.
29. R. Z. Aliber, *The International Money Game*, 5th edn (New York: Basic Books, 1987) p. 153.
30. Aliber, *The International Money Game*, p. 153.
31. J. A. Ritter, 'The Transition from Barter to Fiat Money', *American Economic Review*, 85 (1995) 134.
32. P. Krugman, 'The Confidence Game', *The New Republic*, 5 October 1998, 23–5.
33. See, for example, S. H. Hanke and K. Schuler, *Currency Boards for Developing Countries: A Handbook* (San Francisco: Institute for Contemporary Studies, 1994). For additional discussion and references, see Cohen, *The Geography of Money*, pp. 52–5.
34. As quoted in *The Economist*, 7 March 1998, 43.
35. B. Eichengreen, 'International Monetary Arrangements: Is There a Monetary Union in Asia's Future?', *The Brookings Review*, 15 (1997) 33–5.
36. R. A. Mundell, 'Forum on Asian Fund', *Capital Trends*, 2 (1997) 13.
37. N. Walter, 'An Asian Prediction', *The International Economy*, 12 (1998) 49.
38. A notable exception was the head of the Hong Kong Monetary Authority, Joseph Yam, who in early 1999 made a spirited plea for 'our own Asian currency' to reduce the region's vulnerability to speculative attack (as quoted in *Financial Times*, 6 January 1999).
39. Cohen, *The Geography of Money*, pp. 84–91.

40. Perhaps most ambitious was EMEAP (Executive Meeting of East Asia and Pacific Central Banks), a self-described 'vehicle for regional cooperation among central banks' encompassing Australia, China, Hong Kong, Indonesia, Japan, Malaysia, New Zealand, Philippines, Singapore, South Korea and Thailand. Other examples include SEACEN (South East Asian Central Banks) and SEANZA (South East Asia, New Zealand, Australia), both of which provide for regular meetings of central-bank officials as well as a variety of training programs.
41. *The New York Times*, 27 April 1996, 20.
42. For detail, see E. Altbach, 'The Asian Monetary Fund Proposal: A Case Study of Japanese Regional Leadership', *JEI Report*, 47A (1997) 1–14; A. Rowley, 'International Finance: Asian Fund, R.I.P.', *Capital Trends*, 2 (1997) 1–4.
43. Privately, of course, Washington also feared a loss of political influence in the region, since the AMF, if implemented, would obviously have been dominated by Tokyo. In economic terms, Washington's response to the AMF proposal was remarkably reminiscent of a similar episode a quarter of a century earlier, when an agreement to create a Financial Support Fund in the OECD (Organization of Economic Cooperation and Development, based in Paris) was torpedoed by the US Government on almost identical grounds. For detail, see B. J. Cohen, 'When Giants Clash: The OECD Financial Support Fund and the IMF', in V. Aggarwal, *Institutional Designs for a Complex World: Bargaining, Linkages, and Nesting* (Ithaca, NY: Cornell University Press, 1998) ch. 5.
44. S. Awanohara (ed.), 'A Yen Bloc?', *Capital Trends*, 3 (1998). Most notably, in October 1998, Finance Minister Kiichi Miyazawa offered some $30 billion in fresh financial aid for Asia in a plan soon labeled the 'New Miyazawa Initiative'.
45. J. Bhagwati, 'The Capital Myth', *Foreign Affairs*, 77 (1998) 8–9.
46. Special Functions Minister Diam Zainuddin, as quoted in R.Wade and F. Veneroso, 'The Gathering Support for Capital Controls', *Challenge*, 41 (1998) 20.
47. As quoted in *The New York Times*, 24 October 1998, B15.

5 Shrinking States? Globalization and National Autonomy

GEOFFREY GARRETT

Throughout the world today, politics lags behind economics, like a horse and buggy haplessly trailing a sports car. While politicians go through the motions of national elections – offering chimerical programs and slogans – world markets, the Internet and the furious pace of trade involve people in a global game in which elected representatives figure as little more than bit players. Hence the prevailing sense, in America and Europe, that politicians and ideologies are either uninteresting or irrelevant. (Roger Cohen, 'Global Forces Batter Politics', *The New York Times Week in Review*, 17 November 1996, p. 1)

One of the most widely held beliefs about the globalization of markets is that it has substantially decreased the autonomy of the nation-state, resulting in a 'race to the bottom' – a dismantling of welfare states – by governments competing for mobile economic resources. For many, globalization threatens the prosperity and stability that has characterized the advanced industrial countries since the Second World War, if not the legitimacy of the democratic state itself. Visions of widespread social upheaval abound, and they are often accompanied by pleas for international political cooperation to regulate global capitalism. The bottom line of the conventional wisdom is that there is a fundamental mismatch between the global scope of markets and the national level at which politics are organized. Something has to give, and most commentators assume that it will be the nation-state, de facto if not de jure.

This chapter assesses the merits of the globalization thesis, both theoretically and empirically. First, three discrete mechanisms are discussed through which market integration might influence domestic politics – increasing exposure to trade, the multinationalization of production, and the integration of financial markets. I will then develop rebuttals to the notion that each of these systematically erodes national policy autonomy. The claim being advanced is that the globalization of markets imposes fewer constraints on the range of feasible economic policies than is commonly thought. Most importantly, there are numerous types of government interventions in the economy that are compatible with globally competitive markets. These certainly include the policies emphasized in the 'new growth' literature, such as the provision of education and training and physical infrastructure.[1] But they can also be conceived more broadly to encompass many aspects of the traditional welfare state, particularly when these policies are pursued in countries with dense networks of socio-economic institutions ('corporatism').

The second half of the chapter is empirical and makes three basic points about developments in the industrialized or OECD countries.[2] First, globalization is a multidimensional phenomenon. In particular, one must distinguish between exposure to trade and openness to international financial markets. Although both forms of market integration have increased rapidly in recent years, there remains a tendency for countries that are highly exposed to trade to have less open capital markets.

Second, the evidence is far from clear that even the globalization of finance has exerted systematic 'race to the bottom' pressures on national policies in the advanced industrial democracies. As I have shown elsewhere, capital market integration has been associated with increasing divergence in most facets of tax and spending policy.[3] Moreover, much of this variation continues to be explained by traditional domestic politics variables such as government partisanship and the strength of organized labour. Whereas governments in countries with strong conservative parties and weak organized labour movements have reacted to financial openness with cut backs in the public economy, strong left-labour regimes have done precisely the opposite.

Third, real macroeconomic performance (growth and unemployment) has deteriorated badly in most OECD countries in the past two decades (as price stability has largely been achieved). There is, however, little evidence that these outcomes can be attributed to globalization – even in countries where governments have reacted to market integration with more interventionist economic policies.

Needless to say, there is a marked disjuncture between the analysis of this chapter and the dire predictions about the mismatch between the global economy and national policy autonomy that are so common in the rhetoric of politicians, journalists and academics. It is argued here that the problems confronting interventionist governments in the OECD – slower growth, higher unemployment and the ageing of populations – have little to do with the globalization of markets. It is possible to reap the benefits of market integration without being forced to pay a heavy domestic price. Indeed, government intervention in the economy may play an invaluable role in stabilizing an open international economy by shoring up domestic support for liberalization.[4]

The conclusion argues that this is the lesson of globalization that should be drawn by governments in the OECD, and that should be preached by the World Bank and the IMF. This conclusion may seem at odds with the apparent crisis of the welfare state in Europe and with the havoc wrought by the contagious financial crises in Mexico, East Asia, Russia and Brazil since 1995. European developments in the 1990s, however, were largely driven by the move to monetary union and the creation of the euro was driven by politics (the desire for more integration, above all by Helmut Kohl) not by globalization pressures. With respect to financial crises in developing countries, it is clear that these crises were not precipitated by profligate government policies. Moreover, instability created by financial crises makes it even more important that developing country governments use economic policies to cushion the dislocations generated by globalization.

How constraining is globalization on national autonomy?

Three globalization mechanisms

In economic policy, the term 'globalization' is used to describe three different pressures on government policy: competitiveness pressures in international goods and services markets; the multinationalization of production regimes; and, the integration of financial markets. These conceptions differ in terms of who the relevant actors are in the international economy, the facets of domestic politics they are purported to affect, and the speed with which their behavior affects the activity of governments within nation-states.

The first and oldest argument about the domestic effects of market integration concerns trade. Attention in recent years has been focused on the question: can the welfare state compete? For many, the answer is 'no'. Modern welfare states comprise two basic elements – the public provision of social services (most importantly, education and health) and income transfers (pensions, unemployment benefits, family allowances and some other smaller programs). Both facets of the welfare state reduce market disciplines on labour, creating wage-push pressures. Moreover, government spending must be funded, either by higher taxes or by borrowing. Taxes add to the costs of doing business. Borrowing results in higher inflation and higher interest rates, depressing investment. If borrowing also increases the real exchange rate, the competitiveness of national producers is further decreased. Over time, output and employment will stagnate. Since no government can afford these outcomes, the conventional view about trade integration is that it forces governments to roll back the public economy.

It is important to note, however, that the feedback from competitiveness pressures to changes on national arrangements is likely to be quite slow. There is no reason to expect deeply-rooted domestic institutions to be radically altered because they adversely affect the profitability of firms. This is particularly true of the welfare state, which remains extremely popular among most citizens across the OECD.[5] Only if macroeconomic performance were to deteriorate significantly as a result of outmoded policies would there be sufficient incentives for governments to act. Even then, substantial political obstacles to institutional reform are likely to remain.[6]

The second globalization mechanism is the multinationalization of production. News stories and academic commentary these days are replete with examples of the 'exit' threats of multinational firms to move production from one country to another in search of higher returns. This was the 'giant sucking sound' of lost jobs US-Presidential candidate Ross Perot predicted to result from NAFTA; it was also given considerable play in Europe when Hoover decided to move some production back to Britain after John Major's government chose to opt out of the EU's social protocol at Maastricht. The logic behind these assertions is very similar to that for trade competitiveness. Firms want to minimize the costs of production; government interventions in the economy raise the costs of doing business. The big difference, of course, is the availability of exit as an option for firms: the multinationalization of production allows firms to evade these costs, rather than to be forced to lobby governments to change policy.

One would thus expect that the constraints imposed by the multinationalization of production on government autonomy would be felt more quickly than the effects of trade. Obviously multinational enterprises (MNEs) cannot close a plant in one country and open a new one in a foreign location instantaneously, nor can they 'exit' without incurring significant startup costs. But downsizing one facility and expanding another existing one is a feasible short-term strategy for many multinationals. Thus, governments will likely respond more quickly to their exit threats than to the protests of less mobile businesses about their eroding competitive positions.

The final and most prevalent argument made about globalization concerns the domestic effects of the international integration of financial markets. Traders operating 24 hours a day instantaneously moving mind-boggling amounts of money around the globe in ceaseless efforts to arbitrage profits. For many commentators, the potential for massive capital flight acts as the ultimate discipline on governments that may want to pursue autonomous economic policies. The logic that underpins all of these assertions is the same. Governments are held to ransom by mobile capital, the price is high and the punishment is swift. If the policies and institutions of which the financial markets approve are not entrenched in a country, money will haemorrhage until they are. Of course, financial capital is widely thought to disapprove of all government policies that distort markets, from counter-cyclical demand management all the way down to programs to support single mothers. Governments that disobey the dictates of the market will be forced to pay ever-higher interest rates, retarding domestic economic activity. Unless policies are changed, rising mountains of debt will cripple countries.

How many degrees of freedom are there in the global economy?

Having outlined the basic arguments that underpin conventional view about the damaging effects of globalization on national policy autonomy, I will now present a series of rebuttals, focusing on the front line of the globalization debate – the mobility of multinational firms and financial capital. In addition to arguing that the constraints imposed on interventionist government by capital mobility are in fact quite weak, I also highlight the importance of entrenched socio-economic institutions (particularly organized labour) to the viability of interventionist government in the global economy.

Let us begin with the multinationalization of production. There is no doubt that MNEs today have credible exit threats. But should we expect firms' production decisions to be primarily – if not solely – influenced by cost considerations, and that they will always choose to locate where market conditions most closely approximate the free-market ideal? The evidence hardly supports this view. As Chapter 2 details, most flows of foreign direct investment (FDI) are to and from countries within the OECD where wages and taxes are relatively similar, rather than to the lower-cost developing world. Furthermore, once productivity is taken into consideration, 'unit labour costs' (or costs relative to productivity) cannot be taken as lower in less developed economies than in the OECD.

In fact, as John Dunning argues in Chapter 2, patterns of foreign direct investment are determined by a number of other facts such as the desire to gain access to new technology, new distribution channels and new markets.[7] As Paul Krugman has argued, there are thus good reasons to believe that market integration will not inexorably lead to the movement of production and jobs out of the OECD.[8] Indeed, the flows may be in the opposite direction – as firms take advantage of the complementarities and positive externalities offered by clustering in advanced market economies.

Costs, of course, are not irrelevant to multinational firms. Relative costs may also be a tiebreaker between otherwise equivalent locations. Consider, for example, the recent decisions by Mercedes Benz and BMW to build automobile plants in the American south. The companies chose to locate in the US, rather than say, Mexico, because being physically located inside the large American market for luxury cars was of paramount importance. Having chosen to build in the US, however, the firms were in a position to seek tax concessions from the southern states that were competing for foreign investment. But BMW's choice of South Carolina over other southern states as a production site is a far cry from the apocalyptic visions of multinational mayhem that often characterize the globalization debate.

Turning to the domestic effects of financial integration, there is only one clear case where globalization vitiates national policy autonomy: monetary policy where there are no barriers to cross-border capital movements and where a country's exchange rate is fixed. For all countries (except the anchor in the system), efforts to run expansionary monetary policies will result in capital outflows until domestic interest rates rise sufficiently to hold capital at home. This is currently the case in Euroland, but not the rest of the OECD.

Many scholars seem to believe, however, that under conditions of high capital mobility, governments – fearing wild swings in exchange rates caused by unwarranted speculative attacks in the currency markets – have little choice but to fix exchange rates, and hence to give up monetary policy autonomy (see the related discussion in Chapter 4). But the costs of floating under conditions of high capital mobility are often significantly overstated. Untenable commitments to fixed exchange rates were important determinants of the headline currency crises of the 1990s.[9] Moreover, the countries whose currencies were forced out of the European Monetary System (EMS) in 1992 – notably sterling and the lira – did not suffer as a result. Indeed, the British and Italian economies thrived under the relatively smooth and sensible depreciations of their currencies that followed their governments' very public U-turns away from fixed rates.

Now consider the ability of governments to run budget deficits in a world of global capital. Many assume that deficits signal fiscal recklessness that will be severely punished by the financial markets with the imposition of higher interest rates. But how much higher? Globalization has created a very large and competitive pool of lenders willing to fund government debt, easing the monetary costs of fiscal expansion.[10] At some point, of course, higher debt burdens may trigger fears among the financial markets of governments defaulting on their loans – resulting in dramatic reductions in the availability of credit. Unlike the Latin American debt crises of the 1980s, however, this limit manifestly has not been reached by any industrial democracy.[11]

What about the size of government, *per se* (that is, assuming new spending is balanced by increased revenues)? The conventional view is that the threat of capital flight will lead governments to cut taxes and spending. This assumes that capital will always choose to exit in the face of a large public economy – because government spending is inefficient and because taxes are distortionary. But some facets of

public spending are good for business, such as the provision of services
that promote the rule of law. Equally, it might also hold for the
production of other collective goods that are undersupplied by the
market, such as highly-skilled workers, cooperation between labour
and capital, and overall social stability. If this is the case, paying
taxes might be a reasonable investment for firms.

In sum, the conventional view about the impact of the multinationalization of production and financial integration on national
economic policy regimes is overly simplistic. Managers of multinational enterprises and mutual funds are not unsophisticated capi-
talists whose reaction to interventionist government is everywhere
and always the same. Mobile capital may well choose to invest and
produce in economies with interventionist govenments. As a result,
governments may retain considerably more autonomy in the era of
global markets than is often presumed.

Corporatism in the global economy

I do not want to suggest, however, that all governments can intervene
in the economy at will. Rather, I wish to develop a notion of
'institututional comparative advantage'[12] in which the effects of
different policies depend upon the institutions that exist in a country.
In particular, the large literature on corporatism suggests that the
combination of interventionist government and highly organized
labour generates macroeconomic outcomes that are at least as strong
as in more free market-oriented systems.[13] The potential costs of
interventionist government are more than offset by the combination
of generalized wage regulation (geared to the competitiveness of the
exposed sector of the economy) and the upgrading of workers' skills
through active labour market policies.[14]

This argument dovetails with the large body of recent research in
economics which views an increasing stock of human capital as an
important engine of increasing productivity and output ('endoge-
neous growth theory'). Moreover, government interventions of the
kind described above can enhance stability and thus stimulate
investment and growth in an open economy[15] – in contrast with
the uncertainty which can result from the volatility of trade under
free market conditions and which is damaging to investment.

Of course, not all government interventions in the economy can be
justified under the rubric of corporatism. Good policies include those

which produce economically-important goods that are undersupplied by the market such as education and training. Bad intervention would include defensive industrial policies designed to prop up declining sectors. Moreover, the positive effects of intervention depend upon deeply entrenched institutions that provide mechanisms for coordinating economic activity. These institutions do not exist in all countries, and many would suggest that they are under attack even in their historical bastions of northern Europe.[16] None the less, the existing evidence suggests that corporatism still offers an alternative to the free market that is well suited to a world of mobile capital.

Globalization in the OECD

The proliferation of cross-border transactions in recent decades has been concentrated within the advanced industrial democracies. The OECD's share of world trade was 81 per cent in 1970; it had risen to 84 per cent two decades later. Two-thirds of inward flows of foreign direct investment in the 1980s were into the US and the European Union (with, not surprisingly, much higher percentages for outflows). In contrast, the developing countries' share of the world FDI stock fell by one-third from the late 1960s to the late 1980s.[17] The intra-OECD concentration of more liquid capital movements – in bonds, currencies and equities – is even more pronounced.

The point of this section, however, is one that is often overlooked. It is true that all facets of market integration within the OECD have increased appreciably in recent decades. But at the same time, it is equally true that substantial cross-national variations across different market segments remain. This continued variation has significant implications for our analysis of the domestic effects of globalization.

Trade flows, trade policy and trade volatility

The average exposure to trade of the OECD countries (exports plus imports as a percentage of GDP) increased consistently from less than 50 per cent in 1960 to almost 70 per cent by the mid-1980s, before stabilizing in the following decade (see Figure 5.1). Over the same period, the various rounds of the GATT reduced average tariff rates from around 25 per cent to under 5 per cent.[18] These tariff reductions, however, coincided with increasing uses of non-tariff barriers

FIGURE 5.1   OECD Average Trade Volume and Trade Volatility

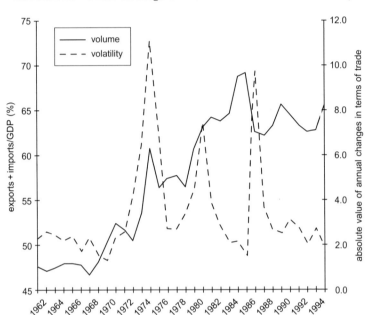

Notes: Data are unweighted annual averages for all available countries.
Sources: OECD, *Main Economic Indicators. Historical Statistics. Prices, Labour and Wages* (Paris: OECD, 1960–94).

(at least until the Uruguay Round). Figure 5.1 also demonstrates that the growth of trade has not been associated with increasing volatility in trade. There have been short periods when the OECD countries' terms of trade have changed dramatically, coinciding with the oil price hikes of the second half of the 1970s and then with the halving of oil prices in the mid-1980s. But there is no evidence of a secular trend toward less stability in trading patterns. Among other things, this reflects the high degree of intra-industry trade within the OECD.

Even among the OECD countries, however, there are significant cross-national variations in exposure to international market forces (see the left-hand panel of Table 5.1 for the period 1985–94). A country's size and its reliance on trade have always been inversely correlated. In turn, year-to-year variations in trade balances have been greatest in countries that are heavily dependent on raw materials, either as importers (Japan) or exporters (Australia and

Norway). Volatility does not increase with exposure to trade; in fact the correlation between the two is negative and quite strong – again a likely artifact of the growing importance of intra-industry trade.

Now consider trade policy. Even after the completion of the Uruguay Round, average tariff rates in Australia and New Zealand were more than twice as high as those in the EU and the US. However, in the former, non-tariff barriers covered a negligible portion of goods and services. This was far from the case in Europe and the US. Moreover, the relationships between trade policy and trade flows are not very strong. As trade economists have long known, geography, wealth and factor endowments are more important determinants of trade than is government policy.

There are no doubt many other observations that could be made about the trade data in Table 5.1. For my purposes, however, only two basic points need to be highlighted. First, cross-national variations stand out in all the data. Second, there are no systematic relationships among trade flows, trade volatility and trade policy. Even though trade has become increasingly important throughout the OECD in the past 30 years, it is neither equally important across countries nor reinforcing across different indicators. As a result, using the passage of time as a simple proxy for increasing market integration is a

---

Notes to Table 5.1 (overleaf)

[a] Standard deviation of annual changes in terms of trade

[b] MFN tariff rates (binding on all merchandise trade) after Uruguay Round (J. Finger, M. Ingco and U. Reincke, *The Uruguay Round* (Washington, DC: *World Bank*, 1996) 67).

[c] Percentage of all products subject to non-tariff barriers in 1993: Indicators of Tariff and Non-Tariff Trade Barriers (OECD, *Economic Outlook* 59 (Paris: OECD, 1996) 52–55).

[d] FDI and portfolio investment only for 1985–93.

[e] Financial openness index only for 1985–93.

[f] 3-month interest rate differential less forward exchange-rate discount (local minus Eurodollar), for 1982–88 only (J. Frankel, *On Exchange Rates* (Cambridge: MIT Press, 1993) 59).

[g] Percentage of cabinet portfolios held by left parties, 1950–95 (D. Swank, 'Funding the Welfare State', *Political Studies* 46 (1998) 671–92).

[h] Percentage of trade unions members in total labour force, 1960–89 (J. Visser, 'Trends in Trade Union Membership', *OECD Employment Outlook* (Paris: Organization for Economic Cooperation and Development, 1991); data for Greece, Ireland, Portugal and Spain only for late 1980s (A. Ferner and R. Hyman (eds), *Industrial Relations in the New Europe* (Oxford: Blackwell, 1992).

TABLE 5.1   The Dimensions of Globalization (1985–94 averages except

| Country | Trade in goods and services | | | |
	Total trade	Volatility of trade[a]	Average tariff rates[b]	Coverage of NTBs[c]
Australia	36.0	9.88	10.4	0.7
Austria	76.2	3.78	6.3	15.1
Belgium	140.7	2.52	4.6	22.1
Canada	54.6	1.92	5.7	8.3
Denmark	65.1	2.11	4.6	22.1
Finland	53.3	4.79	9.2	7.9
France	43.7	4.01	4.6	22.1
Germany	50.6	5.18	4.6	22.1
Greece	45.4	3.95	3.2	22.1
Iceland	67.7	—	4.2	3
Ireland	115.2	2.61	4.6	22.1
Italy	41.3	4.89	4.6	22.1
Japan	19.1	10.90	3.7	11.4
Luxembourg	191.1	—	4.6	22.1
Mexico	30.8	—	13.4	2
Netherlands	101.8	1.98	4.6	22.1
NZ	56.5	4.78	10	0.4
Norway	71.7	8.24	3.1	5.9
Portugal	66.6	—	4.6	22.1
Spain	39.5	5.12	4.6	22.1
Sweden	62.0	3.62	3.3	3.7
Switzerland	71.5	3.68	2.4	3.6
Turkey	33.6	—	9.8	0.2
UK	51.7	2.28	4.6	22.1
US	20.6	2.16	4.5	23
average	64.2	4.4	5.6	14.0
correlation with:				
trade volatility	−0.44			
tariff rates	−0.26	0.22		
NTB coverage	0.29	−0.46	−0.52	
fdi	0.43	−0.25	−0.10	−0.02
portfolio	0.43	0.22	0.44	−0.23
financial openness	0.03	−0.44	0.10	−0.02
interest rate differentials	0.30	0.07	−0.49	0.08
left power[g]	0.22	0.09	−0.07	−0.30
trade union members[h]	0.27	0.00	0.23	−0.42

where noted)

| Foreign direct investment[d] | International capital | | |
	Portfolio investment	Financial openness[e]	Covered interest rate differentials[f]
3.2	56.0	11.1	−0.75
0.9	13.1	12.1	0.13
6.0	45.7	11.8	0.12
1.5	8.7	13.5	−0.10
1.7	21.6	12.8	−3.53
1.9	14.0	11.3	—
2.6	9.0	11.8	−1.74
1.5	10.7	14.0	0.35
—	—	8.2	−9.39
—	—	—	—
0.3	25.6	11.2	−0.79
0.9	10.3	12.1	−0.40
0.9	11.2	10.6	0.09
—	—	—	—
—	—	—	−16.47
5.3	18.7	14.0	0.21
—	—	12.8	−1.63
2.0	16.3	11.3	−1.03
—	—	9.9	−7.93
—	—	11.7	−2.40
3.4	21.6	11.7	−0.23
4.4	14.3	13.0	0.42
—	—	13.0	—
5.1	19.0	14.0	−0.14
1.3	2.5	13.7	—
2.5	18.7	12.1	−2.26

0.45			
0.29	−0.36		
0.25	−0.07	0.71	
0.12	0.23	−0.27	−0.22
0.09	0.34	−0.01	0.13

very imprecise methodology that should be supplemented wherever possible with cross-national research that can take into account the very different market positions of different countries.

Foreign direct investment and international financial capital

Figure 5.2 demonstrates three simple points about international capital markets since 1960. First, annual foreign direct investment (combined inflows and outflows) and international portfolio investment remain a much smaller percentage of GDP among the OECD countries than trade. This should not be surprising for inflows and outflows of foreign direct investment (FDI), but the portfolio data require some explanation. Foreign exchange transactions are by far the largest international capital flows but these are excluded from the portfolio measures (which primarily track international bond and

FIGURE 5.2   Capital Flows and Capital Liberalization

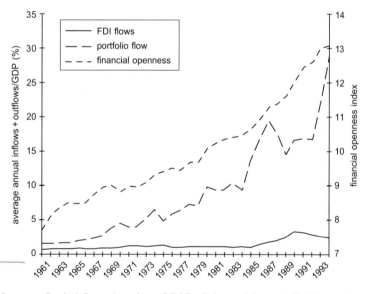

Sources: Capital flows data from OECD, *Balance of Payments Statistics*, various. Financial openness index from D. Quinn and M. Yoyoda, 'Measuring International Financial Regulation', unpublished manuscript (Washington DC: Georgetown University, 1997).

equity transactions). One can, however, gain some insights into currency movements by analysing the extent of capital controls and interest rate data (see below).

Second, the growth of capital flows – most notably portfolio investments, but also FDI – rapidly increased after the Bretton Woods system of fixed exchange rates collapsed in the early 1970s. One interpretation of the mushrooming of capital flows, therefore, is that they simply reflect hedging against currency risk through international diversification. Third, the growth of international capital flows has been very closely correlated with the reduction in government restrictions on international capital movements.[19]

Professional economists, however, are sceptical about the extent of capital market integration in the OECD. In a now seminal paper, in 1980 Martin Feldstein and Charles Horioka argued that capital was not internationally mobile in the 1970s because domestic investment was highly correlated with domestic savings.[20] This finding has subsequently been replicated for the 1980s.[21]

The Feldstein-Horioka approach, however, has been trenchantly criticized. It assumes that anything that affects a nation's investment rate (except the real interest rate) does not also affect its savings rate. This is most implausible. Factors as diverse as government policies, productivity growth and demographic conditions manifestly affect both savings and investment. A better measure of capital mobility is provided by differences in the costs of capital. In a truly global market, interest rates around the world would converge. The difficulty here though lies in which interest rates to use because differences in nominal rates (and even real rates of interest) might be due to expectations about future movements of exchange rates and all the things that affect exchange rates.

The most appropriate indicator for isolating the extent of capital mobility is the 'covered' interest rate, which Richard Marston has demonstrated declined significantly for the G-5 economies during the 1980s and early 1990s.[22] Hence, to the extent that the major five economies are representative of trends throughout the OECD (see below for qualifications to this assumption), it does seem greater capital flows and the removal of capital controls have resulted in significant real integration of financial markets in the OECD. At the same time, Jeffrey Frankel's data[23] reveals that financial markets in the least-developed OECD countries (Greece, Mexico and Portugal) were all very closed in the 1980s, and that capital was also considerably less mobile in Australia, Denmark, France, Ireland, New Zealand, Norway and Spain than in the remaining OECD countries. In other words, the correlation between capital mobility and the liberalization of capital markets was high, whereas international capital flows bore no real relation to effective rates of return on investments.[24]

In summary, international capital movements have increased at least in part due to the fact that governments have reduced their restrictions on capital movements. However, the over-time trend towards globalized production and finance has not been associated with a diminution in cross-national differences (see the right-hand panel of Table 5.1). Indeed, in the past decade, there were substantial differences in the magnitude of FDI flows into and out of the different OECD countries and on Quinn's financial openness index, however, none of these variables was very highly correlated with each other. Having discussed the manifestations of the globalization of markets in the OECD, let us now to assess their impact on economic policy regimes in these countries.

Globalization, economic policy and economic performance

The previous sections have rebutted the conventional wisdom about globalization: that it puts downward pressures on interventionist economic policies; that it creates incentives for economic policies to converge around those that facilitate the free market; and that governments who seek to buck these globalization imperatives will preside over deteriorating macroeconomic performance. This section presents rudimentary tests of the contending arguments. The first sub-section presents the evidence of indicators of economic policies and macroeconomic performance in OECD countries and asks whether market integration has caused economic policies: to become less interventionist; to converge over time; or, where a 'race to the bottom' has not occurred, to cause a deterioration in economic performance. The second sub-section then moves to cross-national comparisons, comparing various indicators of globalization, economic policies and performance in the past decade to policy and performance in previous periods. Finally, other explanations for economic performance are presented such as government partisanship and union density throughout the postwar era.

Spending and deficits

Figure 5.3 presents annual data on OECD averages for total government spending, government consumption expenditures (most importantly education and health), income transfers (mostly pensions and unemployment benefits) and public-sector deficits, all as a portion of GDP. Total government spending doubled from 1960 to 1994, constituting more than half of GDP in the early 1990s. By the end of the period, transfers had replaced consumption spending as the largest component of the public economy, reflecting the ageing of many societies as well as increasing unemployment. The average size of public-sector deficits increased from under 1 per cent of GDP in the 1960s to over 4 per cent in the early 1980s and over 6 per cent in the early 1990s. Governments were clearly unable or unwilling to increase taxes to match greater spending.

FIGURE 5.3   Government Spending and Public-Sector Deficits, 1960–94

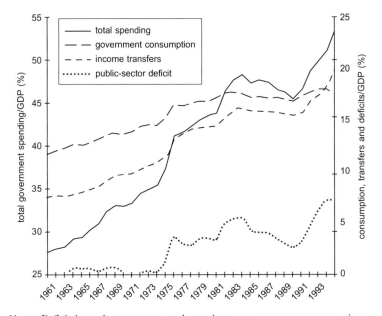

Note: Deficit is total government outlays minus current government receipts.
Sources: Unweighted annual averages for all available countries from OECD, *Main Economic Indicators.*

Taken together, Figures 5.1–5.3 demonstrate that globalization and public-sector expansion have moved more or less in step since the 1960s. But correlation does not prove causation. Following Wagner's 1883 law, for example, few would dispute that increasing prosperity has been a major factor behind the growth of the OECD public economies in the postwar period.[25] The data may give a better insight into the causal dynamics which are of interest in this chapter.

Total government spending, transfers and deficits all increased most rapidly during widespread recessions in the OECD (periods such as 1973–75, 1980–82 and 1989–93) because downturns in the business cycle put upward pressures on entitlement programs (for example, more people claim unemployment benefit) while tax receipts are reduced. What may be more of more interest is the fact that the public economy did not subsequently contract during economic recoveries. The conspicuous exception to this was the mid-1980s when slower public-sector growth stimulated the whole notion that globalization constrains national autonomy and prosperity. Of course, this view fails to acknowledge the rapid pace of spending growth in the 1990s. The depth of the European recession after the end of the Cold War certainly had a lot to do with this; nonetheless the first half of the 1990s should give pause to those wishing to draw facile conclusions about the constraining effects of globalization.

Figure 5.4 presents a rudimentary analysis of the notion that globalization has led to convergence in fiscal policies among the OECD countries. The figure plots annual standard deviations in the same indicators presented in Figure 5.3 – smaller numbers indicate more cross-national convergence in policies. Of essence to the argument being made here is the evidence that fiscal policies have become more heterogeneous over time – as markets have become more internationally integrated. Again, the figure also indicates that the 1980s was an unusual decade – when policies did converge somewhat – but it was preceded and followed by (recession) periods when cross-national differences in fiscal policy increased.

Figures 5.3 and 5.4 are thus consistent with the argument of this chapter that globalization increases the demands on governments to cushion market dislocations but that some governments are more likely to respond to these demands than others. Let us now move to cross-national comparisons. In addition to taking into account differences in the extent of market integration, these comparisons also give

FIGURE 5.4   Cross-National Variations in Government Spending and Public-Sector Deficits, 1960–94

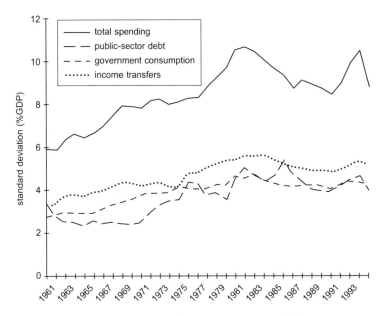

Source: Calculated using data from OECD, *Main Economic Indicators.*

some insight into the importance of domestic determinants of policy choice.

Table 5.2 breaks down the spending and deficits data by country for the period 1985–94 (or the last available year), and then compares the figures with each country's historic averages (1960–84). The results show dramatic differences in the size of the public economy and the financing of government spending in the past decade, and also show significant changes from the previous decades. Sweden's public economy has been fully twice as large as that of Japan's. Spain's government spending grew more than five times as much as the US. With respect to budget balances, Japan, Luxembourg and Norway all ran surpluses in the 1985–94 period, maintaining or improving their fiscal performance from their historic averages. On the other hand, double-digit deficits were the norm in Greece and Italy, representing significant increases from the 1960s and 1970s.

TABLE 5.2 Globalization, Partisan Politics and Government Spending

Country	Total government spending		Public-sector deficit		Government consumption expenditures		Income transfers	
	1985–94	change[a]	1985–94	change	1985–94	change	1985–94	change
Australia	37.9	8.9	3.5	2.1	17.9	2.8	9.9	3.0
Austria	51.5	8.5	3.9	2.5	18.5	2.8	20.6	4.1
Belgium	57.9	10.7	7.4	2.1	15.4	0.5	24.1	6.2
Canada	47.9	11.9	6.7	3.8	20.3	2.6	13.3	3.9
Denmark	59.8	17.1	1.9	1.2	25.4	4.3	18.3	6.2
Finland	51.2	16.5	1.3	3.8	21.7	5.9	18.4	9.4
France	51.6	10.0	4.9	3.4	18.8	2.8	22.0	5.0
West Germany	47.5	5.3	2.6	1.1	20.0	2.0	15.7	1.1
Greece	51.2	16.5	13.8	6.6	14.5	4.4	15.4	7.0
Iceland	39.6	8.1	3.7	4.3	19.4	5.4	5.9	−0.8
Ireland	46.3	5.5	5.6	−1.4	16.2	1.1	15.6	5.9
Italy	52.8	14.3	10.9	4.5	17.0	2.9	18.1	4.6
Japan	32.6	8.2	−0.3	−1.8	9.4	0.7	11.4	4.7
Luxembourg	51.4	9.6	−3.1	−2.1	13.1	2.1	21.9	4.8
Mexico	—	—	—	—	13.1	2.1	—	—
Netherlands	59.0	10.9	5.1	2.4	15.0	−0.4	25.8	3.0
New Zealand	—	—	—	—	16.2	2.1	—	—
Norway	52.4	10.7	−2.8	0.3	20.6	3.7	17.7	5.6
Portugal	43.2	15.6	5.8	3.6	15.6	3.0	12.0	5.6
Spain	43.7	18.4	6.1	4.7	15.8	5.3	16.4	7.0

Sweden	64.2	16.5	3.8	4.0	27.2	4.2	20.8	7.8
Switzerland	32.4	8.1	-2.4	1.7	13.5	2.1	14.7	4.9
Turkey	—	—	—	—	10.4	0.5	—	—
UK	43.7	3.1	4.3	1.0	21.1	1.8	13.3	3.9
US	36.8	5.5	5.1	2.5	17.8	0.0	11.5	3.3
average	47.9	10.9	4.0	2.3	17.4	2.6	16.5	4.8
correlation with:								
trade[b]	0.38	-0.09	-0.25	-0.43	-0.06	-0.16	0.52	0.07
FDI flows[c]	0.18	-0.04	-0.01	0.16	-0.04	-0.26	0.37	0.01
financial openness[d]	0.02	-0.47	-0.29	-0.26	0.20	-0.44	0.15	-0.57
left-labour power[e]	0.58	0.51	-0.31	0.11	0.66	0.63	0.33	0.51

Notes:

[a] Change from historic average (1960–84, with later starting dates for some countries).

[b] Average 1985–94.

[c] Average 1985–93.

[d] Average 1985–93.

[e] Standardized sum of the percentage of cabinet portfolios held by left parties, 1950–95 (D. Swank, 'Funding the Welfare State', *Political Studies* 46 (1998) 671–92) and the percentage of trade unions members in total labour force, 1960–89 (J. Visser, 'Trends in Trade Union Membership', *OECD Employment Outlook* (Paris: OECD, 1991)). Data for Greece, Ireland, Portugal and Spain only for late 1980s (A. Ferner and R. Hyman (eds), *Industrial Relations in the New Europe* (Oxford: Blackwell, 1992)).

These cross-national variations in fiscal policy have been influenced not just by market integration but also by domestic political conditions. These conditions have been studied by political scientists and sociologists who have shown a positive relationship between the political power of the left and organized labour on the one hand, and larger public economies on the other.[26] The effects of left-labour power have been more apparent for consumption expenditures than income transfer programs.[27] These relationships continued to hold for the 1985–94 period and it is also worth noting that left-labour power has not been associated with larger budget deficits.[28] The combined power of the left and organized labour has also been associated with faster public-sector expansion when one moves from the 1960s–1970s to the 1980s–1990s. Moreover, the data in Table 5.2 amply demonstrate that strong left-labour regimes were able to expand the public economy without generating budget deficits out of line with those in other countries. Deficits increased across the board, not only in countries with powerful left parties and trade unions.

How did cross-national variations in trade, FDI and financial openness affect government revenue and expenditure? Surprisingly (for those embracing the free market thesis) market integration tended to be positively correlated with large public economies – in other words, more open economies tended to have more interventionism governments in the post-1985 period. Furthermore, market integration was negatively correlated with the size of budget deficits – in other words, more open economies tended to have smaller budget deficits. Both these findings are discordant with the globalization thesis which would expect market integration to have put downward pressures on public spending and, even more so, on taxes (i.e. leading to bigger deficits).

A second correlation which bears on the relationship of market integration with government activity is that emerging from the data on changes in the public economy from historic averages to the 1985–94 period. Here the data lend more support to the globalization conventional wisdom. In almost all cases, globalization was accompanied by a decrease in spending while the growth of public sector deficits was also slower in countries that were more integrated into global markets.

Finally, the data reveal that the correlation between globalization and the public economy varied considerably across market segments.

In trade, openness was positively associated with higher spending levels in the past decade but bore no relation to changes in spending. In marked contrast, financial openness had little correlation with spending levels in the 1985–94 period, but was consistently and strongly negatively correlated with changes in spending.

Table 5.2 thus gives mixed signals regarding the relationships among globalization, domestic politics and fiscal policy. On the one hand, the correlations between left-labour power and greater government spending were strong in the 1985–94 period, stronger than they were in the preceding twenty-five years. It would thus be hard to argue that domestic autonomy, understood as the ability of citizens to influence economic policy, has been reduced by globalization. But on the other hand, financial openness in the contemporary period was correlated with smaller growth in the public economy which is indicative of the 'race to the bottom' pressures commonly alluded to in the globalization literature.

One way to reconcile these findings would be to endogenize capital mobility, hypothesizing that strong left-labour regimes have chosen to protect their public economies by retaining significant controls on the mobility of capital. But, as Table 5.1 showed, the correlations between the power of the left and the strength of trade unions and financial openness have been very weak in recent years. A more plausible interpretation is that even though most governments, including many on the left, have come to accept the globalization of finance as a reality, this has not constrained their fiscal autonomy. Indeed, partisan considerations have become even more important as the potential dislocations associated with market integration have increased.[29]

This analysis suggests that there is still a compromise of 'embedded liberalism'[30] – in other words, an open international order is accepted since it is combined with domestic policies that cushion short-term market losers. Today, however, the compromise is increasingly dependent upon the political power of the left and organized labour. In social-democratic-corporatist regimes, governments seek simultaneously to enjoy the benefits of market integration, but also to shield their most vulnerable citizens with extensive public provision of social services and income transfers. In contrast, under more 'market liberal' regimes, the insulating effects of the public economy against market-generated risk and inequality are being eroded.

Capital, labour and consumption taxes

Figure 5.5 presents data on trends in effective average rates of taxation on capital, labour and consumption for all available OECD countries.[31] Average effective rates of capital taxation tended to increase from 1970 to the early 1990s, even taking into account business cycle effects (rates went up significantly during recessions when profits declined). Taxes on labour grew yet more quickly. In 1970, labour was taxed less than capital (at an effective rate about five percentage points lower than capital). By the latter half of the 1980s, the two rates had become virtually indistinguishable. In the early 1990s labour rates were increasing while capital taxation was declining. Consumption tax rates have always been considerably lower than capital or labour tax rates. After increasing steadily from the mid-1970s through the mid-1980s, however, consumption taxes began to decline.

FIGURE 5.5   Effective Rates of Taxation

Source: Data are unweighted annual averages for all available countries, from E. Mendoza *et al.*, 'On the Effectiveness of Tax Policy in Altering Long-Run Growth', *Journal of Public Economics*, 66 (1997) 99–126.

This evidence seems to lend some support to the notion that the globalization of finance has shifted the tax burden away from capital and towards labour. But two other facts need to be considered: capital tax rates have tended to increase in recent years, whereas consumption taxes have, if anything, fallen. An increase in capital tax rates is surprising because the conventional view is that mobile capital should have been able to bid down its tax rate, not only relative to other forms of taxation but in absolute terms. Equally, it is surprising that consumption taxes have not been increasing since one would expect these to be the preferred method of raising revenues in the global economy. The owners of capital (and free-market economists) favour consumption taxes because they do not distort investment decisions. Critics, however, point out that consumption taxes disproportionately tax the poor since much of their income is spent on consumption as opposed to investment or savings.

Figure 5.6 plots changes over time in the standard deviations of tax rates. As was the case for spending, these figures do not support the

FIGURE 5.6   Cross-National Variations in Rates of Taxation, 1970–92

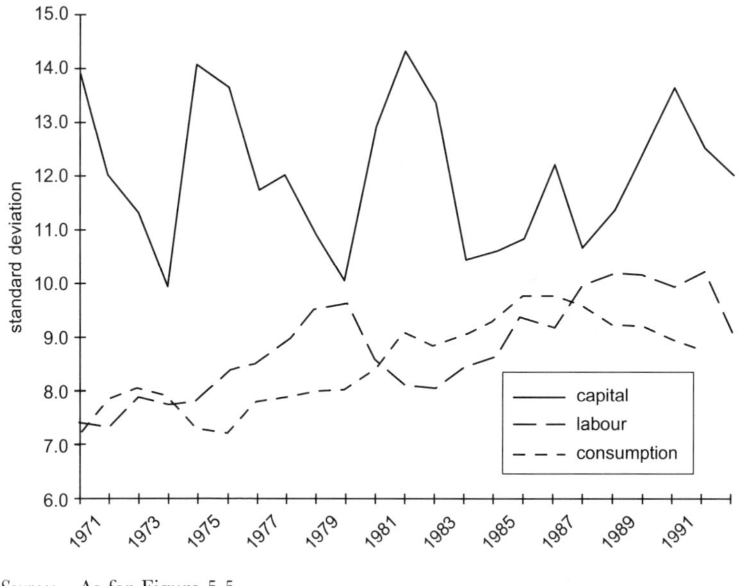

Source: As for Figure 5.5.

notion of cross-national convergence in tax policy. If anything, countries have come to pursue increasingly divergent policies with respect to the taxation of labour and consumption. The taxation of capital has been very volatile over time, with spikes in cross-national divergence corresponding to the deep recessions when governments have reacted very differently to sharp reductions in corporate profits.

Rates of taxation for individual countries are presented in Table 5.3. The first two columns concern capital tax rates since 1985 and changes in these rates from the 1970–84 period (earlier data are not available). There is considerable dispersion in these national data, often belying traditional characterizations of regime types. For example, even though Sweden and Austria both have long histories of interventionist and redistributive government, Sweden's effective capital tax rate was more than three times as high as that in Austria. In 'dirigiste' France, capital taxes were less than half as high as those in Thatcher's Britain; and effective rates in the US were considerably higher than in Germany. Since the 1970s, America was the only country in the OECD that cut its effective capital tax rate, whereas Sweden witnessed one of the greatest increases. But capital taxes rose fastest of all in Japan, notwithstanding its small public economy and the close relationship between the ruling party of the time and business.

The basic pattern of relationships for the correlations between capital taxation and globalization was similar to that for government spending, although the evidence is more supportive of the conventional wisdom about globalization. Left-labour power was only weakly positively correlated with capital tax rates after 1985 and with changes in capital taxation from the previous 15 years, whereas financial openness was strongly negatively correlated with changes in effective rates of taxation from the 1970s and early 1980s to the most recent period. The pace of growth in capital tax rates (which, it should be remembered, continued to rise) was significantly lower in countries with more internationally integrated capital markets.

It should be noted that these findings differ from those of recent studies by Quinn and Swank respectively.[32] Using narrower definitions that focus solely on corporate income taxes, they find no negative relationships between financial integration and capital taxation. Furthermore, I have argued elsewhere that, like spending, the effects of openness on capital taxation are heavily mediated by

TABLE 5.3   Globalization, Partisan Politics and Taxation

Country	Effective rate of taxation on:					
	Capital		labour		consumption	
	1985–92	change[a]	1985–92	change	1985–92	change
Australia	46.8	8.3	18.3	3.5	8.7	0.6
Austria	22.6	2.3	40.5	4.7	21.3	0.9
Belgium	36.7	2.9	47.8	7.7	16.3	−1.4
Canada	41.4	0.7	29.2	8.0	12.5	0.0
Denmark	34.8	1.6	44.1	4.5	35.4	2.5
Finland	44.4	14.4	33.9	6.9	30.1	6.6
France	26.0	3.2	45.6	8.6	19.8	−1.8
Germany	28.5	2.4	42.2	6.9	15.6	−0.3
Greece	—	—	—	—	—	—
Iceland	—	—	—	—	—	—
Ireland	—	—	—	—	—	—
Italy	28.1	3.9	40.9	4.8	13.9	2.0
Japan	48.8	19.4	27.3	8.0	5.5	0.3
Luxembourg	—	—	—	—	—	—
Mexico	—	—	—	—	—	—
Netherlands	30.5	—	52.0	—	18.3	1.1
New Zealand	36.7	2.6	25.7	−0.8	16.5	7.0
Norway	39.2	0.7	39.5	0.7	36.1	4.0
Portugal	—	—	—	—	—	—
Spain	13.9	0.2	34.3	2.4	12.1	4.9
Sweden	60.6	14.0	50.0	6.0	24.6	4.5
Switzerland	28.2	6.2	32.9	6.4	8.1	1.1
Turkey	—	—	—	—	—	—
UK	57.5	1.9	25.7	0.6	16.9	3.1
US	40.5	−2.7	28.8	4.8	4.9	−0.9
average	37.0	4.8	36.6	4.9	17.6	1.9
correlation with:						
trade	−0.13	−0.18	0.59	0.08	0.34	−0.09
FDI flows	0.19	−0.03	0.21	−0.11	−0.05	−0.04
financial openness	0.08	−0.61	0.06	−0.12	−0.15	−0.18
left-labour power	0.27	0.16	0.32	−0.34	0.76	0.56
government spending[b]	0.01	−0.09	0.82	0.04	0.72	0.45

Notes:
[a] Change from historic average (1970–84, with later starting dates for some countries).
[b] Total government spending (1985–94).

domestic politics. My econometrics suggest that left-labour regimes have responded to the globalization of financial markets by increasing the rates at which they effectively tax capital; only countries with more conservative politics have chosen to cut back capital taxation as financial integration has increased.[33]

How could it be that capital taxes have not been reduced by capital mobility? This relationship is at the core of the conventional wisdom about globalization. For most analysts, the only solution to this puzzle is that countries that have persisted with high capital taxes have had to endure damaging capital flight and ultimately poorer macroeconomic performance. I assess this proposition in the next sub-section. But there is another possibility: the changes in capital taxation that have taken place in recent years have been more or less consistent with the interests of mobile investors and multinational firms. This seems very plausible when one delves into changes in the incidence of corporate taxation. Marginal rates of corporate income taxation have been cut significantly in most countries.[34] But at the same time, investment incentives – long favoured by social democrats – have been taken out of the tax code because they have been judged to be ineffective.[35] The net effect of this restructuring has been an increase in the tax take from capital – expanding the tax base – while the methods of taxation have become more consonant with business preferences.[36]

Turning to cross-national variations in effective tax rates on labour, the differences in rates correspond more closely with traditional views about relative tax burdens. For example, the effective taxation of labour was universally low among the Anglo-American democracies, even though this was not the case for the taxation of capital. This suggests that these regimes are relatively more influenced by populist desires to reduce tax burdens on individuals than by the interests of businesses. In contrast, the northern European countries relied heavily on labour as a source of revenues for their large public economies.

The data on changes in labour taxation from the 1970–84 period are very interesting. Taxes did not increase most in the latter 1980s and early 1990s in the big spending countries of northern Europe, but rather in Canada and Japan. At the other end of the spectrum, the laissez-faire revolution in New Zealand was clearly evident with respect to taxes on labour – it was the only country that actually lowered effective rates between the two periods. The Thatcher decade was not quite as successful, but nonetheless successive conservative governments in Britain were able to stabilize labour taxes.

As these individual cases suggest, average effective rates of labour taxation were very strongly and positively correlated with government spending in the 1985–92 period, although there was no correlation between the size of government and the growth in labour taxation. Big spending regimes have always levied very high taxes on labour. The data also suggest that big traders and strong left-labour regimes have relied heavily on labour taxes (but the growth of labour taxes was slower in left-labour regimes).

Perhaps the most interesting facet of the labour taxation data is that the financial openness was not correlated with significant increases in the rate of growth of labour taxation. This refutes Dani Rodrik's contention about the kinds of changes in taxation globalization brings about. However, it may still have been the case that reductions in capital taxes were offset by an increasing use of consumption taxes.

The data on effective rates of consumption taxation are very interesting. Four countries who do not use consumption taxes to any great degree have quite different political economies: Austria, Japan, Switzerland and, above all, the US. In contrast, consumption tax rates in the period 1985–91 were above 30 per cent in Denmark, Finland, Norway and Sweden, all well above average rates for European Union members (for whom consumption taxes are partially 'harmonized', with a lowest common floor).

These cross-national variations in consumption taxation have been quite stable over time. There were only two cases where consumption taxes increased markedly after the mid-1980s. On the one hand, New Zealand's introduction of a generalized sales tax is yet another demonstration of the free-market fever that infected the country. On the other hand, Finland dramatically increased not only consumption taxes but also capital and labour taxes to fund its rapid expansion of the public economy (particularly after 1989 with the collapse of its export markets in the former Soviet Union).

Two broad trends stand out in the consumption tax correlations. First, there was only one positive correlation between any facet of globalization and consumption taxes – the level of trade and the level of taxes in the past decade. Financial openness was associated with both lower rates of consumption taxes and with smaller increases in them from the 1970s. This stands in marked contrast with the

expectations of the conventional wisdom concerning the attractiveness of consumption taxes to mobile capital.

A second trend highlighted by the consumption tax correlations is
that left-labour power was strongly and positively associated both
with consumption tax levels in the post-1985 period and with faster
increases since the 1970s. One interpretation of this relationship is
that left-labour regimes could only feed their appetites for ever-higher
levels of public spending by relying on the most regressive form of
taxation. This interpretation is clearly consistent with the conventional wisdom about taxation in the global economy. But it should be
remembered that consumption taxes are only regressive to the extent
that they fall disproportionately on poor people. In practice, most
governments exempt numerous consumer staples – such as food,
clothing and medicine – from consumption taxes.[37] Thus, one should
not make too much of the reliance of corporatist northern Europe on
this form of taxation.

At this point, it is important to acknowledge that there are many
aspects of the political economy of taxation that require further
investigation. The above data ought to be supplemented with
information on the incidence of taxes, asking, for example, whether
the progressivity of income taxes has been affected by globalization;
whether tax evasion by firms increased or diminished with market
integration; and on whom the burden of consumption taxes primarily
falls. Unfortunately, this information cannot be obtained from traditional national accounts, it requires survey research. The preliminary
work I have done in this area, however, suggests that there is no
evidence that the incidence of taxation has shifted from mobile assets
holders to less mobile wage and salary earners.[38]

Taking all the tax data as a whole, the most important developments in recent years concerning globalization have to do with the
taxation of capital. While the overall effect of financial integration
has been to reduce tax on capital, this correlation masks very strong
partisan effects that may well have strengthened in recent years. With
respect to broader debates about the fate of national policy autonomy
in the era of global markets, people may differ whether this glass is
half full or half empty. Either way, conventional views about
globalization suggest that interventionist governments with high rates
of capital taxation should have suffered macroeconomically under
conditions of integrated markets, and particularly financial markets.
The next subsection examines this contention.

Macroeconomic outcomes

Figure 5.7 plots OECD average macroeconomic performance with respect to per capita GDP growth, inflation and unemployment for the 1961–94 period. There were three major recessions in the period. Smoothing these cycles, however, it is clear that the OECD growth rate has been more or less halved (and unemployment rates have more than doubled) in the past thirty-five years, but inflation rates have been cut dramatically since the late 1970s.

It is often suggested that capital market integration explains the changing emphasis on real aggregates versus price stability in the OECD. According to this view, the markets care less about output and employment than they do about inflation, and their exit power has allowed them to impose their preferences on captive governments. Few if any mainstream economists, however, accept this argument.

FIGURE 5.7 Macroeconomic Performance

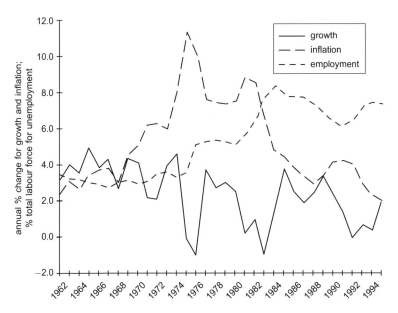

Source: All data from OECD, *Main Economic Indicators*. Growth is per capita GDP growth; inflation is change in the GDP deflator (excluding Iceland, Mexico and Turkey); unemployment rates are based on national definitions.

Comparative advantage and scale economies remain virtually un-challenged concepts with respect to the benefits of trade. Interna-tional capital markets reduce borrowing costs and promote efficient allocation of investment.[39]

This argument could be modified, however, in the light of the preceding subsections in ways that might make it more persuasive. Globalization may be indirectly implicated in changes in OECD economic performance because it has affected the distribution of wealth and risk, to which democratic governments are very sensitive. Where governments have not responded to globalization by curtail-ing their interventions to market-friendly policies, or worse where they have increased the size and scope of government to cushion the effects of global market disciplines, macroeconomic outcomes should have deteriorated. As this chapter argues, however, there is an alternative perspective which contends that globalization, big government and buoyant macroeconomic performance can all coexist.

The simplest way to explore the determinants of macroeconomic performance is to move from OECD-wide trends over time to cross-national comparisons (see Table 5.4 for the past decade, and relative to the 1961–84 period). There is some evidence that growth perfor-mance has been better in more globalized economies. But at the same time, both inflation and unemployment grew more rapidly in coun-tries with greater FDI flows. Finally, financial openness was asso-ciated with lower and faster declining rates of inflation (excluding the very high inflation cases), but with slightly higher and faster growing rates of unemployment.[40]

Turning to the correlations between economic policy and macro-economic performance, there is no strong evidence that countries with larger public economies have suffered more than other OECD economies. This finding has been confirmed in more comprehensive studies,[41] suggesting that the costs of big government are offset by the benefits of the collective goods provided by the public economy. But this is not the case for countries that have been less able to match tax revenues to government spending. Higher deficits have been asso-ciated with high and faster rising inflation and unemployment rates and low and faster declining growth rates. It would be simple to argue that this reflects the costs of deficits, in terms both of tempta-tions for governments to inflate away debt and the higher interest rates markets charge on borrowing. Certainly, there is an element of

TABLE 5.4 Globalization, Economic Policy and Economic Performance

Country	Economic growth 1985–94	change[b]	Inflation 1985–94	change	Unemployment[a] 1985–94	change
Australia	1.7	−0.7	4.7	−2.7	8.5	4.4
Austria	2.0	−1.4	3.3	−1.9	—	—
Belgium	1.8	−1.5	3.5	−1.9	9.2	3.6
Canada	1.2	−1.7	2.8	−3.1	9.5	2.9
Denmark	1.7	−1.0	3.2	−5.0	—	—
Finland	0.9	−2.6	4.0	−4.8	8.3	4.7
France	1.6	−1.5	3.2	−4.4	10.3	6.1
Germany	1.9	−1.0	3.0	−1.3	6.1	3.5
Greece	1.1	−3.5	15.8	5.2	—	—
Iceland	1.1	−2.5	15.1	−13.1	—	—
Ireland	4.0	0.8	3.1	−7.0	15.5	0.8
Italy	2.0	−1.6	6.3	−4.4	10.5	4.0
Japan	2.9	−2.8	1.2	−4.7	2.5	0.8
Luxembourg	2.6	0.2	4.6	−1.1	—	—
Mexico	0.0	−2.6	47.8	28.5	—	—
Netherlands	2.0	−0.5	1.5	−4.5	8.1	3.7
New Zealand	1.0	−0.7	6.4	−2.2	7.4	—
Norway	2.2	−1.4	3.1	−4.0	4.3	2.3
Portugal	3.2	−0.9	12.9	1.2	6.0	−2.1
Spain	2.7	−1.2	6.7	−4.4	19.4	13.0
Sweden	0.6	−2.0	5.6	−1.7	4.2	2.0
Switzerland	1.1	−0.8	3.3	−1.5	3.1	—
Turkey	2.1	−0.4	62.3	39.1	—	—
UK	2.0	0.1	5.0	−3.8	9.4	4.2
US	1.7	−0.4	3.2	−2.2	6.4	0.4
average	1.8	−1.3	9.3 (4.8)[c]	−0.2 (−2.7)	8.3 (7.6)[d]	3.4 (2.7)
correlation with:						
spending	−0.21	−0.07	−0.09 (0.03)	0.13 (0.31)	0.12	0.11
deficit	−0.07	−0.26	0.46 (0.56)	0.25 (0.05)	0.59 (0.66)	0.15 (0.06)
capital tax	−0.30	−0.11	−0.03	0.05	−0.52	−0.64
labour tax	−0.06	−0.18	−0.19	−0.04	0.00	0.02
consumption tax	−0.20	−0.18	0.00	−0.32	−0.07	0.02
trade	0.31	0.41	−0.26 (−0.12)	−0.22 (0.02)	0.15 (0.36)	−0.14 (−0.02)
FDI flows	−0.35	0.16	0.07	0.33	−0.13	0.41
financial openness	−0.18	0.56	−0.04 (−0.66)	0.02 (−0.43)	−0.03 (0.05)	0.14 (0.35)

Notes:
[a] OECD standardized unemployment rates.
[b] Change from historic average (1961–1984, with later starting dates for some countries).
[c] Excluding Iceland, Mexico and Turkey.
[d] Excluding Spain.

truth to this story. But it is equally clear that the causal arrow goes in the other direction as well. Countries with slower growth rates and higher unemployment rates will run larger deficits as a percentage of GDP because there will be greater demands on spending and less output on which to levy taxes.

The correlations between performance and taxation are generally quite weak. Indeed, the only strong relationship was between effective capital tax rates and unemployment. But the correlations went in the opposite direction to those one might have expected – higher capital tax rates were associated with lower and less quickly increasing rates of unemployment. Clearly, this relationship had to be mediated by other factors, such as perhaps the spending purposes to which capital tax revenues were put.

The most prudent conclusion to draw from the data in Table 5.4 is that it is very difficult to make strong claims about the effects of globalization and economic policy on macroeconomic performance without engaging in much more complicated econometric tests than the bivariate correlations presented here. The simple tools used in this chapter are unable to delineate the complex interactions among market integration, economic policy and macroeconomic outcomes.

Conclusion

This chapter has sought to paint in broad strokes the impact of the globalization of markets on national autonomy between the OECD countries. The core argument is that the relationships among globalization, domestic political conditions and economic policy regimes in the past decade belie common predictions of national autonomy in decline. Although on balance, financial openness has been recently associated with marginally less interventionist government, this masks growing differences among countries with respect to most facets of economic policy. An important explanation of this lies in domestic political factors such as the partisan balance of political power and the strength of organized labour movements, both of which still strongly influence economic policy. Moreover, there is little evidence that countries that have chosen to expand their public economies in the era of global markets have suffered the dire macroeconomic consequences predicted by most analysts.

Sceptics might make at least two observations that could potentially under-cut the thrust of this analysis. First, they could claim that the euro is the ultimate manifestation of globalization in Europe, and that this has radically reduced national autonomy on the continent. Second, they could argue that even if the argument holds with respect to the OECD, things are very different in the developing world – one would seem to need to look no further for evidence than to the contagious Asian financial crises of the past two years. Yet, neither point is nearly as damning as some might think.

In respect of globalization in Europe, the sceptical view of this chapter would favour a history of the past two decades in which globalization figures prominently as a constraint on national autonomy. The creation of the single market and the euro would be attributed to the interests of capital – exporters, multinationals and financiers. European governments, the argument would suggest, have been under heavy pressure to deregulate, cut spending and balance budgets – thus losing their macroeconomic independence. Yet there is another way of explaining the causes and consequences of monetary union.[42] EMU is a political creation – ultimately reflecting the longstanding commitments of French and German governments (and above all, Helmut Kohl) to 'Europe' as the key to peace and stability in the continent. The Maastricht criteria were certainly constraining on some countries for a few years, but creative accounting to get under the wire highlighted the dominance of political expediency over economic rigour: Belgium and Italy were both admitted, notwithstanding the fact that public debt in both countries was 200 per cent of the Maastricht threshold.

More importantly perhaps, governments within 'Euroland' may find it in many ways easier to expand their public economies. The delegation of monetary authority to the European Central Bank has increased the fiscal freedom of national governments. This is why the Bundesbank insisted on the straitjacket of the stability pact. But no one believes the stability pact's brutal schedule of fines will be imposed on deficit-spending countries. Rather, there is now fear of a weak Euro due to the dominance of centre-left governments in Europe which may act as a powerful counterweight to the ECB (even if it adheres faithfully to its conservative price-stability mandate). If these governments are able to realize longstanding French desires for the creation of a political body to stand alongside the Central Bank, this inter-institutional balance could be entrenched for a long time.

In respect of developing countries and globalization, the argument of sceptics is perhaps equally weak. Dani Rodrik's important book (1997) demonstrates that the positive relationship between trade and the size of government holds throughout the world, not only in the OECD.[43] At the same time, however, Rodrik contends that this relationship is likely to be undermined by capital mobility – a contention he does not test empirically. My own research suggests there is scant empirical support for this view and that there are marked similarities in the relationships between globalization and government policy – for all countries of the world – to those reported in this paper for the OECD.[44]

But perhaps this has changed since the financial crises in East Asia and elsewhere in the late 1990s? Not in the sense that although there is still considerable debate about the causes of the Asian meltdown, influential analysts – notably Paul Krugman and Jeffrey Sachs – argue strongly that bad government policies were not to blame. Something the East Asian crisis does show is just how unstable – and crippling for broad segments of society – the global economy can be. The lesson that can be drawn from this is that if the open international economy is to be preserved amid massive market volatility, the role of government in cushioning market dislocations will be more important than ever. There may be some room for the reimposition of capital controls, but severe doubt must be cast on the ability of governments to control the financial markets in this way. Adaptation, in the form of policies that redistribute wealth and risk so as to cushion the effects of global markets, seems the more appropriate response.

Having dealt with two important possible objections to my argument, let me briefly conclude with some reflections on the economic role of government in the era of global markets. There is little support these days for traditional industrial policies that prop up declining sectors. Public-sector deficits should be avoided. Taxation systems seem to be 'flattening' on many dimensions. But none of this should obscure the fact that the scope of 'market-friendly' government is considerably broader than the popular wisdom often seems to suggest. Indeed, for markets to work well, governments need to maintain institutions that secure property rights and enforce contracts. Furthermore, the new growth literature argues that the government provision of health, education, research and development, and physical infrastructure is all 'good for growth'. Going yet further, some economists (notably Alberto Alesina[45]) have gone so far as to claim that the welfare state is good for growth because is reduces inequality and increases social stability.

It should also be emphasized, however, that interventionist economic policies are better suited to countries where socioeconomic institutions facilitate the coordination of economic activity among business, labour and government. Rather than being characterized by short-termism, opportunism and free-riding, these political economies are based on the notion that cooperation to manage market forces will benefit all segments of society. Of course, this should be contrasted with the Anglo-American variant of capitalist democracy, where the lack of coordinating institutions in society and the promotion of individualism means that market disciplines must be imposed in the manner envisaged by Adam Smith.

None of this is to deny that big government faces real problems. In the OECD in particular, deteriorating macroeconomic performance coupled with the ageing of society is a very dangerous cocktail for the contemporary welfare state. Governments must take bold measures that may well displease powerful constituencies if these challenges are to be met. But these problems have little to do with globalization. In turn, if societies are to reap the benefits of globalization without paying the high costs of the past – in terms of social instability, nationalism and war – it is essential that governments ameliorate the unequalizing effects of markets. This is something democratic governments have always done and can continue to do even in a globalizing world economy.

Notes

1. R. Barro and X. Sala-I-Martin, *Economic Growth* (New York: Macmillan, 1995).
2. For a preliminary analysis of developments in the rest of the world, see Geoffrey Garrett, 'Governing in the Global Economy', Annual Meetings of the American Political Science Association, Boston, MA (1998).
3. Geoffrey Garrett, *Partisan Politics in the Global Economy* (New York: Cambridge University Press, 1998). Studies that have focused on microeconomic policies (deregulation, most importantly) lend no more consistent support to the globalization thesis than does my evidence on macroeconomic policy. See, for example, Suzanne Berger and Ronald Dore (eds), *National Diversity and Global Capitalism* (Ithaca: Cornell University Press, 1996); D. Vogel, *Trading Up: Consumer and Environmental Regulation in a Global Economy* (Cambridge, MA: Harvard University Press, 1995); S. Vogel,

Freer Markets, More Rules: Regulatory Reform in Advanced Industrial Countries (Ithaca: Cornell University Press, 1996).

4. Of course, this is an old argument that goes back at least to K. Polanyi, *The Great Transformation* (Boston: Beacon Press, 1944). John Ruggie, 'International Regimes, Transactions and Change: Embedded Liberalism in the Postwar Economic Order', in Stephen D. Krasner (ed.), *International Regimes* (Ithaca: Cornell University Press, 1983) believes that this was at the core of the Brettons Woods system. More recently, it has been argued that the mix of domestic interventionism and international openness is still critical throughout the world: Dani Rodrik, *Has Globalization Gone Too Far?* (Washington, DC: Institute for International Economics, 1997).

5. P. Pierson, 'The New Politics of the Welfare State', *World Politics*, 48 (1996) 143–79.

6. Geoffrey Garrett and P. Lange, 'Internationalization, Institutions and Political Change', *International Organization*, 49 (1995) 627–55.

7. See also R. E. Caves, *Multinational Enterprise and Economic Analysis*, 2nd edn (New York: Cambridge University Press, 1996).

8. Paul R. Krugman, *Geography and Trade* (Cambridge, MA: MIT Press, 1991).

9. Barry Eichengreen, *Toward A New International Financial Architecture: A Practical Post-Asia Agenda,* (Washington: IIE Press, 1999).

10. G. Corsetti and N. Roubini, 'Political Biases in Fiscal Policy', in Barry Eichengreen, J. Frieden and J. von Hagen (eds), *Monetary and Fiscal Policy in an Integrated Europe* (New York: Springer, 1995).

11. G. Corsetti and N. Roubini Fiscal Deficits, 'Public Debt and Government Insolvency Evidence from OECD Countries', *Journal of the Japanese and International Economies*, 5 (1991) 354–80.

12. David Soskice, 'Divergent Production Regimes', in H. Kitschelt, P. Lange, G. Marks and J. Stephens, *Continuity and Change in Contemporary Capitalism* (New York: Cambridge University Press, 1999) 101–34.

13. R. M. Alvarez, G. Garrett and P. Lange, 'Government Partisanship, Labour Organization and Macroeconomic Performance', *American Political Science Review*, 85 (1991), 541–56.

14. Garrett, *Partisan Politics*, Chapter 5.

15. Alberto Alesina and R. Perotti, 'The Welfare State and Competitiveness', *American Economic Review*, 87 (1997) 921–39.

16. T. Iversen, 'Power, Flexibility and the Breakdown of Centralized Wage Bargaining', *Comparative Politics*, 28 (1996) 399–436; J. Pontusson and P. Swenson, 'Labour Markets, Production Strategies and Wage – Bargaining Institutions: The Swedish Employers' Offensive in Comparative Perspective', *Comparative Political Studies*, 29 (1996) 223–50.

17. Robert Wade, 'Globalization and Its Limits', in S. Berger and R. Dore (eds), *National Diversity and Global Capitalism* (Ithaca: Cornell University Press, 1996), pp. 67–76.

18. Wade, 'Globalization and its Limits' at p. 69.

19. D. Quinn and M. Yoyoda, 'Measuring International Financial Regulation' (Washington DC; Georgetown University, manuscript, 1997).

20. M. Feldstein and C. Horioka, 'Domestic Savings and International Capital Flows', *The Economic Journal*, 90, (1980) 314–29.

21. T. Bayoumi, 'Savings-Investment Correlations', *IMF Staff Papers*, 37 (1990) 360–387; M. Dooley, J. Frankel and D. Mathieson, 'International Capital Mobility: What Do Savings–Investment Correlations Tell Us?', *IMF Staff Papers*, 34 (1987) 503–30.

22. The covered interest rate is typically measured as a differential against some

numeraire such as the offshore rate for short term US debt (i.e. Eurodollar rates): Richard Marston, *International Financial Integration* (New York: Cambridge University Press, 1995).

23. Jeffrey Frankel, *On Exchange Rates* (Cambridge, MA: MIT Press, 1993) pp. 58–9. Frankel analyses average covered interest rate differentials for the 1982–8 period (the local three month interest rate minus the Eurodollar rate, less the forward discount on the local currency). Countries with negative covered interest rate differentials were able to offer lower effective rates of return than were available in the euromarkets undoubtedly because their domestic conditions created impediments to outflows of capital.

24. Perhaps the prudent conclusion to draw from these data is that flow measures are at best 'noisy' indicators of real capital mobility because they may simply reflect short-term volatility in market condition. This 'noise' might be muted when countries are aggregated, resulting in a strong correlation between capital flows and the reduction of barriers to capital movements (see Figure 5.2).

25. A. Wagner, 'The Nature of the Fiscal Economy', in R. A. Musgrave and A. R. Peacock (eds), *Classics in the Theory of Public Finance* (London: Macmillan, 1958) 1–15.

26. D. R. Cameron, 'The Expansion of the Public Economy: A Comparative Analysis', *American Political Science Review*, 72 (1978) 1243–61; D. R. Cameron, 'Social Democracy, Corporatism, Labour Quiescence, and the Representation of Economic Interest in Advanced Capitalist Society', in J. H. Goldthorpe (ed.), *Order and Conflict in Contemporary Capitalism* (Oxford: Oxford University Press, 1984); Geoffrey Garrett and P. Lange, 'Political Responses to Interdependence: What's "Left" for the Left?', *International Organization*, 45 (1991) 539–64.

27. Garrett, *Partisan Politics*, chapter 4; E. Huber and J. Stephens, 'Political Power and Gender in the Making of the Social Democratic Service State' (Canberra: Research Committee 19, International Sociological Association, Australian National University 19–23 August 1996).

28. Garrett, *Partisan Politics*, chapter 4.

29. Elsewhere, I have presented more sophisticated analysis (using panel regressions with multiplicative interactions between globalization and partisan politics) that supports this interpretation: Garrett, *Partisan Politics*. Essentially, strong left-labour regimes have mitigated the distributional asymmetries generated by capital market integration with ever-higher levels of public spending. In contrast, governments in countries with much weaker left parties and trade unions have chosen to exacerbate the effects of market forces by combining openness to international financial markets with cut backs in the public economy.

30. Ruggie, 'International Regimes'.

31. E. Mendoza, G. Milesi-Ferreti and P. Asea, 'On the Effectiveness of Tax Policy in Altering Long-Run Growth', *Journal of Public Economics* 66 (1997) 99–126.

32. D. Quinn, 'The Correlates of Change in International Financial Regulation', *American Political Science Review* 91 (1997) 531–52; D. Swank, 'Funding the Welfare State', *Political Studies*, 46 (1998) 671–92.

33. Geoffrey Garrett, 'Globalization and Taxation' (New Haven: Yale University/manuscript, 1997).

34. J. G. Cummins, K. A. Hassett, and R. G. Hubbard, 'Tax Reforms and Investment: A Cross Country Comparison', *NBER Working Paper Series* No. 5232 (1995).

35. Swank, 'Funding the Welfare State'.
36. A. Auerbach and J. Slemrod, 'The Economic Effects of the Tax Reform Act of 1986', *Journal of Economic Literature*, 35 (1997) 589–632.
37. OECD, *Consumption Tax Trends*, 2nd edn (Paris: OECD, 1997).
38. Garrett, *Partisan Politics*.
39. Dani Rodrik has recently sought to challenge both of these shibboleths of mainstream economics: F. Rodriguez and Dani Rodrik, 'Trade Policy and Economic Growth: A Sceptic's Guide' (Cambridge, MA: Harvard Kennedy School of Government Manuscript, 1999). Dani Rodrik, 'Who Needs Capital Account Convertibility?' (Cambridge, MA: Harvard Kennedy School of Government Manuscript, 1998).
40. See also Quinn, 'The Correlates of Change'.
41. J. Slemrod, 'What Do Cross Country Studies Teach Us about Government Involvement, Prosperity and Economic Growth?', *Brookings Papers on Economic Activity*, 2 (1995) 373–431.
42. Geoffrey Garrett, 'The Transition to Economic and Monetary Union' in Barry Eichengreen and J. Frieden (eds), *Forging an Integrated Europe* (Ann Arbor: University of Michigan Press, 1998); and Geoffrey Garrett, 'The Politics of Maastricht', in Barry Eichengreen and J. Frieden (eds), *The Political Economy of European Monetary Unification* (Boulder: Westview Press, 1994) 47–66.
43. Rodrik, *Has Globalization Gone Too Far?*
44. Garrett, 'Governing in the Global Economy'.
45. Alesina and Perotti, 'The Welfare State and Competitiveness'.

6 Globalization as a Mode of Thinking in Major Institutional Actors*

THOMAS J. BIERSTEKER

Globalization has become part of our everyday vocabulary. References to the 'forces of globalization' are commonplace in business, in politics, in leading newspapers, and in academe, and there is already a large and extensive literature on its consequences and implications. Many accept the apparent centrality of globalization, and a great deal is attributed to it – both good and ill. Indeed, globalization is increasingly characterized, or even asserted, as an irreversible trend: as the *Wall Street Journal* declared in a special supplement about globalization, 'this is one buzzword that's here to stay'.[1]

One reason for the apparent pervasiveness of globalization is its very ambiguity. Some concepts are like vessels: the more ambiguous they are, the more meanings can be poured into them. Globalization is able to contain multiple meanings: ranging from the economic to the cultural and the political. Some authors define globalization in terms of a cluster of simultaneous contemporary trends. Gordon Laxer has identified globalization with the internationalization of production, the harmonization of tastes and standards, greatly increased mobility of capital, liberalization, deregulation, privatization, new information technologies, and trends toward a universal

* The research assistance of Jalal Alamgir and extensive comments and suggestions of Penelope Walker are gratefully acknowledged.

147

world culture and the erosion of the nation-state.[2] In a similar vein, James Mittelman has described globalization as the spatial reorganization of production, the interpenetration of industries across borders, the spread of financial markets, the diffusion of identical consumer goods, massive transfers of population, resultant conflicts between immigrant and established communities, and an emerging worldwide preference for democracy, concluding that 'the concept of globalization interrelates multiple levels of analysis – economics, politics, culture and ideology'.[3]

However, the vast majority of scholars writing about globalization define it in terms of a dramatic increase in the magnitude of international transactions. Most concentrate on increases in economic exchanges such as trade, financial, or investment flows, or on related technologically driven transfers of information, ideas, and culture.[4] Some of the macroeconomic trends are indeed quite striking, and there is a convergence around the indicators which best illustrate globalization, largely taken from the realm of international finance.

As discussed in Chapter 4, capital flows have increased dramatically. For example, the magnitude of the flow of foreign exchange across national boundaries exceeds $1.5 trillion per day, a figure that surpasses the foreign exchange holdings of all the major central banks of the OECD economies added together.[5] Increasingly common in many discussions of globalization is the powerful imagery of capital 'ricocheting across the globe' instantaneously, on an around-the-clock, twenty-four-hour-a-day-basis. During the early 1990s net capital flows to developing countries averaged more than $130 billion a year, nearly four times the level of flows during the 1980s. Capital flows to emerging markets have fallen since the onset of the Asian financial crisis of the late 1990s, but aggregate flows of capital across national boundaries continue at previous levels.[6]

There has also been a significant increase in international trade transactions as a percentage of world gross national product.[7] Cross-border transactions have more than doubled since 1970,[8] and every OECD country (except Japan) exports a higher percentage of its GDP today than it did in 1960.[9] World trade has been increasing more rapidly than world production since the end of the Second World War. In his textbook, *Global Shift*, Peter Dicken argues that '[i]n 1988, total exports were more than four times greater than in 1960, while total world output was a little under three times greater than in 1960.'[10] Trade in services grew by 12 per cent a year between 1970 and 1990,[11] and the increase in intra-firm trade, in both goods and services, is especially striking.[12]

Increases in foreign direct investment (FDI) have been equally dramatic. The world stock of FDI nearly tripled during the 1980s (from $504 billion to $1402 billion),[13] while worldwide outflows of investment grew by an average of 29 per cent annually between 1983 and 1989, nearly three times faster than trade, and almost four times faster than GNP.[14] With regard to portfolio investment flows, one equity trade in five worldwide involves a foreign share, and in continental Europe, this figure is one in three.[15]

The ease with which transactions can take place has also increased substantially in recent years. The cost of a three-minute telephone call between London and New York fell (in constant terms) from $31 to $3 between 1970 and 1990,[16] and there was a doubling of international phone traffic between 1988 and 1993 alone, a rate of increase that has continued.[17] In a similar vein, airline operating costs per mile fell by about 60 per cent between 1960 and 1990.[18]

It is easy to continue with additional empirical examples, but the striking point that emerges from the preceding evidence is that the vast majority of authors talking about the extent of globalization conceptualize it in terms of increases in transactions: in flows of capital, of goods, of investment, of technology, of information, or of decreases in the costs of these transactions.

This is not significantly different from the 'discovery' of the growth of international interdependence in the late 1960s and early 1970s, a phenomenon that contributed to the emergence of the sub-field of international political economy in North American scholarship. Accordingly, this way of defining or thinking about globalization is not significantly different from interdependence (or internationalization), and is consequently subject to many of the same critiques that befell interdependence theorists in the past.

Critics of interdependence pointed out that an increase in the magnitude of transactions did not necessarily imply any significant change in the behaviour or in the relationships of major actors. It follows from this that if globalization is defined as the growth of international transactions then there is little that is really new here. Indeed, these critics point out that the degree of interdependence (or 'globalization') today is not much different from the degree of interdependence experienced at the beginning of the twentieth century, in the years immediately preceding the First World War: 'Whether measured by levels of trade, international investment, and capital flows (as a percentage of GDP), the world now finds itself at roughly the same point as in 1913.'[19] In a similar vein, others argue that individual states remain the principal location of accumulation in the world economy and that a globalized world economy simply does not yet exist.[20] Moreover, states can always reverse tendencies toward globalization, and most likely will, when threatened.[21]

There is a great deal of truth and insight in these critical reactions, but like the literature they are criticizing, they also tend to concentrate on the transactional aspects of globalization and overlook the potential significance of qualitative changes that may be underway in the way in which major institutional actors think about their role in the contemporary world.

An alternative, and more useful, way to think about globalization is as a basic change in the way in which major institutional actors think and operate across the globe. Changes in the thinking and modes of operation of institutions, in their ways of conceptualizing their mission, or in their basic rules and decision-making procedures and routines could in the end turn out to be far more significant than simple increases in the magnitude of transactions. It is harder to describe and track changes in orientation and mode of operation empirically, but they may turn out to be the most important dimensions of globalization.

This conceptualization of globalization implies that it entails a reorientation away from the local or national level of analysis toward the regional or supranational level (analogous to the transformation of world views triggered by the first photographs taken of the earth from the moon – something which created a vivid image, not of separate states, but of the entire globe, a geosphere). Following Roland Robertson, globalization should therefore be conceptualized not in terms of increases in transactions, but as a change of 'the form in terms of which the world becomes united . . . as a conceptual entry into the problem of world order in the most general sense'.[22]

If processes of globalization (as a re-orientation away from the nation-state) are underway, there should be visible evidence in major institutional actors on the world stage today: in firms, in non-governmental organizations (NGOs), in international institutions, and in the foreign economic and political policies of states themselves.

Changes in thinking and modes of operation of major institutional actors

Changes in thinking and modes of operation of major institutional actors are most visible in the structure of individual firms. Globalization within firms is noticeable when they begin to change their basic modes of operation from a principal concern with national markets toward a concern with planning, production, servicing and competing on a regional and global scale.[23] As Robert Reich has illustrated with his now classic example of a Japanese-owned multinational with a subsidiary in the USA seeking American government support against the unfair trading practices of an American-owned multinational exporting from East Asia, the idea of 'national capital' is increasingly problematic.[24]

There is tremendous variation in the different organizational forms global production can take. The chain of production from research and development to final product distribution and servicing 'can be articulated in different organizational and geographical ways'.[25] In organizational terms, this means that research, production, and service might be contained within a single firm, or they might be subcontracted in a variety of different ways to other firms. As discussed in Chapter 2, in geographical terms, while the location of research, production, or services might once have been contained within a single state, they are increasingly likely to be dispersed across different parts of the globe. When organizational change (the move to subcontracting and alliances of major multinational enterprises) is combined with increased geographical dispersal of activity beyond the limits of a single state, it is possible to derive a virtually unlimited variety of different corporate organizational forms.

Until the 1970s, most of the transnational activity of large corporations was contained within a single entity which might take different organizational forms (from globally concentrated production within one country to host market production in different countries, product specialization for a regional market, or different types of transnational vertical integration).[26] While different branches of this firm might be spread across different countries, they were all part of the same corporate entity. This was the classic model of the formerly national firm that became a multinational (or transnational) enterprise when it began to cross national boundaries during the post-Second World War period. With the recent moves toward much greater use of subcontracting and the initiation of international business alliances in the 1980s, the picture has become far more complicated. At the outset, most firms began to subcontract parts of their activity to firms within their home country in an effort to contain costs and remain competitive. Over time, however, more of this outsourcing was contracted to different producers located at sites dispersed across the globe. Figure 6.1 illustrates, in a simplified and schematic form, the emergence of one form of the new organization of global production.

Many firms have developed networks of global production locations and investment strategies that spread corporate risk (and tax liability) on a global scale.[27] In industries like textiles, apparel, and footwear, many firms have embarked on flexible accumulation on a global scale, increasing their use of subcontracted production sites dispersed across the globe, shifting industrial organization to 'just in time' delivery systems, pursuing flexible production, and introducing a variety of different types of 'buyer-driven' commodity chains.[28] Companies like Nike or Benetton exemplify this new type of production organization.[29] These companies, and firms like them, are transforming consumption patterns worldwide by homogenizing global tastes and accelerating product turnover, introducing new product lines with ever shorter life spans (from 18 to 12 months or even less). This tendency is not restricted to the largest corporations, but is increasingly found in small and medium-sized firms as well.[30]

FIGURE 6.1   The New Organization of Global Production

O r g a n i z a t i o n a l f o r m		Geographical Dispersion of Enterprises	
		National (within one country)	Transnational (across national boundaries)
	Intra-firm	Most US firms (before 1950)	Classic MNCs (1960s and early 1970s)
	Inter-firm	Subcontracting within one country	Multinational Alliances and Transnational Subcontracting (Nike, Benetton)

This change in the organization of production has been accompanied by a corresponding change in the organization of international finance.[31] There has been a major shift away from sharply demarcated national financial boundaries (with effective currency controls in place) from the 1930s to the 1970s toward increased financial liberalization, the elimination of currency controls, and an increased ease of cross-border financial transactions. Even though the Asian financial crisis has put the issue back on the agenda, most countries have avoided sweeping controls or imposed them on only a temporary basis. This tendency toward financial liberalization, which accelerated during the 1980s, has facilitated the emergence of new financial actors in the 1990s – bond traders, currency traders, and major money market fund portfolio investors – who have developed global hedging strategies and operate on an around-the-clock and around-the-globe basis. As a result, the emerging world financial market 'is not comprised of linked national markets; in fact, it is not comprised of geographic locations at all. It is a network integrated through electronic information systems that entails . . . more than two hundred thousand electronic monitors in trading rooms all over the world that are linked together.'[32] This network has itself increasingly become a location of financial power and authority in the world, with an ability to reward countries that pursue policies it deems prudent, and to discipline those that pursue policies it deems unsustainable.

The combined effect of these changes in the organization of global production and finance has 'rendered ambiguous' the traditional territorial imagery of international political economy.[33] As John Ruggie has argued, we need to 'unbundle' our concept of territoriality.[34] Control over flows and networks is becoming more important than hierarchical control over physical territorial space, as Timothy Luke demonstrated with reference to Kuwait (where royal family control over the flows of oil and wealth continued, even after the loss of control of all of the physical territory of the country).[35] The emergence of the 'region-state' – 'natural' economic zones with integrated industrial investment and information systems that straddle national boundaries in an increasingly borderless world – is another manifestation of this blurring of traditional conceptions of territoriality.[36]

There are a number of empirical indicators that reflect the growing significance of the global and regional dimensions of the activities of firms. A number of major companies have chosen to target international markets for major growth, and they are increasingly relying on them for their earnings. For example, AT&T has decided to derive 50 per cent of its business from overseas,[37] while Alcoa Aluminum's foreign sales increased from a third of its total sales to nearly half between 1987 and 1995. There has also been a dramatic increase in strategic alliances among multinational enterprises, particularly in industries where the minimum size of markets to support technological development exceeds the size of most national markets: in automobiles, aviation, banking, pharmaceuticals, biotechnology, aerospace, and information technology.[38] Strategic corporate alliances across national boundaries have even emerged within defense industries.[39]

Even more important, there is a growing perception within firms that principal competitors come increasingly from outside of the domain of the national market. As a result, a growing number of major corporations no longer divide their operations between domestic and international divisions, but increasingly are integrating their activities in technological development, production, marketing, and pricing into single, integrated units, with an eye toward global competition. It is significant to note the number of chief executive officers of major enterprises who have arrived in their positions after extensive careers in the international divisions of their firm, and there is a parallel tendency to favour for promotion to key positions executives who similarly developed their careers within the international sector.

As evident as it is within business, globalization as a change in the mode of operation of institutional actors is not restricted to firms. There is also evidence of a shift in orientation within non-profit non-governmental organizations (or NGOs). As discussed in Chapter 7, they are no longer just 'thinking globally and acting locally,' but many are beginning to act globally as well. Environmental NGOs like Greenpeace have larger annual budgets than the United Nations Environmental Program (UNEP) and have begun to play a significant role in influencing the agendas of international environmental negotiations. Greenpeace has used 'client states', like small Pacific islands with an interest in the potential consequences of global warming, to place items on the negotiating table at inter-governmental meetings. Other environmental NGOs like Friends of the Earth have been credited with pressuring the World Bank to take environmental impacts into consideration in its development projects.[40]

At the same time, NGOs operating in the area of humanitarian intervention have been called upon in recent years to deliver vast quantities of services as part of international relief operations. Nongovernmental organizations disbursed over 10 per cent of all public development aid in 1994 (approximately a total of $8 billion), 'surpassing the volume of the combined UN system ($6 billion)' excluding the international financial institutions.[41] Finally, human rights NGOs have created issue networks that operate on a global scale, and have managed to put effective pressure on states accused of violating individual and group rights, as well as on those states that might sanction them.[42] These networks have the power to draw attention to issues, to mobilize their transnational networks of support, and like Greenpeace, even to place issues on national, regional, and global agendas.

In addition to the globalization of firms and NGOs, inter-state organizations have also altered their orientation and become increasingly intrusive into what have been viewed (at least in the recent past) as issues that were principally the prerogative of individual sovereign states. The International Monetary Fund, the World Bank, the World Trade Organization, and regional institutions have increased the frequency, the depth, and the scope of their interventions. While they have always operated on a global scale, they have never before gone so far into the 'internal' affairs of states (see Chapter 8). In the 1990s, there is an apparent acceptance of their intrusiveness on the part of most states. Accordingly, defences of state behaviour based on claims of 'state sovereignty' are increasingly rare, with the important recent exceptions of China and Serbia.

The International Monetary Fund has introduced more extensive economic conditionalities with its system of 'enhanced surveillance'. The requirement that Mexico post its foreign exchange reserves on the Internet on a weekly basis following the 1994 peso crisis is indicative of this kind of enhanced scrutiny. Similar kinds of requirements have been imposed on Asian economies in the name of increased 'transparency', during the working-out of the Asian financial crisis. The IMF has also entered the realm of security policy for the first time, with its recent explicit criticism of the military and defence spending of member states. The World Bank has flirted with political conditionalities with the 'new conditionality' it introduced in the early 1990s. The European Bank for Reconstruction and Development joined the World Bank in this exercise, by imposing political conditions on the provision of assistance to countries in east and central Europe. The World Bank has also introduced the idea of 'green' conditionality, linking some of its assistance to provisions for environmental protection.

Not to be outdone, the World Trade Organization has pressed the frontier of trade liberalization by becoming ever more intrusive into the historic domain of domestic politics. In the 1960s, the GATT focused on lowering tariffs. It moved progressively into non-tariff barriers during the 1970s, and then proceeded to focus on trade in services in the 1980s. The remaining challenge for trade liberalization is to move into modifications in domestic labour and environmental policies. The US–Japanese 'structural impediments initiative' may have been one of the first illustrations of this general development. Finally, the growing willingness of the international community to address, rather than ignore, emergencies within the borders of war-torn states (as indicated by the increased number of multinational peacekeeping operations under UN auspices during the early 1990s or the use of NATO at the end of the decade) are illustrations of the increased intrusiveness of international institutions in the political and military realm.

While firms, NGOs, and international institutions have changed their orientations in basic ways, there has been an equally profound change in the way in which states organize and think about their relationship with the global economy in recent years. Most states have gone from an inward-oriented focus on the domestic economy (from import substitution industrialization or Keynesian counter-cyclical policies focused at the national level) to a preoccupation with export orientation and national competitiveness. While states and their publics are still preoccupied with their national welfare (or standing), the means to attain advancement are increasingly perceived to be through greater participation in the world economy, not through insulation from it. This is a profound change, an apparent 'triumph' of neoclassical economic thinking throughout the developing world.[43]

At the most general level, the economic ideas being pursued as policy throughout the world today include a reduction and transformation of state economic intervention, from production and distribution toward increased mediation and a redirection of regulation, an important revision of a principal component of Keynesianism in the postwar developing world.[44] At the end of the 1980s, John Williamson has described this change in discourse as the emergence of the 'Washington consensus' (or a nearly 'universal convergence') around the objectives of fiscal discipline, adjustment of public expenditure priorities, tax reform, financial liberalization, exchange rate adjustment, privatization, deregulation, and support for property rights.[45] While the Asian financial crisis and the election of social democratic coalitions within Europe have led to some questioning of the 1980s neoliberal orthodoxy, its basic components – fiscal discipline, tax and regulatory reform, privatization, and support for property rights – remain unchallenged. While some contend that the revived interest in capital controls in Asia portends the reversal of capital market liberalization,[46] it could just as easily turn out to be the kind of correction needed to reinforce and further institutionalize financial market liberalization worldwide. Rather than reverse globalization, it could prove to be just enough re-regulation to stabilize market capitalism and deepen globalization.

By the 1990s, the basic discourse of development had changed. The once-fundamental opposition between capitalist West and socialist East no longer defined the boundaries of development discourse, being displaced by attention to a variety of forms of development within capitalism, along with some as yet inchoate alternatives emerging from marginalized regions of the capitalist world economy. With the end of socialist development alternatives, the range of national development options has narrowed to choices within capitalism (even while our consciousness of the range of choice within capitalism has broadened appreciably). Thus, although there are national variations, there seems to be no going back from fundamental tenets of economic liberalization. This has accelerated processes of trade liberalization and functional regional integration in Europe, in North America, and even in Asia.

Another indication of change in the ways states think about their relationship with the rest of the world can be found within the foreign economic policy of the OECD countries. Since the end of the Cold War, there has been a major shift in the rationale for providing foreign assistance. In the past, the principal motivation was for the purpose of strengthening foreign policy alliances or pursuing a variety of different moral goals. Today, one of the principal rationales for giving aid is to address regional or global problems, whether it involves the provision of new technologies (as called for in the ozone treaty) or for international strategies to deal with common problems like global warming, the drug trade, or the spread of AIDS.

Another indication of the globalization of economic policy-making can be found in the increasing frequency with which sub-national governments at the regional and state level within different countries have developed international trade strategies of their own in the competitive pursuit of trade and commercial advantage. It is increasingly common to hear reports of state (or even municipal) trade delegations from the United States making official visits to other countries or engaging in comparative research on national development strategies for ideas about how to benefit from the globalization of the world economy. Like the changes described above in the case of national government policy, many of these adaptations of orientation at the state, regional, and local level are reactive, or deliberate responses to widely perceived changes in the global economic environment.

Although the bulk of the discussion of the globalization of state policy falls within the realm of the international political economy, there is also growing evidence of a globalization (as multilateralism) in the domain of national security policy. Major states appear to be less inclined to undertake unilateral actions without some form of international backing, either from regional or global institutions. This has been true even in the case of the United States, when it obtained United Nations backing for the legitimation of its intervention in the Gulf War in 1990 and 1991, for its action in Haiti in 1994, and most recently in the case of NATO support against Serbia. At the same time, more and more states appear to be willing to accept the subcontracting of their military services to both regional and international organizations. US forces have been placed under UN auspices in Macedonia. British, French, Dutch and Bangladeshi forces have served under the UN in Bosnia. Russian troops serve under US command in the Balkans. And the Nigerian military has provided troops for regional peacekeeping operations under OAU mandate in Liberia.

Thus, evidence of globalization is visible in all of the major institutional actors on the world stage today. Firms, regardless of sector or size, have begun to go global, NGOs have begun to identify and mobilize networks across state boundaries, international institutions have become far more intrusive into the realm of the 'domestic' than they ever were in the past, and states have adapted their foreign economic and security policies in response to all of these changes. Globalization as a change in mode of thinking and operation in major institutional actors has gone quite far,[47] and it has the potential to have more far reaching implications than a simple increase in the volume of cross-border transactions.

Consequences of globalization

A great deal of empirical work needs to be undertaken on the extent of globalization, before definitive conclusions about its consequences can be reached. Moreover, the potential implications of globalization as a change in thinking and orientation extend from the economic, to the political, the social, and the cultural domains. However, one of the most widely held views about the consequences of globalization is that it increases inequality in a variety of different areas. As Barnet and Cavanaugh have argued, '(I)n the new world economy, there is a huge gulf between the beneficiaries and the excluded and, as world population grows, it is widening.'[48] The discussion which follows will attempt a preliminary analysis of the issues raised by globalization on this most important aspect of its potential consequences.

The literature on the consequences of globalization is divided along some fairly predictable ideological faultlines: between optimists about its beneficial consequences writing from the liberal internationalist tradition, and pessimists from the critical, post-Marxist tradition. The discussion which follows will draw on insights from both traditions, but it is increasingly apparent that the implications of globalization for inequality are contradictory in important respects.[49]

With the globalization of firms and markets, locations of production can be shifted readily from one production site to another. This means that individual states can be drawn into a competition with each other, as they attempt to maintain their attractiveness to investors (and sustain their global competitiveness) by engaging in competitive forms of deregulation and liberalization.[50] Thus, globalization can have the effect of marginalizing entire countries, at least at its initial stages.[51] In an argument reminiscent of dependency analyses of the 1970s, globalization is criticized by some observers for widening the gap that separates the core from the periphery.[52]

Although it might increase levels of inequality between states, the globalization of production also has the potentially contradictory consequence of spreading production to locations in the developing world that otherwise might not have access to major markets in the wealthiest countries.[53] The physical relocation of firms and, in some cases, entire industries (such as textiles and electronics) to other parts of the world is indicative of this development. Thus, rather than increasing inequality between states, the global dispersal of production may actually reduce it. Like previous debates about the consequences of foreign investment, if the counterfactual alternative to globalization is the absence of comparable production and/or access to markets, then it should be credited with a reduction, not an increase, in inter-state inequality. A great deal of empirical research needs to be conducted on this subject, particularly with evidence about the expansion of international subcontracting and the degree of genuine access to global distributive networks.

The apparently contradictory consequences of globalization for inter-state inequality may explain what otherwise might appear to be paradoxical survey data on middle-class public opinion and optimism versus pessimism about the future in different parts of the world. Recent data have suggested growing degrees of pessimism about future welfare in most OECD countries, while optimism prevails among the middle class in emerging market countries like India and China. It may be that the global dispersal of production in some industries from the OECD to emerging markets plays an important role in explaining different degrees of optimism about the future.

If countries perceive themselves to be increasingly in competition with each other and engage in competitive deregulation to maintain their relative economic position, wage levels are likely to be depressed and abysmal working conditions sustained within individual enterprises. Thus, the globalization of firms might not only increase inequality between states, but might also reinforce levels of inequality within them. In addition to an increase in income inequality, gender and ethnic inequality may also be influenced by the globalization of economic activity. The systems of flexible accumulation typically associated with globalization tend to be negative for women and minority populations, because those two groups tend to predominate in the markets for subcontracting to temporary labour. They also tend to be the last hired during times of economic expansion and the first fired in times of economic recession.

However, flexible accumulation can also provide some formal sector employment experience for many that may increase the probability of their subsequent employment at some future date. Like the issue of inter-state inequality, the contradictory implications of globalization for internal economic, gender, and ethnic inequality also deserve much more extensive empirical analysis. In particular, data on relative wages and changes in wage demands should be obtained, again paying careful attention to counterfactual alternatives arguments.

Accelerated turnover and the constant introduction of new products with shorter and shorter product lives tends to reinforce pre-existing class divisions. This is especially the case in instances where fewer people can afford to keep up with the pace of product change. However, like the other potential implications of globalization already considered, product innovation and accelerated turnover also have contradictory implications. For example, they keep markets growing and provide employment opportunities that might not otherwise have been created (another counterfactual alternatives argument).

Like much of the writing on interdependence during the 1970s, the recent literature on the globalization of firms addresses the inequality between states and multinational enterprises. Once again, there is a great deal of emphasis on the growth of challenges to the state and state sovereignty. For many, globalization is said to limit the capacity and/or autonomy of states, something that is generally perceived to be a very *bad* thing.[54] Not only does it allow multinationals to allocate factors of production, but it also creates a situation where major institutional actors lack accountability for their actions and operate 'largely beyond the control of effective state regulation'.[55] The ease with which money market and hedge fund managers can move massive amounts of capital across national boundaries has prompted some observers to express concern about the ways in which the fragility of international financial markets constrains the room for policy manoeuvre for individual states, and it has prompted some states (for example, Malaysia) to reintroduce capital controls.[56]

However, this perception of a shift in the ability of states to control and regulate firms has already begun to provoke a series of counter-reactions at a variety of different levels. Even as they talk about the power and authority of global markets when justifying the need for cuts in welfare and social spending, political leaders at the national level have attempted to reassert their authority over flows of finance and information. The frequency with which the United States resorts to unilateral measures to extend its rules and laws extraterritorialy (such as the controversial Helms–Burton Act and recent efforts to eliminate sweat shops in the clothing industry) is a good illustration of this reaction. At the same time, local challenges to the homogenizing tendencies of globalization have emerged in a variety of different forms: religious, cultural, ethnic, and national. Even at the supranational (or regional) level, there are growing efforts to reassert controls and regulatory conventions. The regionalization of the global political economy, extending from the European Union to Mercosur and NAFTA, can be viewed as a regional, institutional response to globalization. And the International Monetary Fund has taken the initiative to address the problems induced by global financial fragility with its proposals for 'the dissemination of a clear set of internationally accepted standards . . . for the regulation and supervision of banking systems around the world'.[57] Thus, while it is possible selectively to draw out examples that might suggest a unidimensional shift in the balance of power from states to major multinational firms, a counter-reaction is well underway.

The contradictory implications for inequality can be seen not only from the globalization of firms, but also from the globalization of non-governmental organizations. Non-governmental organizations can have an important effect on reducing inequality within states by giving voice to groups traditionally repressed within them. Local NGOs can team up with their counterparts in more powerful countries who are in a position either to put pressure on their home governments or to exert influence on international institutions to which they have relatively easier access. The environmental and human rights NGO communities have been particularly effective in this regard, from the 'greening' of the World Bank to bringing global attention to the plight of the residents of East Timor or the Ogoni peoples of Nigeria.

Once again, however, there are limits on the influence of these globalizing tendencies. The very attention local NGOs receive from abroad may provoke their governments to repress dissident movements more vehemently. Moreover, while they can empower local groups, NGOs are ultimately accountable only to their members, who tend to be drawn disproportionately from the upper middle classes of the wealthiest countries and inclined to equate their own class and regional interests with those of the rest of the world. Like the globalization of the activities of firms, the globalization of NGOs also has contradictory implications for inequality.

The increased intrusiveness of international institutions also has potentially important and far-reaching implications for inequality. The working out of the global debt crisis of the 1980s – and of the financial crisis of the late 1990s – demonstrated that the international financial institutions have much more leverage with debtor countries than with creditor institutions. As Mexico and other heavily indebted countries learned in the 1980s, the bulk of the costs of debt was borne by the developing countries, and routinely passed on to the most marginal populations located within them. The asymmetries of power were stark in the 1980s, when the IMF and the World Bank were the principal sources of finance (or financial guarantees) for many countries. Moreover, while they are accountable to their major contributors, they are powerful institutions which are not directly accountable to the countries that rely most heavily on their finance.

However, experience from the 1980s also shows that creditor institutions rarely received everything they wanted from debtor countries, something repeated at the end of the 1990s. Conditionalities need to be viewed within a bargaining framework in which debtors and creditors engage in complex, multi-level, iterated rounds of bargaining and negotiation. What a debtor country does not achieve at the stage of the negotiation of a letter of intent with the IMF, it may obtain during a stalled or half-hearted implementation of the agreement. The balance of bargaining power is a function of a variety of different factors, including size, strategic significance to creditors, access to non-conditional sources of finance, and a debtor country's domestic bargaining space.[58]

The increased intrusiveness of institutions like the World Trade Organization is likely to make it more difficult for many developing countries to gain access to the markets of the European Union and the North American Free Trade Association. By exporting standards on working conditions and by increasing their attention to green packaging and labelling, the wealthiest countries are in a position to make it more difficult for many developing countries to gain access for their exports. Regional trade agreements like NAFTA have already marginalized entire regions, such as the Caribbean basin. However, while these trade agreements marginalize some, others located at the immediate periphery of the world's largest markets and increasingly integrated with them (like Mexico, the Czech Republic, Hungary, and Poland) appear to be benefiting disproportionately from increased integration and policy harmonization. Once again, the implications for inequality are not uniform across states.

As individual states respond in a variety of different ways to the globalization of firms, NGOs, and international institutions, there are a number of implications for inequality. The short-term costs of rapid economic liberalization and structural adjustment are routinely negative for much of the population.[59] However, the medium- to long-term outcomes can be favourable, if certain institutional conditions are present (particularly if the reforms are implemented fully and maintained for an extended period of time). In theory, rural populations should benefit from orthodox economic reforms in countries where a majority of the population is still engaged in agricultural production. This alone could contribute to a very significant reduction in domestic inequality. However, there is surprisingly little reliable economic evidence to confirm or challenge this theoretical point. Getting the prices 'right' and taking the state out of production and marketing is not sufficient, unless there are effective markets and other incentives in place.

The institutionalization of market-oriented economic reform appears likely to constrain any further extension or deepening of the welfare state within OECD states, at least for the foreseeable future. However, core aspects of the welfare state, like pension schemes, remain largely intact The narrowing of the discourse of development to a range of choices within the market economy has also removed one of the most powerful bases for mobilization of opposition to globalization. Reactions against globalization are common, but they lack the force of a credible, theoretically based alternative to liberal economic ideas.

In conclusion, globalization produces inequalities for states, regions, genders and ideas, but also produces opportunities to challenge and to overcome them. Figure 6.2 summarizes the contradictory implications of globalization in different institutional actors for different types of inequality (between states, within states, and between states and firms). These implications remind us that it is not only important to specify the meaning of globalization carefully but equally to understand its political uses, for it is both a powerful idea and a useful one for different constituencies.[60]

**FIGURE 6.2 Contradictory Consequences of Globalization
for Inequality**

	Increases Inequality	*Decreases Inequality*
1. The Globalization of Firms		
a. inequality	between states shifts production from one country to another	disperses production and provides access to technology and markets
b. inequality within states	encourages competitive deregulation and accelerated turnover	introduces flexible accumulation, provides employment, and keeps markets growing
c. inequality between states	allows firms to allocate production, and operate beyond state regulation	prompts state counter-reactions at the national regional, and global levels
2. The Globalization of NGOs	may invite increased repression and allows agenda setting by actors who lack accountability for their actions	gives voice to marginalized and repressed groups and enables pressure on powerful states and institutions
3. The Globalization of International Institutions	decreases state ability to determine policy and limits trade access for states excluded from regional arrangements	can be countered by state action and provides preferential access for those included in regional arrangements
4. The Globalization of State Policies	increases austerity in short term and limits capacity to extend the welfare state	sends efficient signals to producers and consumers and increases general welfare

Will globalization continue?

Some tendencies towards globalization could be reversed – at least on a temporary basis – by states or other authorities interested in reasserting sovereign authority.[61] Firms could be re-regulated, currency controls could be re-established, NGOs could be repressed, and international institutions could be ignored. There have been isolated examples of each of these responses by states in recent years. However, reversing globalization at a systemic level would take a gargantuan collective effort, and it is by no means clear that any single state – or any other actor – has the will or the ability to undertake and sustain the effort on its own. To understand whether globalization as a change in thinking and mode of operation of major institutional actors is likely to continue, it is necessary to consider the principal sources of globalization.

Business is, and has been, the principal driving force behind globalization. One of the principal motivations for changes in corporate thinking, strategy, and structure has been increasing competitiveness within the global economy.[62] US-based multinational enterprises had no serious competition immediately following the Second World War, but subsequently found themselves pressured by firms from Germany, Japan, the European Union, and more recently by the newly industrializing countries of East Asia and from China. The successive lowering of trade barriers across the globe over the same period has made it easier for individual firms to contemplate and develop a corporate strategy that transcends the national market in an effort to maintain their competitive position. The pace at which technology has been developed and disseminated has also accelerated significantly in recent years, placing increasing pressures on major enterprises, wherever they are located.

At the same time, the complexity, cost, and risk of development of new technology have rendered even the largest national markets too small to be meaningful economic units.[63] This is particularly pronounced in global financial markets, where financial firms have introduced corporate strategies on a global scale. There is also evidence of this in the case of capital-intensive production, where the technological barriers to entry are relatively high. Taken together, these factors have prompted a great many firms to enter into a variety of different types of mutually beneficial multinational alliances with each other.[64]

New information technologies have also made possible different types of association, described in the first section of this chapter. The ease with which capital can be moved electronically, combined with general policy tendencies toward financial openess have facilitated the emergence of new financial actors (global bond traders, currency traders, money market managers, and portfolio investors). New institutional forms like the Eurocurrency market, electronically integrated global financial markets, and new financial instruments like the euro encourage and reinforce the reorientation of these actors away from the local or national to the possibilities of the regional and global levels. Each of these technological and institutional developments is facilitated by political changes within states, such as deregulation, liberalization, and privatization, which make it easier for firms to think and operate globally.

New information technology has also made it possible for NGOs and the general population to view what is going on in dispersed places, to create new 'virtual' communities, and to mobilize publics throughout the world. The bare outlines of a global civil society have begun to emerge in certain issue domains, particularly in the areas of human rights and the environment.[65] At the same time, states are increasingly withdrawing from a number of social welfare commitments, creating space for NGOs to expand their operations on a global scale.

The weakening of non-conditional sources of finance empowered the international financial institutions during the 1980s, and the resulting policy shifts toward market liberalization in most countries increased the number and range of instruments of influence at the disposal of the IMF and the World Bank. With the end of the Cold War, countries can no longer appeal for exemptions from conditionalities because of their 'critical' role in some aspect of superpower conflict, nor can they play one superpower off against another to increase their levels of foreign assistance. The IMF has already identified financial fragility as the primary economic problem facing the twenty-first century (even before the Asian financial crisis) and recommended a strengthened set of international institutional arrangements to address it.

Policy convergence around liberalization and market-oriented reform within individual states is principally the result of the drying up of non-conditional sources of finance during the 1980s. Indeed, the timing of national financial crises explains when serious economic reforms were introduced in most countries: the debt crisis for Latin America in the early 1980s, the raw material price declines for Africa during the same time period, the oil price collapse in the mid-1980s for the OPEC states, and the Indian financial crisis in the early 1990s. This policy shift has been reinforced in the 1990s by the fragility of the sources of finance that have emerged (largely portfolio investment). It is fragile because it can be moved so easily and with such potentially devastating consequences, as Mexico learned in December of 1994, Thailand in 1997, Russia in 1998, and Brazil in 1999. The end of the Cold War has taken away the logic of bipolar competition, created room for problem-oriented rationales for aid-giving, and raised the costs of unilateral military action.

Many of the sources of globalization are founded in technological changes. Global technological changes have facilitated the emergence of new networks of production, the globalization of financial markets, the ability of NGOs to pursue the struggle for the extension of rights or environmental protection, the perceived need for multilateral intervention, and the ability of international institutions to monitor activities within countries. It is increasingly difficult for governments to block their population's access to outside technological influences. Portable satellite dishes, personal computers with fax modems, the Internet, and short-wave radios confound centralized, state efforts to control communications and information flows. In this respect, individuals and groups have gained considerably in power relative to the state, being limited only by money and ingenuity. Global technological advances have led to greater transparency, facilitated the transmission of norms and values, and helped to reinforce the shifting of authority to a growing number of locations outside the traditional, territorial state.

Transnational networks have begun to displace the territorial state in the organization of global production, the distribution of global finance, the provision of emergency relief and assistance, the protection of individual and group rights, and the defence of the global environment. This development, facilitated by the technological change just described, has redefined state sovereignty (by reducing the number, the range, and the recognition of authority claims made by states) and is likely to continue into the twenty-first century.

Conclusion

In the final analysis, the European experience with international integration may be illustrative when one considers the reversibility of processes of globalization. There is little question that the process of integration in Europe has been halting in important respects (with major institutional achievements routinely followed by major setbacks in political support for continued integration).[66] However, the process of regional integration began with a limited focus on trade liberalization and has both widened and deepened – in spite of repeated declarations of its demise – over the course of nearly forty years. One reason for this continued progression may be that 'once free market access is assured, it becomes much more difficult and expensive for governments to pursue other distortionary policies because they can be undermined by international trade'.[67] As long as imports can move freely into the domestic market, a government will be restrained from reintroducing excessive regulation by its own firms, interested in maintaining their own competitive position. These same dynamics may well be operating with regard to globalization.

There is undoubtedly a great deal of hyperbole about globalization. Exaggerated claims about its scope and its implications tend to prevail in far too many discussions of the subject. Yet, equally there is clearly something significant under way. It is popular among some scholars to dismiss the evidence of changes, proclaim the continued centrality of the state, and assert the profoundly national character of investment decisions.[68] However, the evidence suggests that major institutional actors are changing both their way of thinking and their mode of operation.

Notes

1. Editor's Note, *The Wall Street Journal*, 26 September 1996, p. R2.
2. G. Laxer, 'Social Solidarity, Democracy and Global Capitalism', *Canadian Review of Sociology and Anthropology*, 32, 3 (August 1995) 287–8.
3. J. H. Mittelman, 'The Globalisation Challenge: Surviving at the Margins', *Third World Quarterly*, 15, 3 (September 1994) 427.
4. R. J. Barry Jones, *Globalization and Interdependence in the International Political Economy* (London and New York: Pinter Publishers, 1995).
5. M. Miller, 'Where is Globalization Taking Us? Why We Need a New 'Bretton Woods'', *Futures*, 27, 2 (March 1995) 131.
6. *IMF Survey*, 23 October 1995, 343–4.
7. The implications of which are examined in Chapter 3.
8. J. Dunning, 'Globalization: The Challenge for National Economic Regimes' 24th Geary Lecture, Economic and Social Research Institute, Dublin, Ireland, 1993, p. 4.
9. S. Weber, 'Globalization and the International Political Economy', Paper presented at the Berkeley Roundtable on the International Economy Working Meeting on Globalization, Berkeley, California, March 1996, p. 2.
10. P. Dicken, *Global Shift: The Internationalization of Economic Activity*, 2nd edn, (London: Paul Chapman Publishing, 1992), pp. 16–17.

11. UN Research Institute for Social Development, *States of Disarray: The Social Effects of Globalization* (Geneva: UNRISD, 1995) p. 27.
12. D. Levy and J. Dunning, 'International Production and Sourcing: Trends and Issues', *STI Review*, 13 (December 1993) p. 15 and see Chapter 2 of this volume.
13. J. Maarten De Vet, 'Globalization and Local and Regional Competitiveness', *STI Review*, 13 (December 1993) p. 101.
14. Levy and Dunning, 'Industrial Production', p. 30.
15. H. Wendt, *Global Embrace: Corporate Challenges in a Transnational World*, (New York: Harper Business, 1993) pp. 31–2.
16. UNRISD, *States of Disarray*, p. 29.
17. H. M. Trebing and M. Estabrooks, 'The Globalization of Telecommunications: A Study in the Struggle to Control Markets and Technology', *Journal of Economic Issues*, 29, 2 (June 1995) 535.
18. UNRISD, *States of Disarray*, p. 29.
19. J. Levy, 'Globalization and National Systems', Paper presented at the Berkeley Roundtable on the International Economy, Working Meeting on Globalization, Berkeley, California, 8 March 1996, p. 2.
20. P. Hirst and G. Thompson, 'The Problem of "Globalization": International Economic Relations, National Economic Management and the Formation of Trading Blocs', *Economy and Society*, 21, 4 (November 1992) 365.
21. Robert Wade, 'Globalization and its Limits: Reports of the Death of the National Economy are Greatly Exaggerated', in S. Berger and R. Dore (eds) *National Diversity and Global Capitalism* (Ithaca: Cornell University Press, 1996) p. 86.
22. R. Robertson, 'Mapping the Global Condition: Globalization as the Central Concept', *Theory, Culture and Society*, 7, 2–3 (June 1990) 18.
23. Not all firms in every sector need to be responding identically, for a significant change to be underway.
24. R. Reich, *The Work of Nations* (New York: Knopf, 1991).
25. Dicken, *Global Shift*, p. 225.
26. Ibid., p. 202.
27. The factors which impel such globalization have been examined in Chapter 2.
28. G. Gereffi, 'The Organization of Buyer-Driven Global Commodity Chains: How U.S. Retailers Shape Overseas Production Networks', in G. Gereffi and M. Korzeniewicz (eds), *Commodity Chains and Global Capitalism* (Westport CT: Greenwood Press, 1994) 95–122.
29. P. Knox and J. Agnew, *The Geography of the World Economy*, 2nd edn (London: Edward Arnold, 1994) p. 221.
30. Immediately after the Mexican peso crisis of December 1994, a number of small and medium-sized firms based in the state of Rhode Island had cash flow problems associated with the depreciation of the currency.
31. B. J. Cohen, 'Phoenix Risen: The Resurrection of Global Finance', *World Politics*, 48 (January 1996) 268–96 and see Chapter 4 of this volume.
32. S. J. Kobrin, 'Beyond Symmetry: State Sovereignty in a Networked Global Economy', in J. Dunning (ed.), *Governments, Globalization and International Business* (Oxford: Oxford University Press, 1997) p. 20.
33. S. J. Rosow, 'On the Political Theory of Political Economy: Conceptual Ambiguity and the Global Economy', *Review of International Political Economy*, 1 (Autumn 1994) 473–5.
34. J. G. Ruggie, 'Territoriality and Beyond: Problematizing Modernity in International Relations', *International Organization*, 47, 1 (Winter 1993) 171.

35. T. Luke, 'The Discipline of Security Studies and the Codes of Containment: Learning from Kuwait', *Alternatives*, 16 (1991) 315–44.
36. K. Ohmae, *The End of the Nation State: The Rise of Regional Economies* (New York: Free Press, 1995) pp. 79–82.
37. H. Trebing and M. Estabrooks, 'The Globalization of Telecommunications: A Study in the Struggle to Control Markets and Technology', *Journal of Economic Issues*, 29, 2 (June 1995) 539.
38. Kobrin, 'Beyond Symmetry', p. 8.
39. D. Mussington, *Arms Unbound: The Globalization of Defense Production*, (Washington, DC: Brassey's, 1994) p. 29.
40. P. Wapner, *Environmental Activism and World Civic Politics* (Albany, N.Y.: State University of New York Press, 1996) p. 140.
41. L. Gordenker and T. Weiss, 'Pluralizing Global Governance: Analytical Approaches and Dimensions', in their edited book, *NGOs, the UN, and Global Governance* (Boulder, CO: Lynne Rienner Publishers, 1996) p. 25. They argue that 25% of US assistance is channeled through NGOs and that while he was attending the Social Summit in Copenhagen, US Vice President Al Gore pledged to increase that amount to 50% by the end of the decade.
42. K. Sikkink, 'Human Rights, Principled Issue Networks, and Sovereignty in Latin America', *International Organization*, 47, 3 (Summer 1993) 411–41.
43. T. J. Biersteker, 'The "Triumph" of Liberal Economic Ideas in the Developing World', in Barbara Stallings (ed.), *Global Change, Regional Response* (Cambridge: Cambridge University Press, 1995) 174–98.
44. T. J. Biersteker, 'Reducing the Role of the State in the Economy: A Conceptual Exploration of IMF and World Bank Prescriptions', *International Studies Quarterly*, 34, 4 (December 1990) 488.
45. J. Williamson, *The Progress of Policy Reform in Latin America* (Washington, DC: Institute for International Economics, 1990) p. 59.
46. R. Wade and F. Veneroso, 'The Gathering World Slump and the Battle Over Capital Controls', *New Left Review*, 231, special issue devoted to 'The Crash of Neoliberalism', September/October 1998.
47. While there is a good deal of empirical evidence to suggest that globalization as a conceptual change in major institutional actors has advanced fairly significantly in some areas, the subject merits a great deal of further and more systematic empirical investigation.
48. R. J. Barnet and J. Cavanagh, *Global Dreams: Imperial Corporations and the New World Order* (New York: Simon & Schuster, 1994) p. 18.
49. For a wide-ranging discussion see Andrew Hurrell and Ngaire Woods, *Inequality, Globalization and World Politics* (Oxford: Oxford University Press, 1999).
50. P. G. Cerny, 'The Dynamics of Financial Globalization: Technology, Market Structure, and Policy Response', *Policy Sciences*, 27, 4 (November 1994) 335.
51. P. Krugman and A. J. Venables, 'Globalization and the Inequality of Nations', *Quarterly Journal of Economics*, 110, 4 (November 1995) 857–80.
52. P. Sweezy, H. Magdoff and L. Huberman, 'Globalization – To What End?', *Monthly Review*, 43, 10 (March 1992) p. 18.
53. Mussington, *Arms Unbound*, p. 26.
54. Cerny, 'The Dynamics of Financial Globalization', p. 335.
55. Mittelman, 'The Globalisation Challenge', p. 439.
56. J. A. Winters, 'Power and the Control of Capital', *World Politics*, 46, 3 (April 1994) 450–1.

57. *IMF Survey*, 15 July 1996, p. 236.
58. T.J. Biersteker, *Dealing with Debt: International Financial Negotiations and Adjustment Bargaining* (Boulder, CO: Westview Press, 1993) p. 8.
59. Frances Stewart and Albert Berry, 'Globalization, Liberalization, and Inequality: Expectations and Experience', in Hurrell and Woods, *Inequality, Globalization and World Politics*, pp. 150–86.
60. P. Hirst and G. Thompson, 'Globalization and the Future of the Nation State', *Economy and Society*, 24, 3 (August 1995) p. 414.
61. As suggested in the introduction to this chapter, there are strong countervailing resistances to integration and pressures for local autonomy in many parts of the world today.
62. C. Oman, *Globalisation and Regionalisation: The Challenge for Developing Countries* (Paris: Development Centre of the Organization for Economic Cooperation and Development, 1994) p. 33.
63. Kobrin, 'Beyond Symmetry', p. 4.
64. Ibid.
65. Wapner, *Environmental Activism*, p. 164.
66. This may in part be the product of the historical pattern of decoupling the institutional commitment to further integration from the experience of the stresses of adjustment in Europe. See L. Alan Winters, 'What Can European Experience Teach Latin America about Integration?', Paper presented at the Seminar on The Hemispheric and Regional Integration in Perspective, Santafe de Bogota, 1–3 November 1995, organized by the Departamento Nacional de Planeacion, Republica de Columbia, p. 11.
67. Ibid., p. 15.
68. P. Hirst and G. Thompson, *Globalization in Question* (Cambridge: Polity Press, 1996). See also R. Wade, 'Globalization and Its Limits'.

7
Global Civil Society

JAN AART SCHOLTE

As other chapters in this book have amply demonstrated, globalization has considerably redrawn the contours of the world political economy. Production, trade, investment and finance have acquired different dynamics, as have the regulatory frameworks that order them. What, in the meantime, has happened to the so-called 'third sector' that exists alongside markets and governance arrangements? Has civil society also 'gone global'? If so, what does this development imply for issues such as efficiency, democracy and social cohesion?

The present chapter suggests that, indeed, we have witnessed a growth of global civil society in the late twentieth century and that it has played an important part in recasting politics. Yet we must not exaggerate this expansion and associated changes. Nor should we uncritically assume, with liberal-internationalist naivety, that these developments have been wholly positive. Global civil society certainly offers much potential for enhancing security, equity and democracy in the world political economy; however, a long haul of committed endeavour is still required in order fully to realize those benefits.

To elaborate this argument, the first section of this chapter considers what, more precisely, is entailed by the notion of 'civil society'. The second section identifies the distinctiveness of 'global' civil society. The third section examines the forces that have propelled the growth of global civil society in the late twentieth century. The fourth section assesses the impacts that global civil society has had on contemporary politics, including questions of sovereignty, identity, citizenship and democracy. The fifth section highlights seven potential fruits and four possible perils of global civic association. The conclusion makes five general suggestions regarding ways that global civil society might more fully deliver its promises in the future.

173

What is civil society?

The vocabulary of politics is today strewn with terms such as 'civil society', 'social movements', 'non-governmental organizations' (NGOs), 'non-profit associations' (NPAs), 'private voluntary organizations' (PVOs), 'independent advocacy groups' (IAGs), 'principled issue networks' (PINs), 'segmented polycentric ideologically integrated networks' (SPINs), and more. 'Civil society' is the oldest of these concepts, dating back to English political thought of the sixteenth century.[1] The contemporary proliferation of broadly related terms perhaps in part reflects uncertainty, confusion and disagreement about the meaning of the older notion.

What, indeed, is civil society? The concept has been understood very differently across different time periods, places, theoretical perspectives and political persuasions. Thus, for example, 'civil society' for Hegel, as an academic philosopher in Prussia and Baden in the early nineteenth century, has not been the same as 'civil society' for a grassroots eco-feminist group in India in the late twentieth century. We therefore need not a definitive definition, but a notion of civil society that, with due regard for cultural and historical contexts, promotes insight and effective policy in the contemporary world political economy.

We might begin by stressing what civil society is *not*. For one thing, civil society is not the state: it is non-official, non-governmental. Civil society groups are not formally part of the state apparatus; nor do they seek to gain control of state office. On this criterion political parties should probably be excluded from civil society, although some analysts do include party organizations (as distinct from individual party members who might occupy governmental positions). Other fuzzy cases arise in respect of non-official actors that are organized and/or funded by the state. At what point do such bodies cease to be 'non-governmental'? In addition, some agencies outside government help states and multilateral institutions to formulate, implement, monitor and enforce policies. To what extent can 'civil society' be involved in official regulatory functions? Clearly, the precise boundaries of 'non-governmental' activity are a matter for debate. Nevertheless, it is generally agreed that civil society lies outside the 'public sector' of official governance.

Second, civil society is not the market: it is a non-commercial realm. Civil society bodies are not companies or parts of firms; nor do they seek to make profits. Thus the mass media, the leisure industry and cooperatives would, as business enterprises, not normally be considered part of civil society. To be sure, the distinction between the market and civil society is in practice sometimes far from absolute. For example, companies often organize and fund non-profit bodies, including foundations like Packard and Sasakawa that bear a corporate name. Meanwhile business lobbies like chambers of commerce and bankers' associations promote market interests even though these organizations themselves do not produce and exchange for profit. Many voluntary groups engage a salaried workforce in commercial activities like catalogue sales in order to fund their charitable operations. The environmentalist lobby Greenpeace has considered licensing its name as a brand.[2] At what point does the market presence become so strong that an activity ceases to qualify as 'civil society'? No doubt there are borderline cases, but it is generally agreed that civil society lies outside the 'private sector' of the market economy.

Establishing what civil society is *not* only partly establishes what it *is*. Thus far we have identified civil society as a 'third sector' that, while sometimes being closely related to, is distinct from the state and the market. Yet is this to say that any and all non-governmental, non-commercial activity is part of civil society? Presumably we would not label, for example, the everyday routines of households or idle chatter in a park as 'civil society'. Negative terminology like '*non*-governmental organization' and '*non*-profit body' is in this respect not very precise or helpful. What is the *positive* content of civil society?

For the purposes of the present discussion, activities are considered to be part of civil society when they involve a deliberate attempt – from outside the state and the market, and in some other organized fashion – to shape policies, norms and/or deeper social structures. In a word, civil society exists when people make concerted efforts through voluntary associations to mould rules: both official, formal, legal arrangements and informal social constructs. 'Civil society' is the collective noun, while 'civic' groups, organizations, and so on, are the individual elements within civil society.

Civil society encompasses enormous diversity. In terms of membership and constituencies, for example, it includes academic institutes, business associations, community-based organizations, consumer protection bodies, criminal syndicates, development cooperation groups, environmental campaigns, ethnic lobbies, foundations, farmers' groups, human rights advocates, labour unions, relief organizations, peace activists, professional bodies, religious institutions, women's networks, youth campaigns and more.

In terms of organizational forms, civil society includes formally constituted and officially registered groups as well as informal associations that do not appear in any directory. Indeed, different cultures may hold highly diverse notions of what constitutes an 'organization'.[3] Some civic bodies are unitary, centralized entities, like the Ford Foundation and the Roman Catholic Church. Other civic associations like the International Chamber of Commerce or Amnesty International, are federations where branches have considerable autonomy from the central secretariat. Other civic groups like the Asian Labour Network on International Financial Institutions (which links trade unions in four countries to campaign on labour rights and welfare issues) are coalitions without a coordinating office.[4] Still other civic bodies, like Slum Dwellers International (which arranges periodic exchange visits between community leaders of poor neighbourhoods in major cities of Africa and Asia) are loose networks that maintain limited and irregular contacts.[5]

In terms of capacity levels, civil society includes some bodies that are very generously resourced and others that struggle for survival, frequently without success. Some civic associations are richly endowed with members, funds, trained staff, office space, communications technology and data banks. Other groups lack these material means. Some civic organizations have a clear vision and value orientation, a powerful analysis, an astutely conceived campaign, a set of symbols and language that can mobilize a broad constituency, and an effective leadership. Other groups lack such human and ideational capital. Some civic bodies can exploit close links with elite circles, while others are completely disconnected from established power centres.

In terms of tactics, civic associations use a wide variety of means to pursue their aims. Many groups directly lobby official agencies and market actors. Others also or instead put the emphasis on mobilizing the general public through symposia, rallies, petitions, letter-writing campaigns, and boycotts. Some appeals from civil society aim primarily at the heart (with images, music and slogans), while others aim primarily at the mind (with publications, statistics and debates). Quite a few civic associations are adept users of the mass media (even hiring professional communications consultants for this purpose), while others rely wholly on face-to-face contacts. Some civil society organizations make great use of the internet (including listservs and websites as well as person-to-person e-mail messages), while many others are not connected to cyberspace. On a broader tactical issue, some civic associations pursue their aims through cooperation with public authorities and/or market agents, while others adopt a confrontational stance and reject all engagement with established power centres.

Finally, in terms of objectives, civil society includes conformists, reformists and radicals. The general distinction is important, although the lines can blur in practice. Conformists are those civic groups that seek to uphold and reinforce existing norms. Business lobbies, professional associations, think tanks and foundations often (though far from always) fall into the conformist category. Reformists are those civic entities that wish to correct what they see as flaws in existing regimes, while leaving underlying social structures intact. For example, social-democratic groups challenge liberalist economic policies but accept the deeper structure of capitalism. Many academic institutions, consumer associations, human rights groups, relief organizations and trade unions promote a broadly reformist agenda. Meanwhile radicals are those civic associations that aim comprehensively to transform the social order. These parts of civil society are frequently termed 'social movements'. They include anarchists, environmentalists, fascists, feminists, pacifists and religious revivalists, with their respective implacable oppositions to the state, industrialism, liberal values, patriarchy, militarism and secularism.

The distinction between means and ends needs to be stressed. It would be mistaken to assume that quiet lobbying, painstaking research, and collaboration with authorities ipso facto imply a conformist programme. On the contrary, reformists and radicals can and often do adopt such tactics. Likewise, it would be wrong to suppose that street demonstrations, impassioned television spots, and a refusal to engage with official agencies ipso facto imply a radical vision. Various business associations have sponsored boycotts and strikes, and some academic institutes have declined on principle to work with government bodies. In short, when assessing civil society activity it is important to distinguish between tactics and objectives. The height of the profile sought can bear little relation to the depth of the transformation pursued.

In sum, civil society exists whenever people mobilize through voluntary associations in initiatives to shape the social order. Civic groups have a wide range of constituencies, institutional forms, capacities, tactics and goals. Apart from this broad definition and the acknowledgement that civil society is highly diverse, it is difficult to generalize about the phenomenon.

What is *global* civil society?

While notions of 'civil society' go back to the sixteenth century, specific reference to 'global civil society' has emerged only in the 1990s.[6] Commentators have spoken in a related vein of 'international non-governmental organizations', 'transnational advocacy networks', 'global social movements', a 'new multilateralism', and so on.[7] Such discussions are part of a wider concern with globality (the condition of being global) and globalization (the trend of increasing globality). Our conception of global civil society is thus inseparable from our notion of 'global-ness' more generally.

As any glance at the burgeoning literature on globalization indicates, little consensus exists on the precise character of globality. A new vocabulary has arguably developed in response to changes in concrete social relations. However, analysts disagree, often quite profoundly, on the nature, extent, periodization and direction of these changes. The present chapter is not the place to engage in a full-scale exploration of the character and consequences of globalization,[8] but it is necessary to specify the concept of 'global' relations that is operative here.

Five broad kinds of ideas about globalization can be distinguished. First, many people equate the term 'globalization' with 'internationalization'. From this perspective, a 'global' situation is one marked by intense interaction and interdependence between country units. Second, many commentators take the word 'globalization' to mean 'liberalization'. In this usage, globality refers to an 'open' world where resources can move anywhere, unencumbered by state-imposed restrictions like trade barriers, capital controls and travel visas. Third, many analysts understand 'globalization' to entail 'universalization'. In this case, a 'global' phenomenon is one that is found at all corners of the earth. Fourth, some observers invoke the term 'globalization' as a synonym for 'Westernization' or 'Americanization'. In this context, globality involves the imposition of modern structures, especially in an 'American' consumerist variant. Fifth, some researchers identify 'globalization' as 'deterritorialization'. Here 'global' relations are seen to occupy a social space that transcends territorial geography.

Only the last of these five conceptions captures a distinctive trend that sets the world political economy of the late twentieth century apart from earlier periods. The other four notions merely apply a new word to pre-existent circumstances. Internationalization, liberalization, universalization and Westernization have all figured significantly at previous junctures a hundred or even a thousand and more years in the past. No vocabulary of 'globalization' was required on those earlier occasions, and it seems unnecessary now to invent new words for old phenomena. In contrast, contemporary large-scale deterritorialization is unprecedented, and 'globalization' offers a suitable new terminology to describe these new circumstances.

In the present discussion, then, 'global' relations are social connections in which territorial location, territorial distance and territorial borders do not have a determining influence. In global space, 'place' is not territorially fixed, territorial distance is covered in effectively no time, and territorial frontiers present no particular impediment. Thus global relations have what could be called a 'supraterritorial', 'transborder' or 'transworld' character. (The latter three terms will be used as synonyms for 'global' in the rest of this chapter.)

Examples of global phenomena abound in today's world. For instance, faxes and McDonald's are global in that they can extend anywhere on the planet at the same time and can unite spots anywhere on earth in effectively no time. Ozone depletion, CNN broadcasts and Visa credit cards are little restricted by territorial places, distances or borders. Global conditions can and do surface simultaneously at any point on earth that is equipped to host them (for example, a Toshiba plant or an internet connection). Global phenomena can and do move almost instantaneously across any distance on the planet (as evidenced by telephone calls or changes in foreign exchange rates).

This is by no means to say that territorial geography has lost all relevance in the late twentieth century. We inhabit a global*izing* rather than a completely global*ized* world. Social relations have undergone relative rather than total deterritorialization. Indeed, territorial places, distances and borders still figure crucially in many situations as we enter the twenty-first century. Among other things, territoriality often continues to exert a strong influence on migration, our sense of identity and community, and markets for certain goods. Yet while territoriality may continue to be important, globalization has brought an end to territorial*ism* (that is, a condition where social space is reducible to territorial coordinates alone). Alongside longitude, latitude and altitude, globalization has introduced a fourth, supraterritorial dimension to social geography.

If we identify globality as supraterritoriality, then what does global civil society involve? In a word, global civil society encompasses civic activity that: (a) addresses transworld issues; (b) involves transborder communication; (c) has a global organization; (d) works on a premise of supraterritorial solidarity. Often these four attributes go hand-in-hand, but civic associations can also have a global character in only one or several of these four respects. For example, a localized group that campaigns on a supraterritorial problem like climate change could be considered part of global civil society even though the association lacks a transborder organization and indeed might only rarely communicate with civic groups elsewhere in the world.[9] Conversely, global civic networks might mobilize in respect of a local development like the 1994 genocide in Rwanda.

To elaborate these four points in turn, global civil society exists in one sense when civic associations concern themselves with issues that transcend territorial geography. For example, as well as addressing climate change, various civic associations have campaigned on ecological problems like the loss of biological diversity and the depletion of stratospheric ozone that similarly have a supraterritorial quality.[10] Transworld diseases like AIDS have also stimulated notable civic activity.[11] Many civic organizations have raised questions concerning the contemporary globalizing economy, in relation to transborder production, trade, investment, money and finance.[12] Considerable civic activism has been directed at global governance agencies like the United Nations (UN), the Bretton Woods institutions, the Organization for Economic Cooperation and Development (OECD), and the World Trade Organization (WTO).[13] Human rights groups have promoted standards that are meant to apply to people everywhere on earth, regardless of the distances and borders that might lie between them.[14] Some civil society bodies have also treated armament questions like bans on chemical weapons and landmines as global issues.[15]

A second way that civic associations can be global lies in their use of supraterritorial modes of communication. Air travel, telecommunications, computer networks and electronic mass media allow civic groups to collect and disseminate information related to their causes more or less instantaneously between any locations on earth. Jet aircraft can bring civil society representatives from all corners of the planet together in a global congress. In this way, for example, an NGO Forum has accompanied the various UN issue conferences of the 1990s as well as the Annual Meetings of the International Monetary Fund (IMF) and the World Bank since 1986. Telephone, fax and telex permit civic groups to share information and coordinate activities across the world as intensely as across town. As noted earlier, much civic activism has also become global through the internet.[16]

Civil society is global in a third sense when campaigns adopt a transborder organization. According to the Union of International Associations, there were in 1998 some 16 500 active civic bodies whose members are spread across several countries.[17] As noted earlier, the mode of organization can vary. Some supraterritorial bodies are unitary and centralized: for instance, the World Economic Forum (WEF), which assembles some 900 transborder companies under the motto of 'entrepreneurship in the global public interest'. Alternatively, the transworld association may take a federal form, as in the case of the International Confederation of Free Trade Unions (ICFTU). Meanwhile some transborder organizations take the shape of networks without a coordinating secretariat. Illustrative cases in this regard are the Latin America Association of Advocacy Organizations (ALOP), which links 50 groups in 20 countries, and Peoples' Global Action against 'Free' Trade and the World Trade Organization (PGA), which mainly networks through a website.[18] Other global organizations are ephemeral coalitions that pursue a campaign around a particular policy. For example, on various occasions grassroots groups have combined forces with development and/or environmental NGOs to lobby the World Bank on one or the other of its projects.[19]

Finally, civil society can be global insofar as voluntary associations are motivated by sentiments of transworld solidarity.[20] For example, civic groups may build on a sense of collective identity and destiny that transcends territoriality – on lines of age, class, gender, profession, race, religious faith or sexual orientation. In addition, some global civic activity (for example, in respect of human rights, humanitarian assistance and development) has grown largely out of a cosmopolitan inspiration to provide security, equity and democracy for all persons, regardless of their territorial position on the planet.

Taking these four manifestations of supraterritoriality in sum, global civil society has acquired substantial proportions in the late twentieth century. To be sure, by no means has all civic association acquired a global character. Nor has the global aspect of civic campaigns been equally pronounced and sustained in all cases. Nevertheless, owing to the contemporary growth of global issues, global communications, global organization and global solidarities, civic activity can today no longer be understood with a territorialist conception of state–society relations.

Why has global civil society developed?

Global civil society, like globalization in general, is not completely new to the late twentieth century. For example, abolitionists pursued a transatlantic campaign (albeit without global communications) beginning in the eighteenth century. Pacifists, anarchists, the first and second workers' internationals, Pan-Africanists, advocates of women's suffrage and Zionists all held prototypical global meetings during the nineteenth century. In the area of humanitarian relief, the International Red Cross and Red Crescent Movement dates back to 1863.

However, civil society has mainly acquired supraterritorial attributes since the 1960s. To cite but one indicator that the chief increase has occurred recently, less than 10 per cent of the transborder civic associations active in 1998 were more than 40 years old.[21] In this light Lester Salamon has spoken of: 'a global "associational revolution" that may prove to be as significant to the latter twentieth century as the rise of the nation-state was to the latter nineteenth'.[22] While it seems premature to draw quite such dramatic conclusions, Salamon is right to date the principal growth of global civil society to recent history.

What has prompted this rapid expansion? Insofar as the spread of global civil society has been part of a wider process of globalization, some of the forces behind growing transborder civic activity are the same as those that have propelled globalization in general. I have argued at greater length elsewhere that the rise of supraterritoriality has resulted mainly from the mutually reinforcing impulses of global thinking, certain turns in capitalist development, technological innovations, and enabling regulations.[23]

All four of these conditions have been vital to globalization. Global thinking is crucial since people must be able to imagine the world as a single place in order for concrete global relations to be constructed. Without a global mindset, civic activists cannot 'see' global issues of the kind named earlier. Capitalist development is crucial since globalization has largely been spurred by the strivings of entrepreneurs to maximize sales and minimize costs. In addition, global spaces have offered new opportunities for surplus accumulation through sectors like electronic finance and the internet. Technology is crucial since developments in communications and information processing have supplied the infrastructure for global connections. Finally, regulation is crucial since measures like standardization and liberalization have provided a legal framework that encourages globalization.

Another legal trend has had more specific relevance for the contemporary growth of civil society, both global and otherwise: that is, in the 1990s many governments have rewritten laws in ways that facilitate civic organization. Countries in transition from state socialism provide an obvious example, though some, like Romania and Russia, have made slower and more limited reforms than others. Elsewhere, a new constitution enacted in Thailand in 1997 has explicitly promoted the growth of civil society in various respects.[24] In Japan, too, legislators have recently replaced a highly restrictive code on civic associations with a much more permissive regime.

Further stimulus to civic activity has arisen in the 1980s and 1990s with certain reductions in direct state provision of social security. The finances of many public-sector welfare programmes have come under strain in the late twentieth century. Among the reasons for these difficulties, governments have faced pressures to reduce taxes and labour costs in the name of enhancing 'global competitiveness'.[25] In these circumstances states (and also multilateral agencies like the World Bank and the UN High Commission for Refugees) have often contracted transborder civic associations as more cost-effective suppliers of, for example, development aid and humanitarian relief. In other cases NGOs and grassroots groups have stepped into the breach with private donations and voluntary assistance when public-sector provision of social security has become inadequate. This scenario has arisen, for example, in some countries undergoing neoliberal structural adjustment programmes.

Finally, the contemporary expansion of global civil society can also be ascribed in part to a more general altered position of the state in the face of globalization. To be sure, the rise of supraterritoriality has by no means heralded the demise of the state, but the new geography has ended the state's effective monopoly on governance that developed under conditions of territorialism.[26] Large numbers of people have understandably concluded that, in these changed (one might term them 'post-sovereign') circumstances, elections centred on the state are not by themselves an adequate expression of citizenship and democracy. After all, substantial regulation now also occurs through public multilateral agencies like the IMF and the Bank for International Settlements (BIS) where elected legislators have little direct influence. In addition, some governance of global markets occurs through so-called 'self-regulatory' agencies of the private sector, like the International Accounting Standards Committee. Such bodies are even further removed from party politics. Global civil society has therefore also grown in part as citizens have attempted to acquire a greater voice in post-sovereign governance, for example, by directly lobbying global governance institutions.

In sum, then, global civil society first surfaced in earlier centuries and has greatly expanded since the 1960s owing to several forces. Some of the causes of this growth have at the same time been causes for the spread of supraterritoriality more generally. Other causes have related more specifically to civil society. Taken together, these impulses have created momentum on a considerable scale behind increased transborder civic activism. Hence it seems most unlikely that global civil society will shrink in the foreseeable future and all the more probable that it will further expand.

How has global civil society affected politics?

Having assessed causes, what of the consequences? In what ways and to what extent has the growth of global civil society changed the workings of politics? Several broad repercussions can be highlighted: multilayered governance; some privatization of governance; and moves to reconstruct collective identities, citizenship and democracy.

Together, these five developments have contributed to the end of sovereign statehood. That said, the extent of these changes should not be overstated. For example, the rise of global civil society has on no count brought an end to the territorial state, national loyalties and party politics. The following paragraphs elaborate these various matters in turn.

Taking the first point first, global civic activism has often contributed to the contemporary turn toward multilayered governance. Prior to accelerated globalization – and particularly during the late nineteenth and early twentieth centuries – regulation was focused almost exclusively on national-level laws and institutions. Governance effectively meant government: the centralized territorial state. However, recent decades have brought a general retreat from 'nationalized' governance with concurrent trends of devolution, regionalization and globalization. As a result, agencies at substate and suprastate levels have obtained greater initiative and impact in politics. Governance has shifted from a unidimensionality of statism to a multidimensionality of local, national, regional and global layers of regulation.[27]

The growth of global civil society has not been the sole force behind this development, of course, but civic groups have frequently furthered the trend. Global business associations, grassroots organizations, NGOs, trade unions and so on have directed their lobbying at whatever layer of governance seems relevant to their cause. Thus, for example, transborder development cooperation groups have often engaged with provincial and local authorities in the South. Various women's organizations have engaged at a regional level with European Union bodies. Several trade union federations have engaged with transworld economic institutions like the IMF and the WTO. Almost all of the major regional and global governance agencies have by now established institutional mechanisms for liaison with civil society, both at their head offices and in their member countries.[28] Indeed, it could be argued that, through this engagement, civic associations have – whether intentionally or inadvertently – lent increased legitimacy to suprastate governance.

Regarding the second general consequence, that of privatized governance, global civil society has often become directly involved in the formulation and implementation of regulations. Not only has contemporary governance become dispersed across different geographical levels, but it has also extended beyond the public sector.

Various non-official bodies have thereby acquired regulatory functions. This trend, too, has reduced state-centrism in politics.[29]

Global civil society has contributed to this development on several counts. For one thing, as already mentioned in the preceding section, many official agencies have turned to civic associations to help execute policies, especially social welfare programmes. For example, the share of official development assistance from the OECD countries that is channelled through NGOs rose from 4.5 per cent in 1989 to 14 per cent in 1993.[30] Likewise, much humanitarian relief has come to flow through transborder organizations like CARE (with an income of $586 million in 1995) and the aptly named Médecins sans frontières ('doctors without borders', with an income of $252 million in 1996).[31]

Civil society associations have also on a number of occasions entered official channels of policy-making, thereby further blurring the public/private divide in governance. For example, some civic organizations have accepted invitations from states like Australia and the Netherlands to occupy places on government delegations to UN-sponsored conferences. The African National Congress, the International Committee of the Red Cross, and the Palestine Liberation Organization have held (non-voting) seats in the UN General Assembly. Several proposals in the 1990s have called for a 'People's Assembly' of civil society representatives to be created in the United Nations alongside the General Assembly of states. Certain environmental groups have held observer status in the body that oversees implementation of the 1987 Montreal Protocol on Substances that Deplete the Ozone Layer. The International Council of Scientific Unions played an important advisory role in setting up the Intergovernmental Panel on Climate Change in 1988. Some critics worry that such incorporation into official governance may limit the critical and creative potentials of civil society.

On further occasions global civil society has promoted a full-scale privatization of governance, in which official agencies have little or no involvement. For example, the Ford Foundation has insisted that its grants should not be subject to scrutiny or approval by state authorities. In global finance, business organizations like the International Federation of Stock Exchanges, the International Primary Market Association, the International Securities Market Association, and the International Council of Securities Associations have between them loosely filled the role of a transworld securities and exchange commission. The International Accounting Standards Committee and the International Federation of Accountants have developed the main global accountancy and auditing norms currently in use. Such activities take what others have termed 'governance without government' to an extreme.[32]

A third general way that the growth of global civil society has altered the contours of politics relates to collective identities – that is, the ways that people form group affiliations and communal solidarity. The period of state-centrism in governance (at its height during the late nineteenth and first half of the twentieth centuries) was paralleled by a period of nation-centrism in collective identities. Indeed, the two conditions strongly reinforced each other. Although recent decades of large-scale globalization have not dissolved state-nations (that is, national communities that correspond to territorial states), this form of collective identity has lost its previous position of overwhelming primacy. In the late twentieth century world politics is also deeply shaped by substate solidarities like ethno-nations and by nonterritorial, transborder communities based on class, gender, race, religion, sexual orientation and other aspects of identity.[33]

Global civic activity has clearly contributed to this trend toward pluralism. Many transborder associations have united people on the basis of nonterritorial identity: for example, as workers, people of colour, Muslims or gay men. To take but one specific illustration of this altered identity politics, over 30 000 women in civic groups attended the NGO Forum and Fourth United Nations Conference on Women, held at Beijing in 1995.[34] Meanwhile bodies like the World Economic Forum and the Institute of International Finance (IIF, which links over 300 financial service providers headquartered in 56 countries) have helped to forge something of a global managerial class.

Transborder associations have also in various cases promoted the development of ethnic identities. For example, a number of environmental NGOs have supported indigenous peoples' movements in Africa, the Americas and the Indian Subcontinent. Transborder networks have also helped diasporas of Armenians, Irish, Kurds, Palestinians, Sikhs and Timorese to gain political force. Both across and within states, then, global civil society has promoted increased diversity in the identities that stimulate and shape political action.

Shifts in the shape of collective identities under the influence of globalization have been closely connected with shifts in the construction of citizenship, that is, the set of rights and duties that constitute persons as members of a sociopolitical community.[35] In the statist and nationalist world that prevailed prior to the 1960s, citizenship was a question of legal nationality and the various entitlements and obligations that are associated with that status. Although this national-state framework of citizenship remains important, it has become insufficient by itself in a world of large-scale globalization. For example, the growth of the global human rights regime since the 1940s has institutionalized numerous supraterritorial entitlements. Concurrently, global communications and global ecological changes have heightened senses of duties beyond borders for 'world citizens'.[36] Millions of people have, where possible, resorted to dual or multiple national citizenships to accommodate their post-territorialist lives. Meanwhile some environmentalists, feminists and other radical critics have attacked the very institution of territorial nation-state citizenship, regarding it as antithetical to ecological integrity, gender equality or other vital nonterritorial concerns.

Global civil society has also figured significantly in this reconfiguration of politics. Indeed, many transborder civic activists regard themselves as world citizens in addition to (or even more than) national-state citizens. Such a self-concept has helped, for example, to spur human rights advocates in their promotion of global conventions of children's, women's and worker's rights. More recently, civic groups have spearheaded a campaign to establish a permanent International Criminal Court.[37] Humanitarian relief organizations, development cooperation groups, environmentalists and various other civil society associations have, both implicitly and explicitly, advanced the notion that people have global civic duties.

The various developments described above all raise questions about – and point to changes in – concepts and practices of democracy. Prior to contemporary large-scale globalization, 'rule by and for the people' meant rule of the *state* by and for the *nation*. Yet today governance involves more than the state, community involves more than the nation, and citizenship involves more than national entitlements and obligations. Thus issues of democracy like participation, consultation, open debate, representativeness, transparency and accountability are not adequately addressed in terms of territorial institutions and communities alone.

Global civil society has broadened the scope of democratic practice. Transborder civic associations have created additional channels of popular participation, additional modes of popular consultation, additional forums for popular debate, new sites of popular representation alongside elected councils and legislatures, and new popular pressures for open and responsible governance. These innovations have been especially important in bringing citizens into closer touch with regional and transworld regulatory agencies. That said, global civil society has by no means fully countered the many democratic deficits that exist in contemporary politics, as the next section of this chapter will elaborate.

In sum, the growth of global civil society has, in tandem with the spread of supraterritoriality more generally, shifted the framework of politics away from its previous core principle of sovereign statehood. Multilayered and partially privatised governance, pluralistic identity politics, and new forms of citizenship and democracy all contradict traditional practices of sovereignty. No longer does – or can – one site of authority exercise supreme, comprehensive, absolute and exclusive rule over a discrete jurisdiction. The territorial state has lost the attribute of sovereignty (as it was traditionally understood), and no other institution of governance looks likely to take over this mantle.[38] Hence the expansion of global civil society has – together with parallel developments like the growth of global communications, global markets and so on – figured significantly in the shift from sovereign to post-sovereign governance.

Of course, the end of sovereignty has to be distinguished from the end of the territorial state: a world without sovereignty does not imply a world without states. Indeed, on the whole the post-sovereign state is as robust as its sovereign predecessor. States can no longer exercise sole and total jurisdiction over an assigned territory and population, but they have retained many other capacities and have also gained some new ones like computerised surveillance.[39] Most people and most prevailing laws still define citizenship first of all in terms of state affiliation. Thus states continue to exert major influence over civil society, global and otherwise. (Of course, some governments – such as those in the OECD countries – have considerably greater leverage *vis-à-vis* civil society than others – such as those in much of Africa.) Also, given their persistent significance, states continue to be a prime target of civic activism, both territorial and global.

Similarly, in respect of collective identities, the end of nation-centrism in the face of globalization has on no count heralded the end of nations. On the contrary, state-nations persist across the world, and they have been joined by scores of ethno-nations at a substate level and several region-nations (Arab, European, etc.) at a suprastate level. Indeed, as indicated earlier, global civic associations have often promoted the national projects of indigenous peoples and diasporas. More subtly, many transborder networks have also reproduced the nationality principle by organising themselves in terms of national branches.

Finally, the new forms of collective identity, citizenship and democracy advanced by global civil society have by no means signalled the demise of party politics. True, party memberships and election turnouts have declined during recent years in most liberal democracies. Some global civic associations have followings and funds that dwarf those of most political parties. Many citizens have turned to civic activism at least partly out of disillusionment with traditional party politics. Nevertheless, control of the state still confers substantial power in the contemporary globalizing world, and competition within and between political parties remains a key way to gain governmental office in most countries.

In short, the contemporary growth of global civil society has encouraged several important shifts in political institutions and processes, but the extent of those changes must not be exaggerated. In particular, the post-sovereign world includes ample space for states, nations and parties. Global civil society has not replaced older channels of politics so much as opened up additional dimensions.

The promises and perils of global civil society

Having considered definitions, causes and consequences of global civil society, we have established some basis for normative judgements. In a word, is the growth of supraterritorial civic activity a positive or a negative thing? As one might expect, this straightforward question does not yield a straightforward answer.

In whatever domain – global, regional, national or local – civil society is not inherently good or evil. Some enthusiasts have depicted the 'third sector' as an arena of virtue that counters domination in government and exploitation in the market.[40] Yet civic associations can themselves be oppressive hierarchical bureaucracies, and civic activity can involve violence (both deliberate and unintentional) toward vulnerable persons and groups.

Hence we have both civil and *un*civil society. Civic associations can improve or damage policy. They can increase or reduce human security. They can promote or undermine social equity. They can enhance or impair democracy. In short, we need to assess each association and campaign in global civil society on its own merits.

Of course, we need criteria against which to make such judgements. The following paragraphs first suggest seven general ways that civil society can contribute to a positive course of globalization. Then four potential dangers of global civic activity are highlighted.

One way that civil society can advance a humane course of globalization is by *securing material welfare*. As noted earlier, voluntary associations can offer an alternative to the state and the market in the production and delivery of goods and services. Indeed, sometimes civil society mechanisms have supplied welfare more efficiently and equitably than the public and private sectors. Many of these civic programmes catch vulnerable circles with safety nets related to education, health, housing, and other material needs. However, the economic initiatives of civil society can also extend beyond the soup kitchen. For example, in the late twentieth century many civic associations have developed schemes of so-called 'micro-credits' for groups like women and the rural poor that commercial lenders tend to overlook.[41] In addition, several development cooperation groups have promoted alternative marketing schemes that provide producers (for example, of coffee and textiles) in the South with higher returns than commercial dealers offer.

Second, global civil society can be an important conduit for *civic education*. In particular, transborder civic associations can improve public understanding of the various aspects of globalization, alerting citizens to altered conditions of geography, politics, economics, ecology and culture in the contemporary world. Civic groups can in this vein prepare handbooks and information kits, produce audio-visual presentations, organize workshops, circulate newsletters, supply information to the mass media, maintain listservs and websites on the internet, and develop curricular materials for schools and universities. It is in good part thanks to supraterritorial civil society that the world public has become more (albeit perhaps still not adequately) aware of global issues. As people gain greater cognisance of the new geography and its effects, the chances that globalization undermines human security and social justice can be reduced.

Third, global civil society can make positive contributions by *giving voice*. In other words, supraterritorial civic associations can provide channels through which citizens relay information, testimonial and analysis to each other, to market actors, and to governance agencies. In particular, global civil society can hand the microphone to circles like indigenous peoples, smallholder farmers, the urban poor and women who tend to get a limited hearing through firms and official agencies. In this way transborder civic activity can be a significant force for equity and democracy.

Fourth, while giving voice global civic associations can also *fuel debate*. Inputs from civil society can put alternative perspectives, methodologies and proposals on the agenda. For example, a number of civic groups have been instrumental in questioning orthodox economic theory, raising ecological issues, introducing qualitative assessments of poverty, and promoting various proposals for debt reduction in the South. Thanks to such contributions, discussions of social issues become more critical and creative. Wide-ranging, open debate is vital to a healthy democracy and can, moreover, often produce more clear and effective policy.

Fifth, civil society can enhance politics in the contemporary globalizing world by *increasing transparency and accountability*. Many workings of global markets and global regulation have fallen outside public scrutiny, thereby increasing the dangers of abuse. Initiatives by civic associations can help bring into the open, for instance, global financial dealings, the activities of transborder corporations, and the operations of suprastate governance agencies like the BIS and the UN system. As a result, citizens can make more informed judgements about the world political economy, and actors in positions of power and responsibility must do more to account for their behaviour and policy choices. For example, civil society campaigns have publicized a number of global corporate wrongs, such as the marketing of baby formula milk to poor mothers in the South who were ill able to afford it.[42] Thanks in good part to pressure from a variety of civic organizations, the operations of the IMF and the WTO have since the mid-1990s become far more transparent.[43]

A sixth positive effect of global civil society can be to *promote legitimation*, especially in relation to suprastate governance. Legitimacy exists when people acknowledge that an authority has a right to govern them and that they have a duty to obey its rulings. As a result of such consent, legitimate governance tends to be less violent and more easily executed than illegitimate authority. Legitimacy is also desirable on democratic grounds. In territorial states, legitimacy has traditionally been established mainly through political parties and popular suffrage; however, mechanisms such as referenda and direct elections of representatives are rarely available in respect of regional and transworld governance. Civil society can help to fill this legitimacy gap (that is, so long as the civic groups concerned maintain their own democratic credentials, an important qualification to which we will return later). With consultation and monitoring activities, civic associations can influence the respect accorded (or denied) to the policies of suprastate and private regulatory agencies. Likewise, global civic groups can affect the level of resources allocated to (or withheld from) governance institutions. In a word, then, civil society can act as an important check against dictatorship.

Seventh and finally, in terms of beneficial impacts, global civil society can through the various positive influences described above *enhance social cohesion*. Contributions to material welfare, civic education, public discussion and transparent, accountable, legitimate governance can all help to counter arbitrary inequalities and exclusions in society. As a result, conflict can be reduced and social integration can be increased.

In sum, a variety of major positive potentials make the furtherance of global civil society a worthwhile project for the twenty-first century. However, the operative word throughout the preceding discussion has been 'can'. Civic associations do *not* produce the above benefits automatically.

For one thing, in order to yield its fruits transborder civic activity needs to have adequate capacities in terms of human, material and ideational resources. In many cases to date these means have been lacking. Next to governance institutions and the market, civil society has run a very poor third in terms of supporting staff, funds, equipment and symbolic capital. Compare, for instance, the level of recognition and mobilizing power of national flags and corporate logos with that of civic association insignia. So long as global civil society is underresourced, its benefits will remain largely potential rather than actual.

Furthermore, our endorsement of global civil society must be qualified with a recognition that this activism can under certain conditions have negative effects. Thus it is not only that transborder civic associations may fail, owing to capacity shortfalls, to do good. They may also do actual damage. Civic activity can, in four broad ways, potentially detract from security, equity and democracy in contemporary globalization.

For one thing, elements of 'uncivil society' can be *ill intentioned*. Such associations actively seek to undermine human well-being and social justice. Thus, for example, transborder criminal networks have become significant perpetrators of harm in the contemporary world.[44] Meanwhile various groups of racists, ultra-nationalists and fundamentalists have used global communications to preach intolerance and violence. In short, it must never be forgotten that civil society is not intrinsically virtuous.

Other initiatives in global civil society can have laudable aims but suffer from a second failing, namely *flawed policy*. Like programmes of action in the public and the private sector, civic campaigns need to be carefully conceived and astutely executed. True, an ill-informed and misdirected civil society effort can – in spite of itself – inadvertently produce beneficial results. Conversely, even the best laid plans can go awry. More usually, however, poor policy preparation and implementation runs a greater risk of causing harm, including to vulnerable social circles that well-intentioned civic associations may be aiming to help. For example, some environmentalist groups have hurt their cause through the sloppy treatment of scientific evidence. The arguments of global human rights advocates have sometimes suffered from cultural illiteracy. Some relief organizations have miscalculated client needs. Some business associations have misread public sentiments. Some development advocacy groups have not gone beyond protests to proposals with respect to the workings of the liberal world economy. Some research institutes have not got beyond theoretical models to political practicalities. In sum, global civil society can fall short of its potential – and indeed can have negative impacts – when its inputs are of a low quality.

A third potential fault in transborder civic activity relates to *undemocratic practice*. For reasons noted earlier, global civil society is often championed as a force for democracy: it can give voice, stimulate debate, confer legitimacy, and so on. Yet civic groups – even those that actively campaign for a democratization of official institutions and market operations – can fail to meet democratic criteria in their own internal workings. For example, some civic associations offer their members no opportunity for participation beyond the payment of subscriptions. No less than a government department or a business corporation, a civic organization can be run with 'top-down' managerial authoritarianism. In addition, policy-making in global civic associations can be quite opaque to outsiders: in terms of who takes decisions, by what means, from among which options, and with what justifications. Civic groups can be further deficient in respect of transparency when they do not publish financial statements or even a declaration of objectives, let alone full-scale reports of their activities. Moreover, the leadership of many civic organizations is self-selected, raising troubling questions of accountability and potential conflicts of interest. In short, civil society operations are no more intrinsically democratic than programmes in the public or the private sector.

A fourth potential defect in global civil society – namely, *inadequate representation* – is arguably the most difficult shortcoming to redress and warrants more extended discussion. If civil society is to be suitable to provide welfare, educate citizens, give voice, fuel debate, secure transparency and accountability, establish legitimacy and promote social cohesion, then all stakeholders must have access – and pre-ferably equal opportunities to participate. Indeed, biased access to civil society can reproduce or even enlarge structural inequalities and arbitrary privileges connected with class, gender, nationality, race, religion, and so on. Regrettably, global civil society has in practice all too often manifested these problems, thereby further calling into question its credentials for promoting security, equity and democracy.

Uneven representation in, if not downright exclusion from, trans-border civic activity has taken several general forms. For one thing, residents of the North (the OECD countries) have had a far larger and stronger presence in global civil society than people from the South (the so-called 'Third World') and the East (the current and former state-socialist countries). In terms of civilizational inputs, supraterritorial civic activity has on the whole drawn much more from Western Judeo-Christian traditions than from African, Bud-dhist, Confucian, Eastern Orthodox, Hindu, Islamic and other cultures. In relation to gender and race, parts of global civil society have, it is true, given women and people of colour greater voice than they have generally been able to obtain through the state, the market and political parties. On the other hand, striking gender and racial inequalities have often persisted in sections of civil society like academic institutes, business associations, professional bodies and trade unions. Finally, global civil society has thus far shown a pronounced class bias. The initiative in transborder civic activity has lain disproportionately with urban-based, (relatively) high-earning, university-educated, computer-literate, English-speaking professionals. In sum, participation in global civil society has revealed many of the same patterns of inequality that have marked the globalizing world political economy more generally.

This is not to suggest that people from privileged circumstances cannot use global civic activism to advance the lot of their disadvantaged fellow citizens. As indicated earlier, global civil society has done much to advance human security and social justice. Nevertheless, subordinated groups have often lacked adequate opportunities to speak for themselves through transborder civil society, and civic campaigners from elite circles have frequently been remiss when it comes to closely and systematically consulting their supposed constituencies in vulnerable quarters.

In a welcome trend, recent years have witnessed greater sensitivity in some quarters to issues of representation and participation in global civil society. A new rhetoric of the 1990s has underlined 'dialogue' and 'partnership', particularly between South-based and North-based groups. Illustrating this spirit, a global conference of development advocates in July 1998 produced the Harare Declaration on Development Relationships, with the aim of overcoming a 'parent–child' mode of interaction between Northern and Southern civic activists. Many civic organizations have also become more proactive in promoting women and people of colour to positions of leadership. On the other hand, relatively few initiatives have yet emerged to address civilisational and class inequalities in global civil society. Groups like the International Network of Engaged Buddhists and the Participation Resource Action Network (which has linked poor people across four continents) remain rarities.[45] In this respect, radical critics have grounds to regard global civil society in its current condition as predominantly a 'Western' and 'bourgeois' project.

Clearly, then, there are no grounds for complacency regarding the contemporary growth of global civil society. Although this development holds substantial potential for good, it also carries significant dangers. The challenge is to take global civic activity forward in ways that minimize the potential pitfalls and maximize the potential benefits.

Conclusion

Although its proportions can be overstated, global civil society has become an important feature of contemporary politics. As elaborated earlier, civic engagement with supraterritorial spaces has figured in the emergence of multilayered governance, in some privatization of regulation, and in redrawing the contours of collective identities, citizenship and democracy. In the process, civic associations have revealed significant potentials both to enhance and to undermine security and justice in the globalizing world political economy. On the (it would seem reasonable) assumption that transborder civic activity is unlikely to disappear and quite likely to expand in the future, we need to consider how its further development can be kept on the most positive possible course. Five general suggestions might be offered in this regard.

First, as intimated earlier, much attention needs to be given to *building capacity*, particularly in respect of global civic groups that represent underprivileged circles. Partly this is a question of increasing funds, in order to relieve the precarious position of many worthy civic associations. However, money is not by itself sufficient. After all, small budgets have not prevented, for example, women's groups from making a major impact on official agendas and public attitudes. Capacity-building needs to be carefully targeted, *inter alia*, at staff training in advocacy tactics, public speaking, cross-cultural communication, and leadership skills. In addition, civic associations need to develop modes of organization that most effectively inform and mobilize their constituencies and at the same time most successfully advance their policy goals *vis-à-vis* governance and market actors. Where civic groups currently lack global communications technologies, acquisition of these tools should have a high priority.

Second, increased efforts could be directed at *expanding involvement* in global civil society. Transborder civic activism would better realize the various potential benefits detailed earlier if the campaigns could attract larger followings and higher profiles than most associations have acquired thus far. Greater emphasis on outreach initiatives to the general public would help especially to advance the promise of global civil society in respect of civic education and the development of supraterritorial citizenship.

Third, the future development of global civil society should focus on *enhancing diversity*. As stressed at the close of the last section,

transborder civic activism has to date been insufficiently representative. Existing efforts to expand access for women and people of colour
should continue, and they should be supplemented by greater
attempts to involve rural circles, underclasses and non-Western
cultures. Otherwise global civil society runs grave dangers of serving
as an instrument of social inequality.

Fourth, other potential shortfalls in democratic practice noted
earlier suggest a need for *increasing vigilance* in respect of global civil
society. This is not to support intrusive police-state surveillance of
transborder civic groups, though democratic governance institutions
have as much right and duty to monitor civic associations as vice
versa. In addition, civil society workers can be urged to nurture a
more self-critical attitude toward their practices, thereby catching
and correcting their own democratic deficits. At present most civic
associations lack a programme of regular and systematic evaluation,
conducted either internally or by external assessors (other than
financial auditors).

Finally, for political as well as intellectual reasons, the future
development of global civil society would be advanced by further
research. In part such investigations need to examine the general
dynamics of globalization, in order that transborder civic groups
(and others) can better understand the context in which they are
operating. In addition, much more research is required on global civil
society itself, especially empirical studies that assess the experiences of
concrete associations and campaigns. Particular attention could be
given in this regard to providing more marginalized circles of civil
society with resources to undertake or commission research that
addresses their agendas.

These five suggestions reinforce the theme, expressed throughout
this discussion, that global civil society *can* be a force for security and
justice in the contemporary world *if* it is carefully moulded to serve
those ends. Transborder civic associations have great potential to
help steer globalization toward efficiency, equity, democracy and
ecological sustainability. However, complacency about these activities could lead them to promote the opposite results.

Notes

1. E. M. Wood, 'The Uses and Abuses of "Civil Society" ', in R. Miliband *et al.*
(eds), *Socialist Register 1990* (London: Merlin, 1990) p. 61. For more on the

concept of 'civil society', see J. L. Cohen and A. Arato, *Civil Society and Political Theory* (Cambridge, MA: MIT Press, 1992); K. Kumar, 'Civil Society: An Inquiry into the Usefulness of an Historical Term', *British Journal of Sociology*, 44 (1993) 375–95.

2. The Limits to Growth?', *The Economist* 348 (1 August 1998) p. 79.

3. On these issues more generally, see C. Hann and E. Dunn (eds), *Civil Society: Challenging Western Models* (London: Routledge, 1996).

4. Information provided by Philip Robertson, American Center for International Labor Solidarity, Bangkok, April 1999.

5. J. Bolnick *et al.*, 'Community Exchanges for Urban Transformation', paper for the NGOs in a Global Future Conference, University of Birmingham, January 1999.

6. Cf. R. A. Falk, 'The Infancy of Global Civil Society', in G. Lundestad and O. A. Westad (eds), *Beyond the Cold War: New Dimensions in International Relations* (Oslo: Scandinavian University Press, 1992) 219–39; R.D. Lipschutz, 'Reconstructing World Politics: The Emergence of Global Civil Society', *Millennium*, 21 (1992) 389–420; *Citizens Strengthening Global Civil Society* (Washington: CIVICUS World Alliance for Citizen Participation, 1994); M. Shaw, 'Civil Society and Global Politics: Beyond a Social Movements Approach', *Millennium*, 23 (1994) 647–67; A. C. Drainville, 'The Fetishism of Global Civil Society', in M. P. Smith and L. E. Guarnizo (eds), *Transnationalism from Below* (London: Transaction, 1998).

7. P. Ghils, 'International Civil Society: International Non-Governmental Organizations in the International System', *International Social Science Journal*, 133 (1992) 417–31; J. Smith *et al.* (eds), *Transnational Social Movements and Global Politics: Solidarity beyond the State* (Syracuse: Syracuse University Press, 1997); M. E. Keck and K. Sikkink, *Activists beyond Borders: Advocacy Networks in International Politics* (Ithaca: Cornell University Press, 1998); M. G. Schechter (ed.), *Sources of Innovation in Multilateralism* (Basingstoke: Macmillan, 1998).

8. I undertake such an exploration in *Globalization: A Critical Introduction* (Basingstoke: Macmillan, forthcoming).

9. P. Ekins, *A New World Order: Grassroots Movements for Global Change* (London: Routledge, 1992).

10. J. McCormick, *Reclaiming Paradise: The Global Environmental Movement* (Bloomington: Indiana University Press, 1989); T. Princen and M. Finger (eds), *Environmental NGOs in World Politics: Linking the Global and the Local* (London: Routledge, 1994); P. Wapner, *Environmental Activism and World Civic Politics* (New York: State University of New York Press, 1996).

11. P. Söderholm, *Global Governance of AIDS: Partnerships with Civil Society* (Lund: Lund University Press, 1997).

12. J. Brecher and T. Costello, *Global Village or Global Pillage: Economic Reconstruction from the Bottom Up* (Boston, MA: South End, 1994).

13. T. G. Weiss and L. Gordenker (eds), *NGOs, the UN, and Global Governance* (Boulder, CO: Lynne Rienner, 1996); P. Willetts (ed.), *'Conscience of the World': The Influence of Non-Governmental Organizations in the UN System* (London: Hurst, 1996); R. O'Brien *et al.*, *Challenging Global Governance: Social Movements and Multilateral Economic Institutions* (Cambridge: Cambridge University Press, forthcoming).

14. H. J. Steiner, *Diverse Partners: Non-Governmental Organizations in the Human Rights Movement* (Cambridge, MA: Harvard Law School, 1991).

15. R. Price, 'Transnational Civil Society Targets Land Mines', *International Organization*, 52 (1998) 613–44.

16. Cf. H. Frederick, 'Computer Networks and the Emergence of Global Civil Society', in L. Harasim (ed.), *Global Networks: Computers and International Communication* (Cambridge, MA: MIT Press, 1993) 283–95; E. Lee, *The Labour Movement and the Internet: The New Internationalism* (London: Pluto, 1996); W. Harcourt (ed.), *Women @ Internet: Creating New Cultures in Cyberspace* (London: Zed, 1999).

17. Union of International Associations, *Yearbook of International Organizations 1998/99, Vol. I* (Munich: Saur, 1998), p. 1764.

18. http://www.agp.org.

19. See J. A. Fox and L. D. Brown (eds), *The Struggle for Accountability: The World Bank, NGOs, and Grassroots Movements* (Cambridge, MA: MIT Press, 1998).

20. For more on these issues, see P. Waterman, *Globalization, Social Movements and the New Internationalisms* (London: Mansell, 1998).

21. *Yearbook of International Organizations 1998/99*, p. 1764.

22. L. M. Salamon, 'The Rise of the Nonprofit Sector', *Foreign Affairs*, 73 (1994) p. 109. See also Salamon *et al.*, *The Emerging Sector Revisited: A Summary* (Baltimore: Institute for Policy Studies, Johns Hopkins University, 1998).

23. See further *Globalisation: A Critical Introduction*, ch. 5.

24. J. R. Klein, *The Constitution of the Kingdom of Thailand, 1997: A Blueprint for Participatory Democracy* (San Francisco: The Asia Foundation Working Paper No. 8, March 1998).

25. Cf. G. Esping-Andersen (ed.), *Welfare States in Transition: National Adaptations in Global Economies* (London: Sage, 1996).

26. I elaborate these points in the next section of this chapter and in 'Global Capitalism and the State', *International Affairs*, 73 (1997) 427–52; 'Globalisation and Governance', in P. Hanafin and M. S. Williams (eds), *Identity, Rights and Constitutional Transformation* (Aldershot: Ashgate, 1999) 132–53.

27. I have elaborated this point in 'The Globalization of World Politics', in J. Baylis and S. Smith (eds), *The Globalization of World Politics: An Introduction to World Politics* (Oxford: Oxford University Press, 1997) p. 13.

28. P. Spiro, 'New Global Communities: Nongovernmental Organizations in International Decision-Making Institutions', *Washington Quarterly*, 18 (1994) 45–56; Weiss and Gordenker, *NGOs*; Willetts, *Conscience of the World*; P. J. Simmons, 'Learning to Live with NGOs', *Foreign Policy*, 111 (Fall 1998) 82–96.

29. A. C. Cutler *et al.* (eds), *Private Authority in International Affairs* (Albany: State University of New York Press, 1999).

30. Ghils, 'International Civil Society', p. 422; G. Windsperger, 'NGOs and the IMF: Shared Goals – Different Approaches', *IMF Staff News* (March 1997) p. 7. See also M. Edwards and D. Hulme (eds), *Too Close for Comfort? Donors, NGOs and States* (London: Macmillan, 1996); A. Van Rooy (ed.), *Civil Society and the Aid Industry* (London: Earthscan, 1998); I. Smillie and H. Helmich (eds), *Stakeholders: Government–NGO Partnerships for International Development* (London: Earthscan, 1999).

31. I. Smillie, 'At Sea in a Sieve? Trends and Issues in the Relationship between Northern NGOs and Northern Governments', in Smillie and Helmich, *Stakeholders*, pp. 17–18.

32. J. N. Rosenau and E.-O. Czempiel (eds), *Governance without Government: Order and Change in World Politics* (Cambridge: Cambridge University Press, 1992).

33. I have elaborated these points in 'The Geography of Collective Identities in a Globalizing World', *Review of International Political Economy*, 3 (1996) 565–607.

34. A. Mawle, 'Women, Environment and the United Nations', in F. Dodds (ed.), *The Way Forward: Beyond Agenda 21* (London: Earthscan, 1997) p. 155.
35. B. S. Turner and P. Hamilton (eds), *Citizenship: Critical Concepts* (London: Routledge, 1994) preface.
36. Cf. R. Bauböck, *Transnational Citizenship: Membership and Rights in International Migration* (Aldershot: Edward Elgar, 1994).
37. See the website of the NGO Coalition for an International Criminal Court, http://www.igc.apc.org/icc.
38. Some authors speak of new practices of 'pooled sovereignty', 'joint sovereignty', etc.; however, such notions fundamentally contradict the ideas of supremacy and exclusivity that have marked every previous conception of sovereignty.
39. See sources cited in note 27; and L. Weiss, *The Myth of the Powerless State: Governing the Economy in a Global Era* (Oxford: Polity, 1998).
40. E.g. D. C. Korten, *Getting to the 21st Century: Voluntary Action and the Global Agenda* (West Hartford, CT: Kumarian, 1990).
41. Cf. S. Johnson and B. Rogaly, *Microfinance and Poverty Reduction* (Oxford: Oxfam/ACTIONAID, 1997).
42. A. Chetley, *The Politics of Baby Foods: Successful Challenges to an International Marketing Strategy* (London: Pinter, 1986).
43. J. A. Scholte, ' "In the Foothills": Relations between the IMF and Civil Society', in R. Higgott and A. Bieler (eds), *Non-State Actors and Authority in the Global System* (London: Routledge, 1999); Scholte with R. O'Brien and M. Williams, 'The WTO and Civil Society', *Journal of World Trade*, 33 (1999) 107–24.
44. Cf. P. Williams, 'Transnational Criminal Organizations and International Security', *Survival*, 36 (1994) 96–113; J. H. Mittelman and R. Johnston, 'The Globalization of Organized Crime, the Courtesan State, and the Corruption of Civil Society', *Global Governance*, 5 (1999), 103–26.
45. Cf. Sulak Sivaraksa, *Global Healing: Essays and Interviews on Structural Violence, Social Development and Spiritual Transformation* (Bangkok: Thai Inter-Religious Commission for Development and Sathirakoses-Nagapradipa Foundation, 1999); J. Gaventa, 'Learning across Boundaries: Strengthening Participation in North and South', paper for the NGOs in a Global Future Conference, University of Birmingham, January 1999.

8 The Challenge to International Institutions*

NGAIRE WOODS

Globalization, as already defined in this volume, describes dramatic changes in the transactions and interactions taking place among states, firms and peoples in the world. It describes not just an increase in the flow of goods, services, images, ideas, and people, but a change in the way production, distribution, consumption, and other activities are defined and undertaken. State borders no longer contain and define identities, products, and actors' possibilities. Boundaries are still crucial, but so too are transnational opportunities both for politics and for commerce. As a result, an increasing range of activities require some form of management and regulation at the international level. For this reason, states create international institutions.

This chapter examines the challenges globalization poses to states and the international institutions they create, focusing in particular on recent crises and their implications for existing organizations. The opening section describes the myriad of institutions which have emerged in the past two decades. I then outline the new and difficult challenges these international institutions face, illustrating with the case of globalization in finance. Following this, I detail the problems this poses for governments, not just about how to reform the system, but also about who should reform the system. Having investigated some of the obstacles to necessary reform, I outline the new tasks that

---

* I am indebted to Tony Porter, Macmaster University, for incisive and helpful comments on an earlier draft of this chapter.

governments, through international institutions, need to fulfil in a globalizing world. The last part of the chapter examines the factors which determine whether these tasks are likely to be fulfilled. The conclusion suggests that although globalization necessitates a reform of international institutions, the requisite reforms are severely hampered by specific political interests not just of states but also of transnational and private actors within states.

Globalization and institutionalization

Over the course of the twentieth century, a combination of technological advances and government policies have led to a dramatic increase in the interconnectedness of governments, societies, and private actors in world politics. As the possibilities of travel and communication have opened up to a wider range of people and to a wider range of places, new problems have emerged which most nation-states cannot manage without coordination and cooperation with other governments. For example, drugs and other criminal activities can now move more easily across borders, as can infectious diseases and various kinds of environmental problems such as acid rain or nuclear spillout. At the same time, new kinds of interdependence have emerged which also require governments to act together. The globalization of capital markets, for example, has meant that governments are yet more susceptible to effects from financial crises in other parts of the world. This was illustrated in 1997, when policymakers discussed how to prevent 'contagion' across the world economy as East Asia suffered an economic crisis. Equally, the language of 'contagion' has been applied to security crises and ethnic or tribal violence which in the 1990s showed an equal propensity to spread – be it in the Balkans, or around the Great Lakes of Africa.

One way in which governments have sought to manage and regulate problems arising from transnational activities is through international – or better-said 'inter-governmental' – organizations. This has led to a steady increase in the number of international organizations. At the end of the 1990s, over 250 international organizations (IOs) existed in a world of just over 180 states. This compares to around 30 IOs which existed at the turn of the century in a world of less than 50 states.[1] More broadly, international relations have become characterized by increasing numbers of treaties, regimes, and other cooperative arrangements among states.[2] Together, these arrangements comprise an increasingly institutionalized world politics.

More radically, increasing institutionalization has opened up an arena of politics in which other agencies can play a larger role. Some describe this as the emergence of a new 'global politics'.[3] The globalization of politics permits non-state actors to play a part in forming preferences, making decisions, and influencing outcomes at the international level. Among these actors are multinational corporations and international non-governmental organizations (NGOs). The latter have increased in number from an estimated hundred at the turn of the century to over 5000 at the end of the 1990s.[4] For international institutions this has posed a considerable challenges since many NGOs have demanded recognition in international institutions. These NGOs, claiming a transnational or a subnational constituency,[5] have carved out a role for themselves in several organizations,[6] not to mention having taken a lead in pushing international negotiations on some specific issues such as the environment.[7] It is now the case that NGOs can participate within some international fora, such as the World Bank's Panel of Inspection hearings on environmental issues.[8] As Jan Aart Scholte has detailed in Chapter 7, these developments have the potential to produce either positive or negative consequences.[9]

The problem for states has been how to coordinate their responses and policies in response to globalization so as more effectively to ensure economic growth, security and stability within their own borders. The institutions they have created to do this job now face increasing burdens and challenges, as the transnational flows they are attempting to regulate, facilitate or mitigate become larger and more difficult to control. Adding to the problems of management is the fact that globalization is affecting different parts of the world in highly uneven ways. In some parts of the world, globalization brings a promise of integration into a thriving world economy and society, in others globalization is increasing inequality and the prospects of chaos, disorder and poverty.[10] Not all states wish to participate in international organizations, and when states do participate, there is a difficult question as to how much influence any one state should enjoy. One view suggests that international organizations should be structured in ways that reflect the global hierarchy of power among states. By contrast, critics argue that institutions so structured will no longer be effective in a globalizing world since the tasks they face require a different form of power: soft, persuasive power, as opposed to hard, coercive power.[11] This chapter returns to this issue below. First, however, the new challenges faced by international institutions will be elaborated, using the example of globalization in the international financial system.

The challenges for international institutions: the case of globalized finance

In international finance, globalization has powerful implications for governments and for the international institutions they have created. Globalized international financial markets are more open, more liquid and more internationally integrated than ever before. Equally importantly, globalization describes a change in governments' perceptions of these markets as more powerful and more limiting of government autonomy than in any previous era. For this reason, globalization has turned governments' attention to the role and nature of international financial institutions – and not for the first time this century.

In the aftermath of the Second World War, the International Monetary Fund (IMF) and the International Bank for Reconstruction and Development (which became part of the World Bank) were created in order to ensure stable and equitable growth in the world economy. The IMF would ensure stable exchange rates and adjustment by countries with liquidity problems. The World Bank would channel (predominantly) private-sector funds into investment projects which would ensure growth and development. Yet since the 1970s the foundations of the so-called 'Bretton Woods' system have been swept aside and financial deregulation in the industrialized countries has converged with economic liberalization in developing countries to produce more global capital markets.

It is worth noting that several kinds of government policy have furthered globalization. In the 1960s deregulation in industrialized countries led to the emergence of a 'Eurocurrency' market whereby borrowers could issue bonds in currencies other than their national currency (leading to the currency competition detailed by Benjamin Cohen in Chapter 4). In 1971, the United States came off the gold standard, causing a breakdown of the Bretton Woods exchange rate regime. In 1972 the Chicago Options Exchange was established, a first step towards the huge growth in derivatives trading in the 1980s. Finally, as commercial banks based in the United States and Europe globalized their clientele they opened up new sources of finance for governments across the developing world – sowing the seeds of the debt crisis of the 1980s. In brief, a combination of new technology and US (and other industrialized countries') policies unleashed a globalization of financial markets and currencies within which new actors and new transactions flourished.[12]

Governments responded in a variety of ways to the challenges and threats of the new system. Policy coordination was discussed by leading industrialized countries hankering after the stability of the old exchange rate system. More actively, governments looked to a variety of international institutions in order to seek solutions and stability. These institutions included the Bank for International Settlements (BIS),[13] the International Monetary Fund (IMF),[14] the Group of Ten (G-10)[15] and World Bank,[16] the Group of Seven (G-7),[17] European institutions, and a host of other less formal fora for discussion of regulation in the world economy. During the 1980s these institutions acted in concert with the US Treasury and Federal Reserve to shore up threats posed to banking and economic growth in the industrialized world: managing, for example, the debt crises of Latin American and Eastern European countries which threatened major international commercial banks.

In the 1990s a wave of new financial crises caused world economic policy-makers to think about how to respond to new faultlines in the world economy. At the end of 1994, the Mexican peso plummeted (depreciating by 50 percent within one week) causing reverberations in Washington, DC and New York, as well as in other Central and South American countries worried about a 'Tequila' effect – a contagious loss of confidence in economies across the region which would cause the crisis to spread.[18] In the case of Mexico, the US Treasury and the IMF were able rapidly to put together a large assistance package in order to shore up confidence in the Mexican economy – a reaction facilitated by the magnitude of US interests in Mexico.[19] However, the Mexican case immediately raised concerns about whether the IMF had adequate resources to bolster confidence in Mexico and what would happen if other countries had currency crises. Who would bail them out? Was the IMF to be given a new role in crisis management? And if so, where would the requisite resources come from?

Policy-makers' concerns about financial instability proved well-founded. In 1997 a financial crisis sparked by the devaluation of the Thai baht spread across East Asia. This was soon followed by a crisis in the Russian rouble in the summer of 1998. As discussed by Benjamin Cohen, these crises led many countries to consider alternative exchange rate arrangements: from floating currencies, to currency boards or dollarization. A further financial disaster within the United States – the collapse of an investment group called 'Long Term Capital Management' (LTCM) – focused attention yet more closely on the need to reform the 'global financial architecture'.

All the crises of the 1990s highlighted the vulnerability of national financial systems and the need for countries participating in the global financial system to have strong standards of accounting, prudential regulation, disclosure, exchange and so forth. Equally, the crises demonstrated the capacity of private-sector actors, including banks, investment houses, security brokerages, hedge funds and asset managers to create turmoil. As these actors create profit centres out of currency, derivatives, and emerging market security trading departments, and take large positions in leveraged instruments on proprietary accounts, their frenetic trading activities create what one analyst has described as a 'global whirlpool'.[20] The inability of governments to calm some of the 'whirling' was displayed in Mexico, East Asia, and Russia. This has led to a serious re-evaluation of international regulation and institutions.

The challenges for governments: who should regulate – and how?

In the late 1990s a flurry of proposals on global financial reform focussed attention on two issues: first, who should be in charge of reforming the system?; and second, what should the new system look like – should it be a larger, more powerful IMF, or a new global banking regulator? These questions echoed similar debates in other areas of international relations where intervention has been undertaken. For example, in the wake of crises in Somalia, Rwanda and Bosnia, there has been much debate about who should sit on the

United Nations Security Council,[21] as well as about what the security system should look like – should the Military Staff Committee (MSC) be revived and a standing force created,[22] and should security be redefined to include environmental and demographic concerns?[23]

In the international financial system, the question of *who* should influence reform in the wake of crises in the 1990s, was taken up by the US Treasury which moved swiftly to invite 22 countries to take part in a discussion of reform (the so-called G-22). Other governments, however, soon complained that the initiative was too US-dominated. The French Minister of Finance argued that discussions should be undertaken in the IMF's Interim Committee which at least represents all members of the IMF.[24] In a separate proposal the British Chancellor of the Exchequer, Gordon Brown, argued for an over-arching 'Standing Committee for Global Financial Regulation' which would bring together the IMF, the World Bank, the G-10, and other national and international regulatory institutions.[25] In the end, the G-7 created a 'Financial Stability Forum' (FSF) in February 1999, comprising themselves and representativies of the IMF, the World Bank, the Basle Committee on Banking Supervision, the International Organizations of Securities Commissions, the International Association of Insurance Supervisors, the BIS, the OECD, the Committee on Payment and Settlement Systems, and the Committtee on the Global Financial System (formerly the Euro-currency Standing Committee).[26]

The membership of the forum highlights two things. First, the members reflect the great variety of institutions which has emerged in the international financial system, including networks of regulators and supervisors. Second, the membership of the FSF reflects the degree to which the system is run by the leading industrialized countries. In June 1999, the G-7 broadened representation in the forum by inviting senior representatives from Hong Kong, Singapore, Australia and the Netherlands to participate. However, it has been clear from the start that a universal membership is out of the question. More central to negotiations on the composition of a reform discussion group has been the question of how power should be shared between the United States and Europe. Competition between the two was highlighted at the IMF/World Bank meetings of spring 1999 when the US Secretary of the Treasury Robert Rubin suggested reviewing the constituencies within which countries are grouped in the IMF: a proposal swifly rejected by the German Finance Minister recognizing that it could only result in a reduction of the European countries' positions.[27] Discussion as to reform will thus proceed in a forum dominated by the leading industrialized countries, in spite of the fact that globalization has geographically expanded the regions affected by capital flows, as well as the nature and depth of issues and reforms that any international institutions has to deal with.

The nature and shape of a reformed system has yet to be established. Ideas for a global financial regulator, global bankruptcy court, global money and a global central bank have abounded as the depth of the challenge of globalization has been recognized. However, as Barry Eichengreen has pointed out, they are unrealistic since the length of time and effort required to bring about a single currency and a Central Bank in Europe shows that 'it is fantastic to think that this process could be replicated on a global scale in a few years'.[28] Furthermore, as crises recede (whether in international finance or international security) so too does the zeal with which policy-makers promulgate ideas for reform. They also come to recognise the vested interests with whom they will need to clash in order to take even modest steps in a new direction. In international finance, the nature of conflicting interests demonstrates how difficult it is to create or to reform inter-governmental arrangements and organizations.

Vested interests and international institutions: obstacles to regulation and reform

The international financial crises of the 1990s involved private sector creditors whose loans – whether to governments or the private sector in borrowing countries – went bad as confidence in the government or currency evaporated (as in Mexico, Thailand, Korea, Russia and so forth). Furthermore, the investments were overwhelmingly of a short-term portfolio character, making the effects of a loss of confidence yet more immediate and damaging. Prior to the first of these crises (Mexico in 1994), policy-makers had been complacent about loans (whether short- or long-term) to the private sector, assuming that since they did not involve governments, they did not pose a threat to financial stability. They were wrong. The crises of the 1990s demonstrated that large short-term capital flows, whether to private or public borrowers, could jeopardize international financial stability.

For this reason, in each case intervention was required – using taxpayers' money to bail out private-sector creditors.

Public intervention in the 1990s created a strong political backlash which pressured Finance Ministers and Central Bankers seriously to re-evaluate the alternatives to such intervention. In 1996 the G-10 published a report on the resolution of sovereign liquidity crises arguing for a series of measures which would improve the capacity of debtors to adjust and to deal with a sovereign liquidity crisis: adjusting the rules within which international institutions intervene and reapportioning some of the costs and burdens of adjustment onto private-sector creditors.[29] The private sector's response was swift: a counter-report, authored by William Cline, was published by the Institute of International Finance (a Washington, DC-based lobby-group and research organization for international bankers and investors). The IIF report rejected most of the G-10 proposals, arguing that crises could be averted with increased transparency and information flows from borrowers and a modicum of self-regulation by the private sector. Subsequent crises, however, have increased political pressures for a tougher line to be taken with creditors.

At the G-7 Summit in Frankfurt in June 1999, Ministers agreed principles governing the future involvement of private-sector creditors in the resolution of financial crises, including advocating that the IMF lend moral and financial support to countries imposing capital controls or suspending debt repayments. They also supported the G-10 proposals for majority voting and sharing clauses which prevent individual creditors from resorting to lawsuits or other means of obstructing settlements – hence creating an atmosphere conducive to restructuring negotiations. All of these measures, if implemented, would impose a greater cost on creditors lending to a country which is subsequently forced to reschedule its debts.

The pressures on private investors to shoulder some responsibility for crisis management is already having some effect. In the recent case of Brazil, for example, the IMF negotiated an assistance package which included private creditors as well as governments. The problem for policy-makers was to patch up a crisis in the private sector (because it threatened wider financial stability) which involved a very large (and increasing) number of lenders. Each private-sector creditor had an interest in 'taking the money and running'. Yet if all creditors stayed the course, a crisis could be averted or at least managed with less cost to all. Initially, industrialized countries' governments threatened to compel foreign banks to participate in an assistance package. The private lenders, however, argued that compulsory participation would cause many of them immediately to move to reduce their exposure, thus exacerbating the problem. The end-result was a compromise agreement with the voluntary participation of the private sector. The difficulties inherent in managing such crises have forced policy-makers to look harder at ways to prevent crises.

In seeking to prevent crises policy-makers have bolstered the capacity of the IMF. They increased the Fund's resources by requiring member countries to contribute more through two mechanisms: the 'New Arrangements to Borrow' introduced in November 1998 which expands the countries contributing to this special fund beyond the G-10 members; and by a quota increase approved in January 1999. Furthermore, governments expanded the IMF's capacity to act by enabling it to extend contingent credit lines (CCL) to provide countries undertaking strong economic policies with short-term financing as a precautionary line of defense against balance-of-payments problems that might arise from a crisis in another country (so-called 'international financial contagion'). These CCLs were approved by the IMF's Board in April 1999.

The other key reforms policy-makers have promulgated concern information, supervision, and regulation. On information dissemination, the IMF has taken a lead, although on matters of supervision and regulation it has only limited capacity and expertise and hence other international institutions have been called upon. Under direction of the G-10, for example, the 'Basle Committee on Banking Supervision' (formed in 1975 and comprising the central governors of the G-10 members plus Luxembourg) have drafted new proposals aimed at requiring banks to apportion more resources to cover their own risks. In 1999 the proposals included capital standards not just on banks' loans but also on their operational risk (covering anything – from a hurricane knocking out computer systems to staff fraud). Needless to say, banks have strongly rejected the proposals.[30]

Even if effective, however, the Basle Committee proposals cover only international banks, leaving the vast and growing array of other creditors relatively unregulated. For this reason, policy-makers have begun to look at ways to moderate the destabilizing potential of offshore financial centres, non-bank financial institutions, and transactions involving highly leveraged institutions (HLIs or so-called 'hedge funds'). They have widened the data disclosed to the Bank for International Settlements and guidelines have been drawn up regarding bank dealings with HLIs, and general trading activities of banks and securities firms.[31] Additional forms of regulation are also being examined.[32]

Government policies are now also coming under scrutiny. The IMF argues that governments need to develop and adopt internationally accepted standards or codes of good practice for economic, financial and business activities. A first step in this direction was the creation of a Special Data Dissemination Standard in the IMF in 1996. This is a set of guidelines on the dissemination of economic and financial data to the public for countries seeking access to international capital markets. In 1999 the Executive Board of the Fund agreed that the standard should be strengthened and that the Fund should undertake to monitor it. The Fund is also promulgating a 'Code of Good Practices on Fiscal Transparency' and a code of good practices on 'Transparency in Monetary and Financial Policies'. These codes mirror the 'best practices' and 'core principles' guidelines which have been written by the Basle Commitee on Banking Supervision for banking institutions.[33]

For governments, new codes of practice relating to economic policy reflect a new more intrusive reach of institutions. Governments are now being required not just to justify particular macroeconomic indicators or results, but to shape their domestic policies so as to comply with international standards. In the section below, this extension of the reach of international institutions is discussed further.

A final issue raised by the financial crises of the 1990s is capital controls – or how much control governments can or should have over short-term investments to and from abroad. There is now wide support for the idea that governments might in some way try to raise the barrier to short-term flows of finance and thus mitigate the problems being caused by globalization. In particular, Chile's experiment with taxes to limit short-term foreign borrowing by all domestic entities has attracted attention. In the wake of recent crises even the IMF has relaxed its previous hostility to such measures. In 1999 the Fund is reviewing how financial integration ought to be 'managed' and what role capital controls might play. Private-sector creditors remain strongly opposed to any such measures.

The political result of globalization in capital markets has been to highlight the potential and actual roles of international institutions, but also the clash of interests between the private sector and governments in industrialized countries. Previously, the public and private financial sector enjoyed a fairly cosy, if occasionally tense, relationship. In the mid-1980s, for example, in dealing with the Latin American debt crisis, the US Treasury and the IMF were able to coordinate a fairly small number of influential banks in a strategy for managing the crisis (the 'Baker Plan'). In the 1990s, however, the number of private-sector actors has grown enormously as new kinds of investors, mutual funds, pension funds and such like have entered the global finance market. The old implicit understandings and shared culture which facilitated cooperation between the public and private sectors (such as on Wall Street in the US and in the City of London in the UK) are no longer effective.

New fragilities associated with globalized capital markets are forcing governments and international institutions to carve out a new role for themselves. In international finance, the new role requires governments and inter-governmental institutions to exercise authority over the private sector, and over domestic regulation within other countries. Crucially, however, the authority traditionally enjoyed by governments (and inter-governmental institutions) may no longer be effective in trying to fulfil these new tasks.

The new intrusive reach of international institutions

In a globalizing world, powerful governments are increasingly requiring international institutions to delve into the domestic details of politics, norms, values and organization within states. In the 1990s, this phenomenon was noticeable not only in international finance but in areas as diverse as trade and security.

In international trade, as described in Chapter 3, the requirements of a more global trading order have led not just to the creation of a more powerful international organization (the World Trade Organization) but to the negotiation of rules and standards in matters previously considered clearly 'domestic' and not international. Where negotiators once worked to reduce tariffs and protectionist barriers, they are now concerned with a wide range of economic policies and practices, most of which are still widely considered the preserve of national governments.

In the realm of global security, international institutions have also become more concerned with what happens within states, as opposed to addressing what goes on between states. The change has occurred because governments now face a threat from conflicts which spill over boundaries and engulf contiguous countries and even regions. The new threat of spreading conflicts has come about partly as the result of the end of the Cold War which contained warring parties within a rudimentary balance of power. In equal part, however, the new threat is due to the ease with which belligerents, arms, refugees, aid agencies, propaganda and reporting can cross borders and regions. The widening and deepening of global communications, travel, and cross-border activities permits violence and instability to spread quickly. This requires guardians of security in any one country to pay close attention to what is happening within the boundaries of other countries. Most recently, the fear of spreading conflict has catalysed international interventions in Cambodia, the former Yugoslavia, Somalia, Rwanda and Haiti. As UN analysts have noted, these interventions reflect 'the growing willingness to address, rather than ignore, fundamental problems within the borders of war-torn states'.[34] In the early 1990s, there was much talk of a 'new interventionism' engaging security institutions in domestic issues of human rights, democracy and governance.[35]

In a similar way, in international finance, the possibility that a crisis in one country will spill over into others has created the spectre of global instability caused by events in one (not necessarily very large) country. This spectre has driven policy-makers to focus their attention on the domestic policies of countries integrated into the global financial system. Just as good governance and democracy are seen as preventatives in the security realm, so too sound economic policy is seen as an important moderating influence in the international financial system. This has led to the proposals discussed above for international standards in areas such as banking regulation and supervision, auditing and accounting, corporate governance, and bankruptcy laws. The implication is that globalization requires international organizations to enforce a much deeper level of policy integration or convergence, nudging the international institutions ever more deeply into the preserve of national governments' economic policy-making.

The common problem faced by all international organizations in a globalizing world is one of governance: can inter-state organizations, usually dominated by a small number of states, effectively influence and implement international standards and norms across and within a wide range of countries?

The effectiveness of international institutions in a globalizing world

Traditionally, the effectiveness of international institutions created by states has been explained either in terms of reciprocity and mutual interests which states hope to gain through the institution, or in terms of coercion exercised by the dominant state or states in the institution. The realist view of international order proposes hierarchy as a positive ordering element in the international system. The potential for international institutions to play an independent or autonomous role is relegated to the sidelines.[36] Institutions are described as a way for powerful states to reduce or share the costs of maintaining a particular order. Hence, the effectiveness of a multilateral organization will depend primarily upon the relative power and commitment of its more powerful members.[37]

In contrast to this view, others argue that international organizations reflect shared purposes and interests, not just of states, but of peoples, and of interest groups within states.[38] One such case is the European Economic Community as it emerged in the period following the Second World War.[39] Furthermore, once institutions are created by powerful states, even if the powerful state's position declines, the institutions may well continue, as they did in spite of a decline in US hegemony in the 1970s.[40] On this view, multilateral institutions exist to promulgate rules which reflect shared aims, and to ensure rules are enforced through the participation and mutually recognized interests of all parties. As a result inter-state organizations enjoy some modicum of autonomy. Their effectiveness, however, depends on the continuing commitment of all members to the institutions' aims, and their willingness to participate in the enforcement of them.

The challenge in an increasingly globalized world is of a different order. While previously international rules covered a limited range of issues (such as foreign policy, defence and some matters of commerce), globalization has widened and deepened the international agenda, encroaching on areas which governments and electors have jealously guarded as their own. The extent of political issues which are influenced by international agreements or cooperative regimes grows larger by the day, seriously challenging the autonomy of state leaders. The challenge is particularly pronounced in countries who do not enjoy a dominant position within international institutions. They risk becoming increasingly powerless in the face of standards being set by a small number of powerful states. For international organizations whose jurisdiction is expanding, this poses a deep question of legitimacy: on what grounds can they legitimately formulate policies for distant communities?

The legitimacy question was raised sharply in the 1990s in the above-mentioned areas of security, trade and finance. For example, the IMF attempted to require 'forceful, far-reaching structural reforms' from countries in order to correct weaknesses in domestic financial systems and 'to remove features of the economy that had become impediments to growth (such as monopolies, trade barriers and nontransparent corporate practices)'.[41] These conditions go far beyond the kinds of macroeconomic targets previously required by the IMF. They drive deep into a country's domestic economic policies. Politically, this has caused commentators to question the legitimacy of this approach. For example, in his examination of the IMF's response to the crisis in East Asia published in *Foreign Affairs*, Marty Feldstein wrote: 'The legitimate political institutions of the country should determine the nation's economic structure and the nature of its institutions. A nation's desperate need for short-term financial help does not give the IMF the moral right to substitute its technical judgements for the outcomes of the nation's political process'.[42]

The issue here is a difficult one. The IMF is charged with the role of safeguarding the stability of the international monetary system. Yet in a globalizing world, this is increasingly difficult to do without incursion into the domestic policies of countries. Likewise, as argued in the previous section, in trade, and international security, it is difficult to manage problems created at the regional or international level by increasing flows of goods, people, crime, and violence (and the associated changes in perceptions and politics), without addressing domestic social, economic and security policies. The problem here is that what we might call 'deeply domestic' policies and outcomes can not be altered purely by external pressure or fiat from abroad. The only agency which has the capacity to ensure that human rights, environmental standards, or banking supervision guidelines are systematically respected within any country is the state and the government of that country.

International institutions are now being called upon by their dominant members to find ways to deepen all their member-governments' commitments to international standards so that international rules become vigorously applied *within* all states' borders. This is difficult for existing organizations which are hierarchically organized, with a small cohort of powerful countries making the rules and ensuring that the rules are kept to. In the past, this was a means by which powerful states could enforce norms and rules among states. Globalization, however, requires institutions to enforce rules within states. The new task for multilateral organizations is to bring together governments so as to persuade them of and coordinate internationally-agreed-upon policies. If they do not, governments will simply alter their behaviour for short-term incentives, and revert to their previous national policies as soon as those incentives are exhausted.

So how can international institutions be more effective in implementing international standards? The key is legitimacy: as they encroach more upon the policies of elected governments, international organizations will need to be seen to respect basic principles of democracy. The governments they persuade will have to be able to explain to their own electorates why it is that the rules of international organizations represent their interests and ought legitimately to be implemented. International institutions, in other words, will have to point to more than the power of their dominant members as an argument for obedience from other states. In the first place, intergovernmental organizations will have to pay greater attention to representing all states and ensuring their participation in the formulation of new norms.[43] Beyond this, as discussed in Chapter 7, institutions will have to consider what role non-state actors and transnational groups might play.

The record suggests that the inter-governmental organizations mentioned in this chapter are aware of the need to widen their membership and to alter their ways of working. It is equally clear, however, that they are reluctant to go very far in changing their structures. The BIS opened its doors in 1996 to Brazil, China, Hong Kong, India, Mexico, Russia, Saudi Arabia, Singapore, and South Korea. It bears noting, however, that this change in membership has not been equalled by a change in influence. The real work of the BIS is still done by its Board which comprises just the G-10 Central Bankers. In the United Nations Security Council, some very modest changes in procedure were undertaken in the 1990s,[44] and many members have accepted that the membership of the Council should be enlarged, at least to include Germany and Japan as permanent members and probably also representatives of developing countries.[45] However, the Council remains dominated by the Permanent Five members (China, Russia, the US, France and the UK) who not only have permanent seats but also enjoy an effective veto over Security Council decisions.[46] The blocking of reform is due essentially to the unwillingness on the part of the existing permanent members, and especially the United States, to permit any dilution of their rights.[47] The WTO has been created with equal representation of all countries, however, in reality the 'Quad' which dominated the GATT still dominate the organization (see Chapter 3). The IMF has opened up its work and procedures to a much greater degree of public scrutiny, and is just commencing a review of its voting structure which is weighted heavily towards the large industrialized countries.[48]

The reason for such modest change is obvious. Powerful states are being asked to weigh up proven past effectiveness (through hierarchy which gave them control) against possible future effectiveness (through wider participation). It is only when existing institutions upon which they can stamp their will are manifestly ineffectual, that they will contemplate change. However, for as long as the hierarchically arranged institutions enjoy even limited effect, it is unlikely that their powerful members will give up any control or advantage. However, further change might occur at other levels of international governance.

One level of change which is occurring in the international arena concerns the networking of sub-state actors such as regulators, supervisors, and private agencies and the increasing reliance of existing inter-governmental organizations on these networks. It is notable, for example, that the Financial Stability Forum (discussed above) set up by the leading industrialized countries to discuss reform of the financial system, includes the International Association of Insurance Supervisors (the IAIS, which was founded in 1994 to bring together regulators from a wide range of countries) and the International Organization of Securities Commissions. The latter (IOSCO) comprises national securities commissions and is dominated by the US Securities and Exchange Commission. Self-regulatory bodies have been given associate member status in the IOSCO.[49] International lawyers suggest to us that these organizations represent a new kind of international regulation and enforcement, or even, as one scholar puts it: 'new vision of global governance: horizontal rather than vertical, decentralized rather than centralized'.[50] Other scholars have described this as part of a serious shift in authority from public- to private-sector actors.[51] However, these networks have yet to prove their effectiveness. Indeed, the IOSCO has failed in its attempts to develop capital adequacy requirements for its members. Further-more, it would be wrong to overlook the fact that these new networks do not escape the hierarchy of power present in inter-state organiza-tions – indeed, many participants argue that they largely reflect it.

Sub-state networks are not the only additional form of governance emerging in the international financial system. At the end of the 1990s, many states are showing increasing interest in regional institu-tions. The international financial institutions (or, better said, their most powerful members), however, have shown little enthusiasm for such developments. For example, the countries of East Asia have debated whether a regional institution would better be able to prevent or contain currency and capital market crises in vunerable countries, or to insulate the region as a whole from negative spillover effects from crises in Latin America or Russia. Indeed, they have made several proposals for an Asian Monetary Fund or the like. These proposals have been strongly opposed by the US Treasury and the international financial institutions who recognize immediately that a regional institution would lessen their own control and influence over monetary and financial affairs in the region. At the same time, however, existing institutions cannot ignore the fact that demands for regional bodies have been fuelled by the extent to which the existing international economic institutions exclude smaller, less powerful countries and economies from effective participation in policy- and decision-making.[52]

In summary, although complementary and competing governance structures are emerging, they do not constitute a solution to the problem of effectiveness which international organizations face in an increasingly globalized world.

Conclusion

This chapter has argued that globalization has been accompanied by an increased number of international institutions, many of which represent attempts by states to cooperate and to regulate global issues multilaterally. Yet these new formal and informal organizations have not successfully found ways to manage the challenges and threats emerging as globalization affects finance, trade, and security. Institutional change is hampered by competition among states for power and influence and, in particular, an unwillingness on the part of dominant states to embrace a more participatory system. Change is also hampered by national and transnational non-governmental actors with vested interests in the existing system who therefore resist any attempts to reform it. What does this mean for the effectiveness of international institutions?

Institutions are now being used to effect a more intrusive level of regulation and policy coordination. This requires compliance not just from governments willing to sign agreements, but from their citizens. For this reason, institutions will not be effective while they rely on short-term incentives and the coercion of their strongest members in order to uphold global norms, laws and standards. Rather, international organizations will need to offer a wider range of governments an opportunity for genuine participation and these governments' citizens a better rationale for implementing internationally agreed standards or norms. Many powerful governments have already recognized this imperative. However, as global regulation and reform encroaches more on the vested interests of specific groups within countries (especially in countries who dominate existing institutions), governments will face increasing resistance to change from national and transnational actors aware that any diffusion of their government's power in international institutions is likely to reduce their own influence over global regulation or standards.

Notes

1. Union of International Associations, *Yearbook of International Organizations 1996* (Munich: Saur, 1996).
2. David Held, Anthony McGrew, David Goldblatt and Jonathan Perraton, *Global Transformations: Politics, Economics and Culture* (Cambridge: Polity Press, 1999).
3. A. G. McGrew (ed.), *Global Politics* (Milton Keynes: Open University Press, 1988); Held *et al.*, *Global Transformations*.
4. Held *et al*, *Global Transformations*, p. 54.
5. L. MacDonald, 'Globalizing Civil Society: Interpreting international NGOs in Central America', *Millenium*, 23 (2) (1994) 267–85; Thomas Princen, *Environmental NGOs in World Politics: Linking the Local and the Global* (Routledge, 1994).
6. Thomas G. Weiss and Leon Gordenker, *NGOs, the UN and Global Governance* (Boulder: Lynne Rienner, 1996). Nick Wheeler, 'Guardian Angel or Global

Gangster: A Review of the Ethical Claims of International Society', *Political Studies*, 44, 123–35.
7. John Meyer, David Frank, Ann Hironaka, Evan Schoefer and Nancy Tuma, 'The Structuring of a World Environmental Regime 1870–1990', *International Organization*, 51 (1997) 623–52.
8. R. Bisell, 'Recent Practice of the Inspection Panel of the World Bank', *American Journal of International Law* (1997) 91: 741–4; Ibrahim Shihata, *The World Bank Inspection Panel* (Oxford: Oxford University Press, 1994).
9. See also M. Edwards and D. Hulme, 'Too Close for Comfort: the Impact of Official Aid on Non-governmental Organizations', *World Development*, 24 (1996) 961–73; and Katherine Bain, 'Building or Burning Bridges: The Accountability of Trans-national NGO Networks in Policy Alliances with the World Bank', Paper prepared for the Conference of NGOs in a Global Future (Washington, DC: World Bank, 1999).
10. Andrew Hurrell and Ngaire Woods, *Inequality, Globalization and World Politics* (Oxford: Oxford University Press, 1999).
11. Robert Keohane and Joseph Nye, 'Power and Interdependence in the Information Age', *Foreign Affairs*, 77 (1998) 81ff.
12. Eric Helleiner, *States and The Reemergence of Global Finance: from Bretton Woods to the 1990s* (Ithaca: Cornell University Press, 1994).
13. Created in the interwar period to promote the cooperation among central banks and provide additional facilities for international financial operations see *The Bank for International Settlements: A Profile of an International Institution* (BIA/Profile Basle, Switzerland) June 1991.
14. Created in 1944, see Harold James, *International Monetary Cooperation since Bretton Woods* (Oxford: Oxford University Press, 1996).
15. The G-10 comprises the United States, the United Kingdom, Germany, France, Belgium, the Netherlands, Italy, Sweden, Canada, Japan and Switzerland – the countries which signed the General Agreement to Borrow (GAB) in 1962 which increased the resources available to the IMF.
16. Created in 1944 as the International Bank for Reconstruction and Development: see Devesh Kapur, John P. Lewis and Richard Webb, *The World Bank: Its First Half Century Volumes 1 & 2* (Washington, DC: Brookings Institution, 1997).
17. Comprising the United States, Japan, Germany, the United Kingdom, France, Italy and Canada, who first met as the 'Group of Seven', in 1975. Since the 1986 Tokyo Economic Summit, finance ministers and central bankers from these countries have met (along with the managing director of the IMF) more specifically as an economic forum.
18. Ricardo Ffrench-Davis, 'The Tequila Effect: Its Origins and its Widespread Impact', *Desarrollo Económico: Revista de Ciencias Sociales*, 37 (1997) 195–214.
19. Ngaire Woods, 'International Financial Institutions and the Mexican Crisis, in Carol Wise (ed.), *The Post-NAFTA Political Economy: Mexico and the Western Hemisphere* (Pennsylvania University Press, 1998) 148–70.
20. Percy Mistry, 'The Challenges of Financial Globalisation', in Jan Joost Teunissen, *The Policy Challenges of Global Financial Integration* (The Hague: Forum on Debt and Development, 1998) 83–119.
21. Thomas G. Weiss (ed.), *Collective Security in a Changing World* (Boulder CO: Lynne Rienner, 1993).
22. Boutros Boutros-Ghali, *An Agenda for Peace 1995* (New York: United Nations, 1995); Thomas G. Weiss, 'New Problems for Future UN Military Operations: Implementing an Agenda for Peace', *Washington Quarterly* 15, 1 (1993) 58–66; Benjamin Rivlin, *The Rediscovery of the UN Military Staff*

Committee (New York: Ralph Bunche Institute, Occasional Papers Series No. 4, 1991).

23. Jessica Tuchman Mathews, 'Redefining Security', *Foreign Affairs* 68, 2 (1989) 162–77.

24. Ministère de l'Economie, des Finances et de l'Industrie (Dominique Strauss-Kahn), 'Réforme des institutions financières internationales', presented at Interim Committee Meeting of IMF, Hong Kong, 21 September 1997.

25. Gordon Brown, 'New Global Structures for the New Global Age', Speech delivered at the Commonwealth Finance Ministers Meeting in Ottawa, 30 September 1998, and also delivered at the Annual Meeting of the Governors of the World Bank and IMF, 4 October 1998. See also Gordon Brown, 'Rediscovering Public Purpose in the Global Economy', Speech delivered at the Kennedy School, 15 December 1998: a brief report of this speech is in David Wighton, 'Companies warned on obligations', *Financial Times*, 15 December 1998.

26. This FSF has been described as a logical step in the evolution of a financial regulation regime: Tony Porter, 'Representation, Legitimacy, and the Changing Regime for Global Financial Regulation', Prepared for Annual Meeting of the American Political Science Association, Atlanta, September 1999.

27. Robert Chote, 'Rubin Seeks to Limit Europe's Influence', *Financial Times*, 28 April 1999, p. 4.

28. Barry Eichengreen, *Toward a New International Financial Architecture: A Practical Post-Asia Agenda* (Washington, DC: Institute for International Economics, 1999), p. 93.

29. Group of Ten' 'The Resolution of Sovereign Liquidity Crises', *Report to the Ministers and Governors Prepared under the Auspices of the Deputies* (1996) (www.bis.org/publ).

30. See Basle Committee on Banking Supervision, *Principles for the Management of Credit Risk* (Basle: Bank for International Settlements, 1999); George Graham, 'Banks Unhappy at Basle Risk Proposals', *Financial Times*, 5 March 1999, p. 3; Richard Lapper and Stephen Fidler, 'Investors say no to Crisis "Bail-ins"', *Financial Times*, 17 March 1999, p. 6.

31. Basle Committee: http://www.bis.org/wnew.htm.

32. The 'Financial Stability Forum' mentioned above has created three working groups to look into this. See Press Release, BIS, Ref No. 19/1999E, 11 May 1999.

33. See, for example, the Basle Committee on Banking Supervision publications: *Best Practices for Credit Risk Disclosure, Sound Practices for Loan Accounting and Disclosure, Principles for the Management of Credit Risk* (Basle: Bank for International Settlements, 1999).

34. Thomas G. Weiss, David P. Forsythe, and Roger A. Coate, *The United Nations and Changing World Politics* 2nd edn (Boulder, CO: Westview, 1997) p. 90.

35. James Mayall (ed.), *The New Interventionism: United Nations Experience in Cambodia, Former Yugoslavia, and Somalia* (New York: Cambridge University Press, 1996); Stephen John Stedman, 'The New Interventionists', *Foreign Affairs*, 72, 1 (1993) 1–16.

36. Robert Tucker, *The Inequality of Nations* (London: Martin Robertson, 1977); Kenneth Waltz, *Theory of International Politics* (New York: McGraw-Hill, 1979); John Mearsheimer, 'The False Promise of International Institutions', *International Security*, 19 (1995) 5–49.

37. Mearsheimer, 'The False Promise'; Charles Glaser, 'Realists as optimists: cooperation as self-help', *International Security*, 19 (1995) 50–93.

38. Robert Keohane, *International Institutions and State Power* (Boulder: Westview Press, 1989); Kenneth Oye (ed.), *Cooperation under Anarchy* (Princeton: Princeton University Press, 1986); Volcker Rittberger (ed.), *Regime Theory and International Relations* (Oxford: Oxford University Press, 1993).
39. Early postwar writings include: Ernst Haas, *Beyond the Nation-state: Functionalism and International Organization* (Stanford: Standford University Press, 1964); David Mitrany, *The Functional Theory of Politics* (London: M. Robertson, 1975).
40. Robert Keohane, *After Hegemony: Cooperation and Discord in the World Political Economy* (Princeton: Princeton University Press, 1984). Of course, the claim that hegemony had declined became hotly contested: Joseph Nye, *Bound to Lead: the Changing Nature of American Power* (New York: Basic Books, 1990). Cf. the realist view: Hans Morgenthau, *Politics Among Nations: the Struggle for Power and Peace* (New York: McGraw-Hill, 1967) and Robert Gilpin, *The Political Economy of International Relations* (Princeton: Princeton University Press, 1987).
41. IMF, *The IMF's Response to the Asian Crisis* (Washington, DC: IMF, 1998).
42. Marty Feldstein, 'Refocusing the IMF', *Foreign Affairs*, 77 (1998), p. 24.
43. Ngaire Woods, 'Good Governance in International Organizations', *Global Governance*, 5 (1999) 39–61.
44. Michael Wood, 'Security Council: Procedural Developments', *International and Comparative Law Quarterly*, (1996) 45 150–61.
45. Bruce Russett, Barry O'Neill and James Sutterlin, 'Breaking the Security Council Restructuring Logjam', *Global Governance* (1996) 2 65–80. Note that among the developing countries' regions, there are competing contenders for a permanent seat: India versus Pakistan or Indonesia; Brazil versus Mexico or Argentina; Nigeria versus South Africa or Egypt.
46. When the UN was created many members were opposed to giving the 'Permanent Members' special rights, but ultimately they agreed to give what amounts to a veto in order to secure the major powers' participation. Whilst on procedural matters, the P5 do not have a veto, they can veto the prior question as to whether an issue is procedural or substantive: giving rise to what some call a 'double veto'.
47. Benjamin Rivlin, 'UN Reform from the Standpoint of the United States', *UN University Lectures: 11* (Tokyo: UN University, 1996); Newt Gingrich, Bob Schellhas, Ed Gillespie and Rich Armey, *Contract with America: The Bold Plan by Rep. Newt Gingrich, Rep. Dick Armey and the House Republications to Change the Nation* (New York: Random House, 1994); Ruggie, *Winning the Peace*, p. 172.
48. See IMF, *A Guide to Progress in Strengthening the Architecture of the International Financial System* (Washington, DC: IMF, 28 April 1999). Also published at the website: www.omf.org/external/np/exr/facts/arch.htm.
49. See website at http://www.iosco.org.
50. Anne-Marie Slaughter, 'Governing the Global Economy through Government Networks' (Manuscript, Harvard). See also David Zaring, 'International Law by Other Means: the Twilight Existence of International Financial Regulatory Organizations', *Texas International Law Journal*, (1998) 33: 281.
51. William Coleman and Tony Porter, 'International Institutions, Globalization, and Democracy: Assessing the Challenges', Prepared for 11th Annual Meeting on Socio-Economics, Madison, Wisconsin, USA, 8–11 July 1999.
52. Mistry, 'The Challenges', p. 86.

Index

Africa
  ethnic/tribal violence 203
  level of inbound
    investment 23
  raw material price
    decline 167
African National
  Congress 186
AIDS 158, 180
Alesina, Alberto 143
Aliber, Robert 95
Americanization 178
Andersen, Benedict 85
Andrews, David 78
Angell, Norman 2
Amnesty International 176
Andrews, David 78
Angell, Norman 2
APEC 66, 67, 70
Asia
  capital controls 157
  IMF conditionalities 155
Asia crisis, 1997 55, 60, 63,
    78, 98ff, 109, 141, 142,
    148, 153, 157, 203
Asia, East
  competition to United
    States 166
  and Japan 100
  rate of growth of
    imports 60
  see also Asia and Southeast
    Asia
Asian Labour Network 176
Asian Monetary Fund 101
Association of Advocacy
  Organizations
  (ALOP) 181
Association of South East
  Asian Nations
  (ASEAN) 67
Australia
  capital mobility 122
  and civic associations 186
  participation in FSF 208
  tariff rates 117
Austria
  tax rates 132
  consumption tax 135

balance of payments 211
  and deterritorialization 90
balance of power among
  states, and monetary
  sovereignty 87

Balkans 158, 203
banana dispute 62
Bank for International
  Settlements 82, 184,
    192, 206, 208, 212, 217
banking regulation 214,
    216
Bank of Japan 82
  and Asia crisis 101
Barnet, R.J. 159
Basle Committee on Banking
  Supervision 208, 211
beef hormone dispute 63
Belgium, and Maastricht
  criteria 141
Bhagwati, Jagdish 101
BMW 112
borrowing
  costs of 138
  results of 110
Bosnia 158, 207
Brazil
  financial assistance 210
  portfolio investment 168
Bretton Woods 205
  and civic activism 180
  collapse 121
Britain
  changes in labour tax,
    1970–84 135
  tax rates 131
Brown, Gordon 208
budget deficit
  and global capital 113
  and inflation 138
Bundesbank 141
business associations,
  global 185
business cycle 130
business lobbies 175

Cambodia 214
Canada, labour tax 134
Canada–US Free Trade Area
  (CUSFTA) 64
capital controls 101ff, 142
  in Asia 157
  and China 102
  and financial crisis,
    1990s 212
  and interest rates 121
  removal of, in OECD 121
  and state sovereignty 161
capital flows 148
  and currency risk 121

to developing
    countries 32, 148
  and financial crisis 209
  government
    restrictions 121
  interest rates 121
  and liberalization 120
  and policy flexibility 92
  and rate of return on
    investments 122
capital market integration
    108, 121, 203
capital mobility 80, 111–12
  and constraints on
    states 78, 80
  and the covered interest
    parity 121
  hypothesis 78ff
  and liberalization of
    capital markets 122
  and taxation 131, 134
capital taxation 130ff
  and capital mobility 131,
    134
capital transfers 2, 59
  and growth in trade 59
Cardoso, President 71
CARE 186
Caribbean Basin
  Initiative 64
Caribbean Community
  (CARICOM) 67
Central and East European
  countries
  civil activism 195
  debt crisis 206
  economic system 46
  in global trading
    system 58
  rate of growth of
    investment 23–4
Cerny, Philip 95
Chicago Options
  Exchange 206
Chile
  expansion of NAFTA 71
  tax 212
China
  and capital controls 102
  and claim of state
    sovereignty 155
  competition to the United
    States 166
  and the Internet 168
  welfare 160

citizenship
  construction of 187–8
  and globalization 182–4, 196
  multiple 188
civic associations 190
  and accountability of institutions 192
  and communication 192
civil society 173ff
  and communication 192
  and collective identity 187
  and democracy 188, 194
  and global governance 185–6
  negative effects of 194
  and official channels of policy-making 186
  and regulation 185–6
  and representation 195
  and social cohesion 193
  tactics of 176
  and the UN 186
Cline, William 210
'clustering' 30
CNN 179
Cold War, end of 214, 167–8
  and foreign assistance 157–8
  and trade liberalization 157
  US preponderance 63
collective goods 139
collective identity 181, 184, 187, 196
commercial banks 206
Committee on the Global Financial System 208
Committee on Payment and Settlement Systems 208
comparative advantage 114, 139
competition, global 154, 166
competitive advantage 28
  location-specific advantage 20ff
  and mergers 30
  ownership advantage 20ff
competitive deregulation 160
Conservative parties
  and financial openness 108
  and capital tax 134
consumption tax 130ff, 135
  and financial openness 135
  and left/labour power 136

'contagion' 203
contingent credit lines 211
convertibility guarantees 97
corporate risk 152
corporatism 108, 114ff, 140
  as alternative to the free market 115
  and macroeconomic outcomes 114ff
  and the public economy 128
criminal activity, and globalization 203
creditors, and liquidity crisis 210
currency
  attractiveness of 97
  controls 153
  cross-border competition 80
  deterritorialization 81
  equivalence among national monies 83
  internationalization 80
  physical circulation of 82
  and political authority 86
  ranking of 83
  reputation 97
  scale of cross-border use 82
  stability 79
  substitution 80
currency boards 99, 207
currency competition 81, 205
currency crisis, 1990s 113
customs union, and transaction costs 29
Czech Republic 164

debt crisis 12, 163, 167, 206–7
  and private sector actors 207
debtors, and liquidity crisis 210
decentralization in decision-making 5, 71
  EU 5
  World Bank 5
democracy
  and communication 192
  and global society 173, 188, 194
democratic deficit 198
Denmark
  capital mobility 121
  consumption tax 135
deregulation 79, 167

deterritorialization 179ff, 189
  and balance of payments 90
  winners and losers 93
Deutschmark 82, 84
developing countries 141
  capital inflows 31
  foreign direct investment 32, 39, 59
  and international institutions 163
  liberalization 59
  participation in international trade regime 65–6
  and mergers and acquisitions 30
  and national autonomy 141
development aid 155, 183
dollarization 83, 207
drug trade 158, 203

economies of scale 29, 60
Economic Community of West African States 67
economic liberalization, and the end of the Cold War 157
Eichengreen, Barry 209
'embedded' liberalism 129
environmental NGOs 186, 188, 194
environmental problems 179–80, 203
environmental standards 61, 216
ethnic identities 187
EURO 109, 113, 141, 167, 205, 209
Eurocurrency Standing Committee 208
European Bank for Reconstruction and Development 156
European Central Bank (ECB) 209
European Economic Community (EEC) 215
European integration 168–9
European Monetary System (EMS) 113
European Monetary Union (EMU) 141
European Union 5, 26, 69, 70
  access to EU market 163
  commercial banks 206

European Union (*cont.*)
  consumption tax   135
  foreign direct
      investment   115
  institutions   206
  labour tax   135
  single market   65
  and the United
      States   63–4, 206,
      208
exchange rate
  arrangements   207
  and capital mobility   79
  and the IMF   205
  manipulation of   86
  risk   90
  speculative attacks   113
  volatility   79

Feldstein–Horioka approach
    to capital mobility   121
firms
  globalization within   151
  regional activities   153–4
firm behaviour
  and globalization   152
  in oligopolistic
      markets   95–6
financial market
  integration   3, 77ff, 108,
      111, 157, 168
  domestic effects   113
  see also market integration
financial capital
  mobility   *see* capital
      mobility
financial crisis   63, 109
  and EU   63
  management of   208ff
  of 1990s   209
  prevention of   211
  and private-sector
      creditors   210
  and the United States   63
financial liberalization   153
  see also liberalization
financial openness
  and consumption tax   135
  and growth in public
      economy   129
  and inflation   138
  and labour tax   135
Financial Stability Forum,
    FSF, 1997   208
fiscal policy   79, 157
  convergence of,
      OECD   124
  domestic political
      conditions   128
  and globalization   124
  and power of the
      left/labour   128

Ford Foundation   176, 186
foreign direct investment
    (FDI)   13, 24, 32, 35,
      39, 120, 148
  determinants of   112
  in developing
      countries   59
  distribution of by region
      and country, 1975–80,
      1990–96   *22*
  and factor endowments   29
  geography of   20–4,
      1990–96   *36*;
      explanations   *33*
  and externalities   112
  and inflation   138
  North–South flows   46
  in OECD   120
  and privatization   59
  and productivity   112
  recipients of   *24*
  sectoral concentration
      of   38
  state intervention   57
  stocks of   *34*
  strategic asset seeking, 31
  and wages   112
foreign assistance, and the
    end of the Cold
    War   157–8
foreign exchange market   *see*
    exchange market
foreign policy   150, 157
France
  capital mobility   121–2
  and EMU   141
  tax rates   132

GATT (General Agreement
    on Trade and
    Tariffs)   54, 57–8, 61–2,
      69, 71, 156, 218
  see also WTO
G-7   208
  Cologne summit
      1999   210
G-22   208
GDP, growth in OECD   137
Germany
  and EMU   141
  tax rates   132
  and UN Security
      Council   217
  and the United
      States   166
global central bank   209
global civil society   173ff,
      190
global competition   154,
      159, 183
global conventions on
    rights   188

global finance   82, 207
  and business
      organizations   186
  and international
      institutions   205ff
global production   152
global security   213
global warming   158
globalization   2, 10ff, 59,
      147, 157, 159ff, 166, 169,
      203
  dimensions of   *118–19*
  and economic policy and
      performance   *139*
  expansion of markets   3,
      59
  and government
      spending   *126*
  and growth   161
  and human rights   9
  and inequality   9,
      159, *165*, 204
  institutional arrangements
      of   66
  and national security
      policy   158
  and partisan politics   *126*,
      133
  pressures on government
      policies   109
  and taxation   *133*
  and state sovereignty   4,
      17, 107ff
gold standard   205
Goodhart, Charles   86
governance
  legitimacy   93, 192
  multilayered   185, 197
  privatization of   186
  post-sovereign   189
government control
  of demand side of the
      market   95
  of money supply   94
government intervention
  and capital mobility   111
  and coordination of
      economic activity   142
  and corporatism   114
  and market
      integration   124, 128
  and socio-economic
      institutions   112
government policies
  as determinant of
      investment locations
  in an oligopolistic
      world   96
  and trade   119
government spending
    consumption
      expenditure   123

income transfers 123
and left/labour
power 129
OECD 124
and public sector
deficit *123*; cross-
national *125*
Great Depression 101
Greece
capital mobility 121
public deficit 125
Group of Ten (G-10) 206,
208, 210, 217
growth theory
endogenous 114
and government
activity 142
Gulf War, 1991 63, 68, 159

Haiti, US intervention 158,
214
Hanke, Steve 99
Harare Declaration on
Development
Relationships,
1998 196
Harioka, Charles 121
Heckscher–Ohlin-type
investment flows 48
hedge funds 212
Hegel, G.W.F. 174
Helleiner, Eric 79
Helms–Burton Act 162
Hongkong
currency board 99
foreign direct investment in
China 32
participation in FSF 208
Hoover 110
human capital 114
humanitarian
intervention 214
humanitarian relief 182,
186, 188
Hungary, and regional trade
organizations 164
hysteresis 79

Ibrahim, Anwar, Malaysian
Finance Minister 102
India
welfare 160
financial crisis, 1990s 167
Indonesia
Asian crisis 102
currency board 99
inequality 9, 159ff, 204
and consequences of
globalization *165*
gender and ethnic 190–1
and global civil
society 195

income 160
between states 159, 161
within states 160
inflation
tax 85, 87
credibility 97
and growth 140
in OECD 137
see also seigniorage
infrastructure 13, 39, 40
as determinant for location
of MNE 26–8
Institute of International
Finance 187, 210
interest rates 111, 121
Intergovernmental Panel on
Climate Change
(1988) 186
International Accounting
Standards
Committee 184, 187
International Association of
Insurance
Supervisors 208
International Bank for
Reconstruction and
Development 205
International Chamber of
Commerce 176
International Confederation
of Trade Unions 181
International Council of
Scientific Unions 186
International Council of
Securities
Associations 186
International Federation of
Accountants 187
International Federation of
Stock Exchanges 186
international finance 205,
213
international
institutions 202ff
and global finance 205ff
and inequality 163–4
and international
rules 217
intrusiveness of 163
legitimacy of 217
and policy
coordination 214
reform of 202, 209ff
international market *see*
market
International Monetary
Fund, IMF 155, 162,
167, 184, 205, 206, 208,
210, 216
contingent credit
lines 211
and debt crisis 210, 216

economic
conditionalities 155
and government
policies 212, 216
'international financial
contagion' 211
and Latin America
crisis 213
legitimacy 216
and Mexican crisis 206
'new arrangement to
borrow' 211
resources 211
security policy 155
'special data dissemination
standard', 1996 212
International Network of
Engaged
Buddhists 196
international
organizations 155
and domestic
policies 213–14
internal structure 204
legitimacy 216
number of (1900 and
1990) 203
International Organizations
of Security
Commissions 208
International Primary
Market
Association 186
International Red
Cross 182
international rules 9, 215
international
standards 214ff
international trade 116
composition of 56
direction of 56
industrialized
countries 56
inter-regional 72
intra-industry 57, 116
intra-regional 72
strategies 158
politics of 7–3
regional trade 69
see also trade
internet 168, 177, 179, 181
intervention *see* government
intervention
investment
efficient 138
and financial crisis 209
inbound 23
locations 7
and saving 121
short-term 209
see also foreign direct
investment

Ireland, capital
    mobility 122
Italy
    budget deficit 125
    and Maastricht
        criteria 141

Japan
    budget balance 125
    and civic associations 183
    consumption tax 135
    labour tax 135
    public economy, size 125
    outward direct
        investment 35
    share of inbound
        investment 23
    supply of Yen, total 82
    tax rates 132
    and the United
        States 156, 166
    and the UN 217
joint ventures 58, 69

Kennedy Round,
    GATT 57
Keynes, John Maynard 68,
    157
Kirschner, Jonathan 87
Kohl, Helmut 109, 141
Korea 209
Kosovo War, 1999 63
Krugman, Paul 98, 101
Kuwait 153

labour 39
    low-skilled 8
    minimum wage,
        France 8
    skilled 30
    tax 19, 22, 134
labour-intensive goods 58
Latin America
    debt crisis 113, 206, 213
    imports 60
Latin American Association
    of Advocacy
    Organizations 181
Latin American Integration
    Association 67
'liberal institutional
    view' 55, 173
liberal internationalist
    tradition 159ff
liberalization of markets 30,
    39–40, 79–80, 205
    and capital flows *120*
    multilateral 54
    developing countries 59
Liberia 158
liquidity crisis 210

'Long Term Capital
    Management'
    (LTCM) 207
Luke, Timothy 153
Luxemburg, budget
    balance 125

Maastricht
    criteria 141
    Treaty 110
Macedonia 158
Maghreb Union 67
Major, John 110
Malaysia
    Asian crisis 102
    capital controls 161
market integration 3, 77ff,
    108, 111, 128, 132, 157,
    168
Marshall, Alfred (1920) 30,
    94
McDonald's 179
Médecins sans
    frontières 186
Mercedes Benz 112
Mercosur 67, 70, 71, 162
Mexico 71, 209
    capital mobility 121
    crisis, 1994–95 63, 91,
        163, 206
    IMF requirements 155
    portfolio
        investment 167–8
    regional trade
        organization 164
Mill, John Stuart 85
Mahathir, Mohamad,
    Malaysian Prime
    Minister 102
monetary policy 84, 87–8
monetary sovereignty 77,
    80–1, 84ff, 90, 98
    loss of 94
monetary union, 99–100,
    141
    see also EMU
money 87–98
    functions of 80, 84
    and macroeconomic
        policies 90–1
    production of 84
money demand 94, 98
money supply 86, 94, 98
Montreal Protocol on
    Substances that deplete
    the Ozone Layer,
    1987 186
most-favoured-nation (MFN)
    treatment 66
multilateralism 55–6, 62,
    69
    institutions 69, 72

multinational enterprises
    (MNE) 3, 24ff, 38ff,
    57–8, 110–11, 114, 151,
    204
    aggressiveness of 42
    geography of activity 24ff
    industrial composition 38ff
    and inequality 161
    location of 40
    and market conditions 24
    and R&D 28
    size *44*
    strategy of 40

NAFTA (North American
    Free Trade
    Agreement) 64, 67,
    69–71, 110, 163
national security
    policy 157–8
nation-state
    autonomy 107
    demise 10ff
NATO (North American
    Treaty Organization)
    156
neoclassical economic
    thinking 184
New Zealand
    capital mobility 122
    labour tax 134
    sales tax 135
    tariff level 117
NGO *see* non-governmental
    organizations
NGO Forum 187
Nigeria
    peace-keeping
        operations 158
non-governmental
    organizations 5, 42,
    166, 174, 183, 185, 204
    and development
        assistance 186
    and inequality 161
    and the UN 181
    and the World Bank 181,
        204
non-profit
    organizations 174
non-state actors 5, 208, 217
    see also multinational
        enterprises
North American Free Trade
    Agreement *see* NAFTA
North American Treaty
    Organization *see*
    NATO
Norway
    budget balance 125
    capital mobility 122
    consumption tax 135

OAU (Organization of
    African Unity)   158
OECD (Organization for
    Economic Cooperation
    and Development)   59,
    122–4, 208
    and civic activism   180,
        195
    foreign direct
        investment   115
    foreign economic
        policy   157
    macroeconomic
        performance   108,
        137, 143
    public sector
        expansion   124
    tariff level   57
    terms of trade   116
    trade volatility   *116*
    trade volume   *116*
    welfare   160
    world trade, share
        of   115
offshore financial
    centres   211
oil price shock   116, 167
oligopoly, in monetary
    control   93
Oman, Charles   68
Orwell, George   83
ozone layer   179–80

Palestine Liberation
    Organization
    (PLO)   186
Padoa-Schioppa, Italian
    central banker   85
Participation Resource
    Action Network   196
partisan politics
    and government
        spending   *126*
    and taxation   *130*;
        crossnational   *131*
Pauly, Louis   79
People's Global Action
    against 'Free
    Trade'   181
Perot, Ross   110
peso crisis   155
Poland, and regional trade
    organizations   164
political economy   1, 158
    of trade   54, 56ff
    of regionalism in
        trade   69ff
portfolio investment   12,
    149, 168
Portugal, capital
    mobility   121

Preferential Trade Area
    (PTA) for East and
    South African
    States   67
privatization   167
    and foreign direct
        investment   59
    of governance   186
    of markets   40
production   3
    location of   160
    multinationalization
        of   110
    organization, new   *152*
    specialization   26, 57
    subcontracted   152
    systems   38
production patterns   39
production networks   31,
    168
protectionism   54, 69
public intervention   *see*
    government intervention
public sector
    deficit   123, 142
    expansion   123
    spending   124, 128

Quinn, D.   132
    financial openness
        index   122

R&D sector (research and
    development)
    expansion of   21
    and investment
        patterns   28
'race to the bottom'   107,
    122, 129
Reagan, Ronald   25
recession, and income
    inequality   161
regional assistance   158
regional trade   *69*
    arrangements   66–7,
        71–2, 163–4
regionalism   5, 17, 71–3, 153
    and multilateralism   69ff
    in trade relations   54, 69
regionalization   162
regulation   156–7, 183
    and civil society   185, 197
risk
    coverage by banks   211
    distribution of   138, 142
Robertson, Roland   150
Rodrik, Dani   12, 135
Roman Catholic Church   176
Romania   183
Rubin, Robert, US Secretary
    of the Treasury,
    1999   208

Ruggie, John   153
Russia   183, 209
    and the Balkans   158
    portfolio
        investment   167–8
Rwanda   207, 214

Sachs, Jeffrey   142
security   204, 206
    policy   158
seigniorage   85, 89ff, 93, 97
    international   89, 92
    see also inflation
Serbia   155, 158
Silicon Valley   30
Singapore
    Asian crisis   102
    participation in FSF   208
Slum Dwellers
    International   176
social cohesion, and civil
    society   193
social democratic
    governments   157, 177
social justice, and civic
    activism   196
social service
    provisions   109, 183
    see also welfare state
socialism, end of   157, 183
    see also Cold War
Somalia   207, 214
Soros, George   102
South African Development
    Coordination
    Conference,
    SADCC   67
South Asian Association for
    Regional
    Cooperation   67
Southeast Asia, inbound
    investment   23
Soviet bloc countries   135
    in international trade
        regime   59
Spain
    capital mobility   122
    public economy, size
        of   125
spillover, of crisis   214
stability pact   141
state   93, 156
    autonomy   107, 109
    and institutions   4, 150
    and monetary
        authority   92
    and multilateralism   68
state sovereignty   4, 17, 155,
    161, 184–5, 215
sterling   84
subnational groups   5
Strange, Susan   95

Suharto, President of
    Indonesia 99
Sweden
    consumption tax 135
    public economy, size
        of 125
    tax rates 132
Switzerland, consumption
    tax 135

Taiwan, Asian crisis 102
tariffs
    and Australia 117
    and GATT 115
    OECD 57
taxation 142
    on capital 130ff
    and capital mobility 114
    on consumption 130ff
    costs of 110
    cross-national
        convergence 132
    effective rates *130*;
        cross-national *131*
    on labour 130ff
    and macroeconomic
        performance 140
    and partisan politics *133*
    and unemployment 140
tax evasion 136
technological change 31,
    57, 167, 183
'Tequila effect' (debt
    crisis) 206
territoriality, dismantling
    of 153
Thailand
    constitutional change 183
    devaluation, 1997 207
    portfolio investment 168
Thatcher, Margaret 25, 134
Third World
    and civic activism 31
    see also developing
        countries
Toshiba 179
trade 3, 117, 148, 216
    balance 116
    and country size 116
    exposure 108, 116
    policy 117
    regional *26,* 69
    volatility in 115–6
    see also international trade
trade barriers
    intra-regional 32
    non-tariff 117
    reduction in 72, 166
trade related intellectual
    property (TRIPS) 61

trade related investment
    measures (TRIMS) 61
trade unions 185
transaction costs 27, 29, 149
    and investment
        patterns 29
transnational networks 168

unemployment, in OECD,
    1961–94 137
Union of International
    Organizations 181
United Nations (UN)
    and civic associations 186
    Military Staff
        Committee 208
    and NGOs 181
    peacekeeping 180
    Security Council 208, 217
    and US interventions 158
United Nations Conference
    on Trade and
    Development
    (UNCTAD) 21, 31
United Nations Environment
    Programme
    (UNEP) 154
United Nations High
    Commissioner for
    Refugees
    (UNHCR) 183
United States of America
    (USA)
    and Asia crisis 101
    commercial banks 206
    and EU 63, 208
    extraterritorial laws 64,
        162
    and gold standard 205
    hegemony, decline of 63
    Helms–Burton Act 162
    inbound investment 23,
        115
    and international
        institutions 66
    interventions 158
    and multilateralism 64
    multinational
        enterprises 166
    outward investment 32
    protectionism 64, 66
    public economy, size
        of 125
    security issues 63
    tax rates 132, 135
    trade 64, 158
    and the UN 158
    as a unilateral actor 64
    and the Uruguay
        Round 70

Uruguay Round, GATT,
    1986 61, 65, 70
US–Israel Free Trade
    Agreement 64
US Treasury
    cooperation with
        international
        institutions 206
    and Latin American
        crisis 213
    and Mexico crisis 206

'virtual communities' 167
voluntary export
    restraints 54

Wade, Robert 11
wage regulation 114
Wagner's law of correlation
    between prosperity and
    public economic growth,
    1888 124
'Washington consensus' 157
wealth distribution 138, 142
welfare objectives 7, 183
    maintaining of 11
    and NGOs 167
    'race to the bottom' 7,
        107
    withdrawal from 167
welfare state 108
    and competition 110
    crisis 108
    dismantling of 107
    and growth 143
    income transfer
        programmes 110
    and institutional economic
        reform 164
'Westernization' 179
women
    and collective
        identity 187
    and income
        inequality 160
    organizations in the
        EU 185
World Bank 109, 155, 163,
    167, 183, 204, 205–6
    conditionalities 155–6
    and NGOs 156
World Economic
    Forum 181, 187
WTO (World Trade
    Organization) 54,
    61–2, 64–6, 69–70, 73,
    155, 163, 185, 192, 213
    intrusiveness of 163

Yugoslavia 214